Digital Humanities and Digital Media

Conversations on Politics, Culture, Aesthetics and Literacy

Fibreculture Books

Series Editor: Andrew Murphie

Title Editor: Athina Karatzogianni

Digital and networked media are now very much the established media. They still hold the promise of a new world, but sometimes this new world looks as much like a complex form of neofeudalism as a celebration of a new communality. In such a situation the question of what 'media' or 'communications' are has become strange to us. It demands new ways of thinking about fundamental conceptions and ecologies of practice. This calls for something that traditional media disciplines, even 'new media' disciplines, cannot always provide. The Fibreculture book series explores this contemporary state of things and asks what comes next.

Digital Humanities and Digital Media

Conversations on Politics, Culture, Aesthetics and Literacy

Roberto Simanowski

( )
OPEN HUMANITIES PRESS

London 2016

First edition published by Open Humanities Press 2016

Copyright © 2016 Roberto Simanowski and respective contributors

Freely available online at http://openhumanitiespress.org/books/titles/
digital-humanities-and-digital-media/

The cover image is a visualization of the book's text. Each interview
was algorithmically assessed, paragraph by paragraph, for relevance to
"politics", "culture", "aesthetics" and "literacy" and the result plotted
as a streamgraph. All of the streamgraphs were overlaid to create a
composite image of the book. Made with Gensim and Matplotlib.
© David Ottina 2016 cc-by-sa

PRINT ISBN 978-1-78542-030-6

PDF ISBN 978-1-78542-031-3

OPEN HUMANITIES PRESS

Open Humanities Press is an international, scholar-led open access
publishing collective whose mission is to make leading works of
contemporary critical thought freely available worldwide.

More at: http://openhumanitiespress.org

Contents

*Johanna welcomes governmental regulation on the internet
against 'neoliberal entrepreneurialism,' rejects new
grand narratives 'reconfigured by the pseudo-authority of
computation' and considers the sociality of contemporary
existence an obstacle for 'interior life,' innovation, and
zoophilia. She compares Digital Humanities with the 'cook in the
kitchen' and Digital Media Studies with the 'restaurant critic,'
sees the platform and tool development in the Humanities
as a professional, not academic track, she calls for a visual
epistemology in times of Screen culture and diagrammatic
knowledge production and she explains how to contaminate the
world of quantitative and disambiguating underpinnings with
the virtues of relativism and multi-perspectivism.*

*John Cayley positions 'capta' against 'data', reveals
vectoralization as algorithmic determination within a new
socioeconomic architecture, bemoans the blackmail of 'terms
of service' as well as the infantile misunderstanding of what it
is to be a social human by Mark Zuckerberg and the serfdom
of narcissistic selves to the data-greedy service providers.
He underlines the dumbness and deception of statistics and
algorithmic agency, wonders when the vectoralist class of big
software will, eventually, be 'too big to fail,' speculates about
unrealized artworks with Google Translate, rejects "social
reading" and fears Digital Humanities.*

devalued as thinkers by technological advances. They speak
about the pluriformism of the Digital Humanities movement,
about visualized thinking and collaborative theorization,
about the connection between cultural criticism and Digital
Humanities, they share their mixed experiences with the Digital
Humanities program at UCLA, explain why most innovative
work is done by tenured faculty and muse about the ideal
representative of Digital Humanities.

N. Katherine Hayles discusses the advantages of social and
algorithmic reading and reaffirms the value of deep reading;
she doubts media literacy requires media abstinence; she
underlines the importance of the Humanities for 'understanding
and intervening' in society but questions the idolized 'rhetoric
of "resistance"' and she weights the real problems facing the
Digital Humanities against unfounded fears.

Jay David Bolter talks about the (missing) embrace of digital
media by the literary and academic community, about hypertext
as a (failing) promise of a new kind of reflective praxis,
about transparent (immediate) and reflected (hypermediate)
technology. He compares the aesthetics of information with
the aesthetics of spectacle in social media and notes the
collapse of hierarchy and centrality in culture in the context of
digital media.

Bernard Stiegler speaks about digital tertiary retention
and the need for an epistemological revolution as well as
new forms of doctoral studies and discusses the practice
of 'contributive categorization,' the 'organology of
transindividuation,' 'transindividuation of knowledge' and
individuation as negentropic activity. He calls for an 'economy
of de-proletarianization' as an economy of care, compares the
impact of the digital on the brain with heroin and expects the
reorganization of the digital from the long-term civilization
in the East.

Introduction

Roberto Simanowski

Motivation: Quiet revolutions very quick

There is a cartoon in which a father sits next to a boy of about twelve and says: 'You do my website... and I'll do your homework.' It accurately depicts the imbalance in media competency across today's generations, typically articulated in the vague and paradoxical terms: "digital natives" (for the young) and "digital immigrants" (for the over thirties). Historical research into reading has shown that such distinctions are by no means new: 250 years ago, when children began to be sent to school, it was not uncommon for twelve year olds to write the maid's love letters – an example that also demonstrates that conflicts between media access and youth protection were already in existence in earlier times. Is the father in the cartoon the maid of those far off times? Has nothing else changed other than the medium and the year?

What has changed above all is the speed and the magnitude of the development of new media. Few would have imagined 20 years ago how radically the Internet would one day alter the entirety of our daily lives, and fewer still could have predicted ten years ago how profoundly Web 2.0 would change the Internet itself. Since then, traditional ideas about identity, communication, knowledge, privacy, friendship, copyright, advertising, democracy, and political engagement have fundamentally shifted. The neologisms that new media have generated already testify to this: They blend what were formerly opposites — prosumer, slacktivism, viral marketing; turn traditional concepts upside-down — copyleft, crowdfunding, distant reading; and assert entirely new principles — citizen journalism, filter bubble, numerical narratives.

Twenty years are like a century in web-time. In 1996 the new media's pioneers declared the *Independence of Cyberspace* and asked, 'on behalf of the future,' the governments of the old world, these 'weary giants of flesh and steel,' to leave them alone.[1] Following this declaration others bestowed the new medium with the power to build its own nation. The 'citizens of the Digital Nation,' says a *Wired* article of 1997, are 'young, educated, affluent [...] libertarian, materialistic, tolerant, rational, technologically adept, disconnected from conventional political organizations.'[2] The 'postpolitical' position of these 'new libertarians' has since been coined the Californian Ideology or Cyber Libertarianism – they don't merely despise the government of the old world in the new medium, they despise government pure and simple.

Two decades later Internet activists and theorists are turning to the old nation state governments, asking them to solve problems in the online world, be it the right to be forgotten, the protection of privacy and net-neutrality, or the threatening power of the new mega players on the Internet.[3] Meanwhile the political representatives of the 'Governments of the Industrial World' – which is now called the Information Society – meet regularly to discuss the governance of Cyberspace – which is now called the Internet. Governments, once at war with the Internet, are now mining it for data in order to better understand, serve, and control their citizens.[4]

Theorists have long scaled down their former enthusiasm for the liberating and democratizing potential of the Internet and have begun addressing its dark side: commercialization, surveillance, filter bubble, depoliticization, quantification, waste of time, loss of deep attention, being alone together, Nomophobia and FOMO (i.e. *no mobile-phobia* and the *fear of missing out*). Those who still praise the Internet as an extension of the public sphere, as an affirmation of deliberative democracy, as a power for collective intelligence, or even as identity workshop seem to lack empirical data or the skill of dialectical thinking. Have tables turned only for the worse?

It all depends on who one asks. If one looks for a more positive account, one should talk to entrepreneurs and software developers, to "digital natives", or even social scientists rather than addressing anyone invested in the Humanities. The former will praise our times and produce lists of "excitements": information at your finger tips whenever, wherever, and about whatever; ubiquitous computing and frictionless sharing; new knowledge about medical conditions and social circumstances; the customization of everything; and a couple of ends: of the gatekeeper, the expert, the middleman, even of the author as we knew it. And the next big things are just around the corner: IOT, Industry 4.0, 3D printing, augmented reality, intelligent dust ...

No matter what perspective one entertains, there is no doubt that we live in exciting times. Ours is the age of many 'silent revolutions' triggered by startups and the research labs of big IT companies. These are revolutions that quietly – without much societal awareness let alone discussion – alter the world we live in profoundly. Another ten or five years, and self-tracking will be as normal and inevitable as having a Facebook account and a mobile phone. Our bodies will constantly transmit data to the big aggregation in the cloud, facilitated by wearable devices sitting directly at or beneath the skin. Permanent recording and automatic sharing – be it with the help of smart glasses, smart contact lenses, or the Oculus Rift – will provide unabridged memory, shareable and analyzable precisely as represented in an episode of the British TV Sci-Fi series *Black Mirror*: "The Entire History of You". The digitization of everything will allow for comprehensive quantification; predictive analytics and algorithmic regulation will prove themselves as effective and indispensable ways to govern modern mass society. Not too early to speculate, not too early to remember.

Methodology: Differences disclosed by reiteration

If a new medium has been around for a while it is good to look back and remember how we expected it to develop ten, twenty years ago. If the medium is still in the process of finding and reinventing itself, it is good to discuss the current state of its art and its possible future(s). The book at hand engages in the business of looking back, discusses the status quo, and predicts future developments. It offers an inventory of expectations: expectations that academic observers and practitioners of new media entertained in the past and are developing for the future. The observations shared in this book are conversations about digital media and culture that engage issues in the four central fields of politics and government, algorithm and censorship, art and aesthetics, as well as media literacy and education. Among the keywords discussed are: data mining, algorithmic regulation, the imperative to share, filter bubble, distant reading, power browsing, deep attention, transparent reader, interactive art, participatory culture.

These issues are discussed by different generations – particularly those old enough to remember and to historicize current developments in and perspectives on digital media – with different national backgrounds: scholars in their forties, fifties, sixties and seventies mostly from the US, but also from France, Brazil, and Denmark. The aim was also to offer a broad range of different people in terms of their relationship to new media. All interviewees research, teach, and create digital technology and culture, but do so with different foci, intentions, intensities, and intellectual as well as practical backgrounds. As a result the book is hardly cohesive and highlights the multiplicity in perspectives that exists among scholars of digital media. A key aspect of the book is that the interviews have been conducted by a German scholar of media studies with an academic background in literary and cultural studies. This configuration ensures not only a discussion of many aspects of digital media culture in light of German critical theory but also fruitful associations and connections to less well known German texts such as Max Picard's 1948 radio critique *The World of Silence* or Hans Jonas' 1979 *Search of an Ethics for the Technological Age*.

Another key aspect of this collection of interviews is its structure, which allows for a hypertextual reading. The interviews were mostly conducted by email and for each field, some questions were directed to all interviewees. They were given complete freedom to choose those relevant to their own work and engagements. Other questions were tailored to interviewees' specific areas of interest, prompting differing requests for further explanation. As a result, this book identifies different takes on the same issue, while enabling a diversity of perspectives when it comes to the interviewees' special concerns. Among the questions offered to everybody were: What is your favored neologism of digital media culture? If you could go back in history of new media and digital culture in order to prevent something from happening or somebody from doing something, what or who would it be? If you were a minister of education, what would you do about media literacy? Other recurrent questions address the relationship between cyberspace and government, the Googlization, quantification and customization of everything, and the culture of sharing and transparency. The section on art and aesthetics evaluates the former hopes for hypertext and hyperfiction, the political facet of digital art, the transition from the "passive" to "active" and from "social" to "transparent reading,"; the section on media literacy discusses the loss of deep reading, the prospect of "distant reading" and "algorithmic criticism" as well as the response of the university to the upheaval of new media and the expectations or misgivings respectively towards Digital Humanities.

That conversations cover the issues at hand in a very personal and dialogic fashion renders this book more accessible than the typical scholarly treatment of the topics. In fact, if the interviewer pushes back and questions assumptions or assertions, this may cut through to the gist of certain arguments and provoke explicit statements. Sometimes, however, it is better to let the other talk. It can be quite revealing how a question is understood or misunderstood and what paths somebody is taking in order to avoid giving an answer. Uncontrolled digression sheds light on specific ways of thinking and may provide a glimpse into how people come to hold a perspective rather foreign to our own. Sometimes, this too is part of the game, the questions or comments of the interviewer clearly exceed the lengths of the interviewee's response. The aim was to have the interviewer and the interviewee engage in a dialogue rather than a mere Q&A session. Hence, the responses not only trigger follow-up questions but are sometimes also followed by remarks that may be longer than the statement to which they react and the comment they elicit. The result is a combination of elaborated observations on digital media and culture, philosophical excurses into cultural history and human nature, as well as outspoken statements about people, events and issues in the field of new media.

Media Literacy: From how things work to what they do to us

The overall objective of this book is media literacy, along with the role that Digital Humanities and Digital Media Studies can play in this regard. Media literacy, which in the discourse on digital media does not seem to attract the attention it deserves, is – in the US as well as in Germany – mostly conceptualized with respect to the individual using new media. The prevalent question in classrooms and tutorials is: what sorts of things can I do with new media and how do I do this most effectively? However, the achievement of media competency can only ever be a part of media literacy: competency must be accompanied by the ability to reflect upon media. The other important and too rarely asked question is: what is new media doing to us? As Rodney Jones puts it in his interview: 'The problem with most approaches to literacy is that they focus on "how things work" (whether they be written texts or websites or mobile devices) and teach literacy as something like the skill of a machine operator (encoding and decoding). Real literacy is more about "how *people* work" — how they use texts and media and semiotic systems to engage in situated social practices and enact situated social identities.'

The shift from *me* to *us* means a move from skills and vocational training towards insights and understanding with respect to the social, economic, political, cultural and ethical implications of digital media. Understood in this broader sense, in terms of anthropology and cultural studies, media literacy is not inclined to the generation of frictionless new media usage, but is determined to explore which cultural values and social norms new media create or negate and how we, as a society, should understand and value this. Media literacy in this sense, is, for example, not only concerned with how to read a search engine's ranking list but also with how the retrieval of information based on the use of a search engine changes the way we perceive and value knowledge.

The urge to develop reflective media literacy rather than just vocational knowhow raises the question about the appropriate institutional frameworks within which such literacy is to be offered. Is Digital Humanities – the new 'big thing' in the Humanities at large – be the best place? The qualified compound phrase "sounds like what one unacquainted with the whole issue might think it is: humanistic inquiry that in some way relates to the digital."[5] For people acquainted with the ongoing debate (and with grammar), digital humanities is first and foremost what the adjective-plus-noun combination suggests: 'a project of employing the computer to facilitate humanistic research,' as Jay David Bolter, an early representative of Digital Media Studies, puts it, 'work that had been done previously by hand.' Digital Humanities is, so far, computer-supported humanities rather than humanities discussing the cultural impact of digital media. Some academics even fear Digital Humanities may be a kind of Trojan horse, ultimately diverting our attention not only from critical philosophical engagement but also from engaging with digital media itself.[6] Others consider, for similar reasons, digital humanists the 'golden retrievers of the academy': they never get into dogfights because they hardly ever develop theories that anyone could dispute.[7]

To become a breed of this kind in the academic kennel scholars and commentators have to shift their interest 'away from thinking big thoughts to forging new tools, methods, materials, techniques ...'[8] In this sense, Johanna Drucker proposes an interesting, rigorous distinction of responsibilities: 'Digital Humanities is the cook in the kitchen and [...] Digital Media

Studies is the restaurant critic.'[9] The commotion of the kitchen versus the glamour of the restaurant may sound demeaning to digital humanists. Would it be better to consider them waiters connecting the cook with the critic? Would it be better to see them as the new rich (versus the venerable, though financially exhausted aristocracy) as Alan Liu does: 'will they [the digital humanists] once more be merely servants at the table whose practice is perceived to be purely instrumental to the main work of the humanities'?[10]

The more Digital Humanities advances from its origin as a tool of librarians towards an approach to the digital as an object of study, the more Digital Humanities grows into a second type or a third wave[11], the more it will be able to provide a home for Digital Media Studies or sit with it at the table. The methods and subjects of both may never be identical. After all Digital Media Studies is less interested in certain word occurrences in Shakespeare than in the cultural implications of social network sites and their drive towards quantification. However, interests overlap when, for example, the form and role of self-narration on social network sites is discussed on the grounds of statistical data, or when the relationship between obsessive sharing and short attention span is proven by quantitative studies. The best way to do Digital Media Studies is to combine philosophical concerns with empirical data. The best way to do Digital Humanities is to trigger hermeneutic debates that live off of the combination of algorithmic analysis and criticism.

Summary: digital libertarianism, governmental regulation, phatic communication

Naturally, interviews are not the ideal exercise yard for "golden retrievers." The dialogic, less formal nature of an interview makes it very different from the well-crafted essays shrouded in opaque or ambiguous formulations. A dialogue allows for provocation. As it turns out, there are a few angry men and women of all ages out there: angry about how digital media are changing our culture, angry at the people behind this change. In an article about Facebook you wouldn't, as John Cayley does in the interview, accuse Mark Zuckerberg of a 'shy, but arrogant and infantile misunderstanding of what it is to be a social human.' In a paper on higher education you wouldn't, as bluntly, as Mihail Nadin does, state that the university, once contributing 'to a good understanding of the networks,' today 'only delivers the tradespeople for all those start-ups that shape the human condition through their disruptive technologies way more than universities do.'

There is no shortage of critical and even pessimistic views in these interviews. However, there are also rather neutral or even optimistic perspectives. One example is the expectation that personalization 'becomes interactive in the other direction as well,' as Ulrik Ekman notes, 'so that Internet mediation becomes socialized rather than just having people become "personalized" and normatively "socialized" by the web medium.' However, most interviewees are more critical than enthusiastic. This seems to be inevitable since we are interviewing academics rather than software engineers, entrepreneurs or shareholders. To give an idea of what issues are of concern and how they are addressed, here are some of the findings on a few of the keywords listed above.

1. *Regarding the field of government, surveillance and control*, it does not come as a surprise that obsessive sharing and big data analysis are considered in relation to privacy and surveillance. There is the fear that 'our "personal" existence will become public data to be consumed and used but not to get to understand us as individuals through a daring but not implausible comparison: 'distance reading might become an analogy for distance relationships. No need to read the primary text—no need to know the actual person at all.' (Kathleen Kolmar) As absurd as it may sound, the problem starts with the distant relationship between the surveilling and the surveilled. A fictional but plausible case in point is the Oscar winning German movie *The Lives of Others* by Florian Henckel von Donnersmarck about a Stasi officer who, drawn by the alleged subversive's personality, finally sides with

his victim. Such a switch can't happen with an algorithm as "offi-cer". Algorithms are immune to human relation and thus the final destination of any 'adiaphorized' society. Robert Kowalski's famous definition 'Algorithm = Logic + Control' needs the adden-dum: minus moral concerns.

While there are good reasons to fear the coming society of algorithmic regulation, many people – at the top and at the bottom and however inadvertently – are already pushing for it. Since – as any manager knows – quantification is the reliable partner of control, the best preparation for the algorithmic reign is the quantitative turn of/in everything: a shift from words to numbers, i.e. from the vague, ambiguous business of interpret-ing somebody or something to the rigid regime of statistics. Today, the imperative of quantification does not only travel top down. There is a culture of self-tracking and a growing industry of supporting devices, whose objective is a reinterpretation of the oracular Delphic saying 'Know Thyself,' aptly spelled out on the front page of quantifiedself.com: 'Self Knowledge Through Numbers.' Even if one is part of this movement and shares the belief in the advantages of crowd-sourced knowledge, one can't neglect the 'danger that self-monitoring can give rise to new regimens of governmentality and surveillance' and that 'the rise of self-tracking allows governments and health care systems to devolve responsibility for health onto individuals' (Rodney Jones). The original name of one of the life-logging applications, OptimizeMe, clearly suggests the goal to create 'neoliberal, responsibilized subjectivities'[12] ultimately held accountable for problems that may have systemic roots. It suggests it so boldly, that the name was soon softened to Optimized.

To link back to the beginning of this introduction: It may be problematic to speak of a "digital nation," however, its "citizens" could eventually succeed in changing all nations according to the logic of the digital. David Golumbia calls it the 'cultural logic of computation' and concludes that Leibniz' perspective, 'the view that everything in the mind, or everything important in society, can be reduced to mathematical formulae and logical syllogisms,' has finally prevailed over Voltaire's 'more expansive version of

rationalism that recognizes that there are aspects to reason outside of calculation.' Nadin even speaks of a new Faustian deal
where Faust conjures the Universal Computer: 'I am willing to
give up better Judgment for the Calculation that will make the
future the present of all my wishes and desires fulfilled.'

The redefinition of self-knowledge as statistics demonstrates
that transformation often begins with terminology. However,
the *semiological guerrilla* or *détournement* is not conceptualized as resistance against the powerful but is being used by the
most powerful corporations.[13] An example is the term "hacker"
which is now even found as self-description for members of governments, as Erick Felinto notes. Brazil's 'most progressive former minister of culture, Gilberto Gil, once said: "I'm a hacker,
a minister-hacker".' Regardless how appropriate this claim was
for Gil, Felinto seems to be correct when he holds that 'in a time
when big corporations are increasingly colonizing cyberspace,
we need to imbue people with the hacker ethics of freedom, creativity and experimentation.' However, creativity and experimentation are not inherently innocent as other interviewees state.
'Hackers may maintain an agnostic position concerning the significance or value of the data=capta that their algorithms bring
into new relations with human order or, for that matter, human
disorder,' Cayley holds, assuming that hackers may help the vectoralists of "big software" discover where and how to exploit
profitable vectors of attention and transaction. Golumbia goes
even further in expressing a reservation with regard to hackers
and "hacktivism" pointing out the underlying 'right libertarianism,' the implicit celebration of power at the personal level,
and 'its exercise without any discussion of how power functions
in our society.' In addition one has to remember that freedom,
creativity and experimentation all are terms also highly appre-
ciated in any start-up and IT company. The "big corporations"
that Felinto refers to have already hacked the term hacker:
'many tech business leaders today call themselves hackers; not
only does Mark Zuckerberg call himself a hacker, but Facebook
makes "hacking" a prime skill for its job candidates, and all its

technical employees are encouraged to think of themselves as "hackers"' (Golumbia).

Have they hacked the very independence of cyberspace? For many the Internet today means Google and Facebook: billion dollar companies as the default interface on billions of screens teaching us to see the world according to their rules. The problem is now, as Nick Montfort states, 'that corporations have found a way to profitably insinuate themselves into personal publishing, communication, and information exchange, to make themselves essential to the communications we used to manage ourselves. As individuals we used to run BBSs, websites, blogs, forums, archives of material for people to download, and so on. Now, partly for certain technical reasons and partly because we've just capitulated, most people rely on Facebook, Twitter, Instagram, Google, and so on.'

The next wave of such "counter-revolution" is already on its way and it also starts in the academic realm itself. It is significant and 'intolerable,' as Ekman states, that projects regarding the internet of things and ubiquitous computing 'are pursued with no or far too little misgivings, qualms, or scruples as to their systemic invisibility, inaccessibility, and their embedded "surveillance" that will have no problems reaching right through your home, your mail, your phone, your clothes, your body posture and temperature, your face and emotional expressivity, your hearing aid, and your pacemaker.' One of the things, for which Ekman wishes more qualms and scruples, is 'pervasive healthcare' which, even in a small country like Denmark, a handful of research groups work on. Ekman's warning invokes the next blockbuster dystopia of our society in 30 or 20 years: the 'massive distribution and use of smart computational things and wirelessness might well soon alter our notion of the home, healthcare, and how to address the elderly in nations with a demography tilting in that direction.'

The driving force of progress is, apart from power and money, efficiency and convenience. This becomes clear in light of the success story of two examples of the 'transaction economy' which itself is the natural outcome of social media: *Uber* and *airbnb*. As Nadin points out: 'In the transaction economy ethics is most of the time compromised', i.e. Uber disrupts the taxi services and all labor agreements, benefits and job security that may exist in this field. However, it is useless to blame the Uber driver for killing safe and well-paid jobs: What shall she do after she lost her safe and well-paid job in the hotel business? It is the tyranny of the market that we are dealing with and there is little one can do if one tends more toward Hayek's economic philosophy than to Keynes'. The situation is comparable to that of East-Germany in the early 1990s immediately after the fall of the Berlin wall: people bought the better products from West-Germany undermining their own jobs in archaic, inefficient companies that were not able to compete and survive without the help of protectionism or consumer patriotism. Maybe new media demand in a similar way a discussion of the extent to which we want to give up the old system. If we don't want the market alone to determine society's future we need discussions, decisions, and regulations. We may want 'to put politics and social good above other values, and then to test via democratic means whether technological systems themselves conform to those values,' as Golumbia suggests.

The result could be a state-powered Luddism to fight reckless technical innovations on the ground of ethical concerns and political decisions. The response to the "hacking" of cyberspace by corporations is the "embrace" of the government as the shield against the 'neoliberal entrepreneurialism, with its pseudo-individualism and pro-corporate ideology, and the inequities that intensify with disbalances of economic power' (Johanna Drucker). While in preparation for Industry 4.0 the "homo fabers" involved expect the government to pave the way for economic development, the observing "Hamlets" at humanities departments call for interventions and debate. But it is true, 'the fact that many Google employees honestly think they know what is good for the rest of society better than society itself does is very troubling' (Golumbia). The soft version of Neo-Luddites are Federal Commissions that do not blindly impede but consciously control innovations. Given the fact that computer technologies 'are now openly advertised as having life-altering effects as extreme as, or even more extreme than, some drugs' it is only logical to request a FDA for computers, as Golumbia suggests, or to wish the 'FCC to protect us against the domination by private enterprise and corporate interests,' as Drucker does.

While it appears that the issue of corporations and regulations could be fixed with the right political will and power, other problems seem to be grounded in the nature of the Internet itself – such as the issue of political will and power. The political role of the Internet has been debated at least since newspapers enthusiastically and prematurely ran the headlines: 'In Egypt, Twitter trumps torture' and 'Facebook Revolution'. The neologisms "slacktivism" and "dataveillance" counter euphemisms such as "citizen journalism" or "digital agora". Jürgen Habermas – whose concept of the public sphere has been referred to many times and not only by German Internet theorists – is rather skeptical about the contribution digital media can make to democratic discourse. In his 2008 essay *Political Communication in Media Society: Does Democracy still have an Epistemic Dimension?*, Habermas holds that the asymmetric system of traditional mass media offers a better foundation for deliberative, participatory democracy than the bidirectional Internet, since the fragmented public sphere online and the operational modus of laypeople obstruct an inclusive and rigorous debate of the pros and cons of specific issues. The much objurgated or at least ignored experts once forced us to avoid the easier way and cope with complex analysis of a political issue. Today, after the liberation from such "expertocracy," we register a dwindling willingness to engage with anything that is difficult and demanding such as counter arguments or just complex ("complicated" and "boring") meditations. Not only is the democratic potential of the Internet questionable because now ISIS is using social media to recruit supporters, but also because the Internet 'does not "force" individuals to engage with a wider array of political opinions and in many cases makes it very easy for individuals to do the opposite' – whereas before, in the age of centralized mass media, there was 'a very robust and very interactive political dialogue in the US' (Golumbia).

The Internet not only decentralizes political discussion, it also distracts from it by burying the political under the personal and commercial. Yes, there are political weblogs and yes, the Internet makes it easy to attain, compare, check information free from traditional gatekeepers. However, the applied linguist also underlines the ongoing shift from Foucaultian 'orders of discourse' to Deleuzian 'societies of control': 'Opportunities to "express oneself" are just as constrained as before, only now by the discursive economies of sites like Facebook and YouTube.' (Jones) But how much of the information processed online each day is political anyway? How much of it is meaningless distraction? What Felinto affirms most likely echoes the belief of many cultural critics: 'Instead of focusing on the production of information and meaning, we're moving towards a culture of entertainment. We want to experience sensations, to have fun, to be excited. If silence is becoming impossible, meaning also seems to be in short supply theses days.'

2. *Fun, sensation, entertainment* are effective ways to occupy, or numb, brain time. As Adorno once famously said: Amusement is the liberation from thought and negation. Adorno's equation and Felinto's observation link the political to the psychological and shift the focus to issues of deep reading and attention span. Another very effective form of depolitisization is the subversion of the attention span and the skill of complex thinking, both needed in order to engage thoroughly with political issues. The obvious terms to describe the threat are "power browsing", "multi tasking", "ambient attention". The less obvious, most paradoxical and now quite robust term is "hypertext". It is robust because it doesn't depend on the user's approach to digital media but is embedded in the technical apparatus of these media. The multi-linear structure of the Internet is one of its essential features – and possibly one of the most reliable threats to complex thinking.

This is ironic, since it was precisely hypertext technology which, in the 1990s, was celebrated not only as liberation from the "tyranny of the author" but also as destabilization of the signifier and as highlighting the ambivalence and relativity of propositions. Hypertext was seen as an ally in the effort to promote and practice reflection and critical thinking; some even saw it as a revolution of irony and skepticism[14]. Today hypertext technology – and its cultural equivalent hyper-reading – appears, by contrast, as the practice of nervous, inpatient reading, discouraging a sustained engagement with the text at hand and thus eventually and inevitably hindering deep thinking; an updated version of 'amusement' in Adorno's theory of the culture industry. Jay David Bolter – who agrees that the literary hypertext culture some academics were envisioning at the end of the 20th century never came to be – considers the popularization of hypertext in the form of the WWW 'a triumph of hypertext not limited to or even addressed by the academic community.' How welcome is this unexpected triumph given that it contributes to the trend, noted by Felinto, of ubiqutious 'stupidification' in Bernard Stiegler's characterization?

When it comes to issues such as attention span and deep reading, academics respond as teachers having their specific, anecdotal classroom experiences. While the extent to which Google, Facebook, Twitter, Wikipedia and other digital tools of information or distraction make us stupid is debatable, there is the assertion – for example by neuroscientist Maryanne Wolf as popularized in Nicholas Carr's book *The Shallows: What the Internet is Doing to Our Brains* – that multitasking and power browsing make people unlearn deep reading and consequently curtail their capacity for deep thinking. Such a judgment has been countered by other neuroscientists and popular writers, who hold that new media increase brain activity and equip digital natives to process information much faster. The debate of course reminds us of earlier discussions in history concerning the cognitive consequences of media use. The German keywords are Lesesucht (reading addiction) which was deplored in the late 18th century and Kinoseuche (cinema plague) which broke out in the early 20th century. Famous is the defense of the cinema as preparation for life in the modern world and put forward by Walter Benjamin in his essay *The Work of Art in the Age of Mechanical*

Reproduction. While others complain that the moving image impedes thought, Benjamin applauded the shock experience of the montage as a 'heightened presence of mind' required for the age of acceleration.

Those who have not read other texts by Benjamin may be tempted to refer to his contrary praise of cinema (contrary, relative to all the condemnations of the new medium by conservatives) when insisting on the beneficial effects of new media for cognition. Others may point to the difference between Geistesgegenwart (presence of mind), that Benjamin sees increased by cinema, and Geistestiefe (deep thinking). The shift from deep to hyper reading resembles the shift from deep Erfahrung (interpreted experience) to shallow Erlebnis (lived experience) that Benjamin detected and criticized in other essays. Processing more information faster in order to safely get to the other side of a busy street is very different from digesting information so that it still means something to us the next day. This meaning-to-us is at stake in a medial ecosystem that favors speed and mass over depth.

If the 'templates of social networking sites such as Facebook constitute a messy compromise between information and spectacle,' as Bolter notes, one may, with Bolter, place his hope on text-based media such as WhatsApp and Twitter: 'The baroque impulse toward spectacle and sensory experience today seems to be in a state of permanent but productive tension with the impulse for structured representation and communication.' On the other hand, the templates of these media (140 signs or less) do not encourage the transmission of complex information nor the engagement in deep discussion. These are "phatic technologies"[15] good for building and maintaining relationships, good for fun, sensation, and entertainment. Whether this is reason enough to be alarmed, Bolter will discuss in his next book, *The Digital Plenitude,* arguing that we experience different forms of cultural expressions which are not reconcilable and holding that 'we have to understand that outside our community this discourse [about what kind of cultural standards we have to pursue] isn't necessarily going to make much sense.' Bolter's conclusion is radical beyond postmodernism and contrary to any culture pessimism: 'That's exactly what people like Nicholas Carr on the popular level or some conservative academics on the scholarly level are concerned about when they complain about the loss of reflective reading or the ability to think and make arguments.'

For many addressed by Bolter, Wikipedia is one of the red flags concerning the cultural implications of digital media. The concern is mostly directed towards the accuracy of a crowd-sourced encyclopedia vs. one written by experts. However, several studies suggest that Wikipedia's score compared to "official" encyclopedia is not as bad as usually assumed. There are other worries: What does it mean when Wikipedia "intends to be and has partly succeeded at being *the* single site for the totality of human knowledge" (Golumbia)? What does it mean when an encyclopedia rather than monographs or essays becomes the only source students consult today? How will it change the culture of knowledge when one encyclopedia plus search engines become the prevalent form for presenting and perceiving knowledge?

One result of the new approach to knowledge is known to many teachers who discover that students today have a ,shorter concentration span' and favor audio-visual information over reading (Willeke Wendrich); that they 'want instant and brief responses to very complex questions' (Kolmar); and that their 'moan-threshold' for reading-assignments has fallen from 20 to 10 pages: 'Deep reading is increasingly viewed as an educational necessity, not something done outside the classroom, for pleasure or personal learning' (Diane Favro). Katherine N. Hayles, in her article in *Profession* "Hyper and Deep Attention: The Generational Divide in Cognitive Modes", shares a similar sense of these questions already in 2007. Others may have better experiences or see the reason less in digital media than in the move of higher education towards the type of instrumentalism found in vocational training. They may be convinced that 'the era of deep attention is largely a fantasy that has been projected backwards to romanticize a world that never existed' and point to teenagers playing videogames: 'their rapt attention, complex strategy making, and formidable attention to detail' (Todd Presner). Or

they may remind us that the "deep critical attention" of print literacy did not prevent centuries of war, genocide, and environmental devastation and imagine their students 'rolling their eyes
at being called stupid by a generation that has created the economic, political, social and environmental catastrophe we now
find ourselves in' (Jones).

Stiegler, who translates Carr's concerns into political language and detects a threat to society if the capability of critical attention is compromised, speaks of the digital as opium for
the masses, an expanding addiction to constant sensual stimulation. Stiegler considers the digital a pharmakon – which can
be either medicine or poison depending on its use – ‚prescribed
by sellers of services, the dealers of digital technology.' He does
not accuse Google or other big Internet-companies of bad intentions but blames us, the academics, who did not ‚make it our job
to produce a digital pharmacology and organology.' While the
theoretical implications of this task are ‚new forms of high-level
research' *of* rather than *with* digital instruments, one pragmatic
facet of such digital pharmacology is a certain form of media
abstinence in order to develop real media literacy: 'Children
should first be absolutely versed in grammar and orthography
before they deal with computation. Education in school should
follow the historical order of alteration of media, i.e. you begin
with drawing, continue with writing, you go on to photography,
for example, and then you use the computer which would not be
before students are 15 or 16.'

Other interviewees, however, suggest that all elementary
school kids should learn to program and to 'create and critique
data sets' (Drucker) or object: ‚Stiegler's approach of "adoption—
no!" may be feasible for very young pre-schoolers, it becomes
ineffective, and probably impossible, for children older than five
as they become exposed to school, classmates, and other influences outside of the home.' (Hayles) The notion of peer pressure is certainly operative and it is also true that the tradition
of deep attention always ‚required the support and nurturing of
institutions—intellectual discourse and an educated elite' and
that therefore today the role of ‚educators at every level, from

kindergarten through graduate school, should be to make connections between contemporary practices, for example browsing and surfing the web, and the disciplined acquisition of knowledge' (Hayles). However, one does wonder whether children have to be exposed to computers as early as advocates of classrooms decked with technology maintain, if it is so easy to pick up the skills to use computers and so difficult to learn the skill of "deep reading." It is also worth noticing in this context that those who invent, sell and advertise – 'prescribe' as Stiegler puts is – the new technology partly keep their own children away from it or take measures to ensure it does not turn into a poisoning drug: Executives at companies like Google and eBay send their children to a Waldorf school where electronic gadgets are banned until the eighth grade, and Steve Jobs denied his kids the iPad.[16]

What shall we think of people preaching wine but drinking water? At best, these parents are selling toys they consider too dangerous for their own kids. At worst, they want to ensure their own breed's advantage over people addicted to sensory stimulation and unprepared for tasks that demand concentration, endurance and critical thinking. In a way, what these parents do in their family context is what Golumbia wants society to do on a bigger scale: to check whether new technological tools conform to the values of this society – or family.

No matter what one considers the best age to be introduced to the computer or how one sees the issue of deep reading and deep attention, there is no doubt that today younger generations are immersed in constant communication. They are online before they see the bathroom in the morning and after they have turned off the light in the evening: 'They live entirely social existences, always connected and in an exchange, no matter how banal, about the ongoing events of daily life.' (Drucker) But Drucker is less concerned about the prevalence of phatic communication than the 'single most shocking feature' of the way young people are living their lives nowadays: 'that they have no interior life and no apparent need or use for it.' For Drucker the disregard and discard of reflection, meditation, imaginative musing jeopardizes innovation, change, and invention which 'have always come from individuals who broke the mold, thought differently, pulled ideas into being in form and expression. Too much sociality leads to dull normativity.' The birth of conventionalism out of the spirit of participation; this implicit thesis in Drucker's account is spelled out in Nadin's assessment: 'social media has become not an opportunity for diversity and resistance, but rather a background for conformity.'

One could go even further and say: too much sociality through mobile media and social network sites spoils the cultural technique of sustained, immersed reading. The reason for this is associated with another essential feature of the Internet: its interactivity, its bias to bidirectional communication, its offer to be a sender rather than "just" a reader. 'Feed, don't read the Internet,' this slogan was around before the turn of the century. Today people read as much as they can. They must do so, if they want to keep up the conversation and avoid trouble with their friends. What they mustn't do is: wait too long for their turn. Nobody expects them to listen for long before they are allowed to answer; nobody except their teachers. In his 1932 essay *The Radio as an Apparatus of Communication*, Bertolt Brecht demands a microphone for every listener. It was the Marxist response to the advent of a new medium; a response that exploited the unrealized potential of the medium ('undurchführbar in dieser Gesellschaftsordnung, durchführbar in einer anderen') as an argument to fight for a new social order. The notion of turning the listener into a speaker reappears with the concept of the open artwork and the advent of hypertext. The readers' freedom to chose their own navigation through the text was celebrated as 'reallocation of power from author to reader.'[17] This perspective was later dismissed on the ground that it was still the author who composed the links and that, on the other hand, the feeling of being 'lost in hyperspace'[18] hardly constitutes liberation or power. Who – of all the scholars of literature celebrating the end of linear reading back in the 1990s – would have thought that it actually was the hope for the empowerment of the reader itself that had to be dismissed?

The natural development, following from the demise of patient, obedient readers is their replacement by a machine; the sequel to "hyper-reading" is "distant reading". Nonetheless, the relationship of the reader to the author is similar: one no longer engages in a careful following – or 'listening' to – the author's expression but rather navigates the text according to one's own impulses and interests. The new pleasure of the text is its algorithmic mining. However, for the time being there is still a significant difference between these two alternatives to good old "deep reading": distant or algorithmic reading is not meant as a substitution for deep reading. Rather it 'allows us to ask questions impossible before, especially queries concerning large corpora of texts,' which is why 'we should not interpret algorithmic reading as the death of interpretation' as Hayles states: 'How one designs the software, and even more, how one interprets and understands the patterns that are revealed, remain very much interpretive activities.' The exciting goal is to carry out algorithmic reading in tandem with hermeneutic interpretation in the traditional sense, as Hayles with Allen Riddell does of Mark Danielewski's *Only Revolutions* in her book *How We Think*. Hayles' perspective and praxis counters any cultural pessimism opting for a use of new technologies in a way that does not compromise the old values: 'Instead of "adoption, not adaption" my slogan would be "opening the depths, not sliding on surfaces".'

3. Digital Humanities and higher education is a link that, unsurprisingly, creates certain scepticism among the interviewees. If the Humanities are seen as 'expressions of resistance' that 'probe the science and technology instead of automatically accepting them,' as Nadin does, then the 'rushing into a territory of methods and perspectives defined for purposes different from those of the humanities' does not seem to be a good trade-off. Nadin's anger goes further. He addresses the university as an institution giving in to the mighty IT companies and the deterministic model of computation: 'If you want to control individuals, determinism is what you want to instill in everything: machines, people, groups. Once upon a time, the university contributed to a good understanding of the networks. Today, it only delivers the trades-people for all those start-ups that shape the human condition through their disruptive technologies way more than universities do.'

The criticism of the 'intrusion of capital' into the sphere of higher education (Golumbia) is shared by others who fear that 'differently motivated services outside the institutions of higher education will first offer themselves to universities and then, quite simply, fold their academic missions and identities into vectoralist network services' (Cayley). The assumption is that the digital infrastructure of the university will affect its academic mission: '"cost-effective' and more innovative services provided from *outside* the institution' Cayley holds 'may then go on to reconstitute the institution itself. "Google" swallows computing services at precisely the historical moment when digital practices swallow knowledge creation and dissemination. Hence "Google" swallows the university, the library, the publisher.' Was this inevitable? Is it still stoppable? Golumbia is not surprised 'that academics, who often rightly remain focused on their narrow areas of study, were neither prepared nor really even in a position to mitigate these changes.' Montfort is less reproachful and displays more hope for resistance within academia: The research Google is conducting is, 'by the very nature of their organization as a corporation, for the purpose of enriching their shareholders. That by itself doesn't make Google 'evil,' but the company is not going to solve the scholarly community's problems, or anyone else's problems, unless it results in profit for them. A regulation won't fix this; we, as scholars, should take responsibility and address the issue.'

While Nadin implies that the humanities and the university in general are being rebuilt according to the paradigms of computer science and big business, in Hayles' view 'these fears either reflect a misunderstanding of algorithmic methods [...] or envy about the relatively abundant funding streams that the Digital Humanities enjoy.' She does not exclude the possibility that Digital Humanities is 'being coopted by corporate funding to the extent that pedagogical and educational priorities are undercut' nor does she neglect the need for 'defining significant problems rather than ones tailored to chasing grants.' However, one should, with Hayles, see the exciting prospects of combining algorithmic data analysis with traditional criticism rather than always looking for the dark side of the digital humanities. In the same spirit Montfort underlines the valuable insights that already have been reached from computational humanistic study and points out: 'Fear of quantitative study by a computer is about as silly as fearing writing as a humanistic method – because writing turns the humanities into a branch of rhetoric, or because writing is about stabilizing meaning, or whatever.'

After all, rather than being colonized by technical science, digital humanities can also be seen as the opposite if it brings the 'insights from the humanities that are seldom considered, let alone valued in the sciences, including computer science' to computational approaches: 'that data are not objective, often ambiguous, and context dependent' (Wendrich). The same hope – that 'it will be the humanistic dimensions that gain more traction in the field—not just as content, but as methods of knowledge, analysis, and argument' – is uttered by Drucker who rightly calls on Digital Humanities to overcome its obsession with definitions and start to deliver: 'until a project in Digital Humanities has produced work that has to be cited by its home discipline—American History, Classics, Romantic Poetry, etc.—for its *argument* (not just as a resource)—we cannot claim that DH has really contributed anything to scholarship.'

Conclusion and Speculation: Media ethics from a German perspective

If we don't limit the discussion of media ecology to either the contemporary reinvention of the term in the work of Matthew Fuller or the conservative environmentalism of post-McLuhan writers such as Neil Postman, we may refer to the magnum opus of a German philosopher who discussed the cultural implications of technological advancement and its threat to humanity in the light of the first Club of Rome report. In his 1979 book

The Imperative of Responsibility: In Search of an Ethics for the Technological Age Hans Jonas demanded an 'ethics of responsibility for distant contingencies.'[19] We have to consider the consequences of our actions even though they do not affect us or our immediate environment directly. It is remarkable that Jonas saw the fatality of man lying in the 'triumph of *homo faber*' that turns him into 'the compulsive executer of his capacity': 'If nothing succeeds like success, nothing also entraps like success.'[20] Almost 40 years later it is clear that we have more than ever given in to this imperative of technological success and compulsively create hardware and software whose consequences we barely understand.

Jonas' warning and demand are part of the environmentalism that developed rapidly in the 1970s. The discussion today about big data, privacy and the quantitative turn through digital media, social networks and tracking applications has been linked to the environmental catastrophe in order to broaden the discussion of relations and responsibilities.[21] Just as, at a certain point, one's energy bill was no longer simply a private matter – after all the ecological consequences of our energy consumption affects all of us – the argument is now that our dealings with personal data have an ethical dimension. The supply of personal data about driving styles, consumption habits, physical movement, etc. contributes to the establishing of statistical parameters and expectations against which all customers, clients and employees, regardless of their willingness to disclose private data, will be measured. Generosity with private data is no private issue. In other words: obsessive sharing and committed self-tracking are social actions whose ramifications ultimately exceed the realm of the individuals directly involved.

There is no question that society needs to engage in a thorough reflection on its technological development and a broad discussion about its cultural implications. There is no doubt that universities and especially the Humanities should play an important role in this debate. However, it is also quite clear that the search for an ethics in the age of Web 3.0 and Industry 4.0 is much harder than it was in Jonas' time. While nobody questions the objective of environmentalists to secure the ground and future of all living beings (the point of contention is only the actual degree of the danger), digital media don't threaten human life but "only" its current culture. Data pollution, the erosion of privacy and the subversion of deep attention are not comparable to air pollution, global warming and resource depletion.[22] The ethics of preservation is on less sound ground if this project aims to preserve cultural standards and norms. Even if people agree on the existence of the threat they will not agree on how to judge the threat. After all, this is a central lesson that the Humanities teach: radical upheavals in culture are inherent to society.

Nonetheless, the ongoing and upcoming upheavals and revolutions need to be discussed with scholarly knowledge and academic rigor. According to many interviewees in this book such discussion is not taking place as it should. The reasons are not only political, but also epistemological and methodological. ,We were given the keys to the car with very little driver's education' and hence incur a high risk of 'derailment' on the digital highway, as Favro puts is. To stay with the metaphor: We also lack the time to look beneath the hood. Rather than pulling all the new toys apart in order to understand how they work we just learn how to operate them. There are too many toys coming out too fast. The frenetic pace of innovation has a reason, as Nadin makes clear: 'what is at stake is not a circuit board, a communication protocol, or a new piece of software, but the human condition. The spectacular success of those whom we associate with the beginnings lies in monetizing opportunities. They found gold!' When Nadin speaks of the 'victory of "We can" over "What do we want?" or "Why?"' it is reminiscent of Jonas' comment on *homo faber*. And like Jonas, Nadin addresses our complicity in this affair: 'The spectacular failure lies in the emergence of individuals who accept a level of dependence on technology that is pitiful. This dependence explains why, instead of liberating the human being, digital technology has enslaved everyone—including those who might never touch a keyboard or look at a monitor.' We need a 'reorganization of the digital,' Stiegler accordingly says, because the Web, ,completely subject to computation and automation,' is producing entropy, while the ,question for the future, not only for the Web, but for human kind is to produce negentropy.'

Of course, such negative assessment of the ongoing techno-logical revolution is debatable. It is not only Mark Zuckerberg who, along with his wife in a letter to their newly born daughter, considers the world a better place thanks to digital technology, including of course the opportunity for people to connect and share.[23] Many others too expect advances in health care, social organization, and individual life from computation and automation. Nonetheless, if experts demand the prohibition of certain technological advancement citing predictable devastating consequences – take the *Open Letter from AI and Robotics Researchers* from July 28 in 2015 to ban autonomous weapons – one feels reassured that there is indeed an essential risk that many researchers and entrepreneurs are taking at our expense. This risk is not reduced to weapons and the scenarios of cyber-war (or worse: cyber terrorism) in a world after Industry 4.0 and the Internet of Things. It includes genetically-engineered viruses and self-learning artificial intelligence whose decisions exceed human capacity for comprehension. The questions such consideration raises are pressing: Where does the marriage of intelligence and technology lead us? Who or what are the driving forces? How did they get their mandate? And most importantly: Is it possible to stop them/it?

If we hear scientists who do research on invisible (killer) drones or genetic design we don't hear them refer to Friedrich Dürrenmatt's 1961 tragicomedy *The Physicians* where a genius physicist feigns madness so he is committed to a sanatorium and can prevent his probable deadly invention from ever being used. What we see instead is the excitement to overcome scientific problems with little qualms concerning humanity's ability to handle the outcomes. Technical discoveries, technological advancement will be made, where and when possible, regardless of the benefit to humanity. Some scientists defend their ambition with the notion that not scientists, but society must decide what use it wants to make of the technology made available.

Others, referring to economic and military competition, argue that there is no universal authority that has the power for binding decisions: If we don't do it, the enemy will. It is difficult to ignore this argument, even though dangerous inventions have been successfully banned worldwide, such as blinding lasers, by the UN in 1998. This said, it is also difficult not to consider those scientists opportunists who talk about excitement and competition rather than responsibility, while secretly being in contact with companies interested in producing the perfect embryo or an invisible drone.

Perhaps we mistake the actual problem if we only focus on the "black sheep" among scientists and engineers. Maybe it is really the *human condition* that is at stake here, though in a different way than addressed by Nadin. To turn to another, much older German philosopher: In the third proposition of his 1784 *Idea for a Universal History with a Cosmopolitan Purpose* Immanuel Kant considers the 'purpose in nature' that man go 'beyond the mechanical ordering of his animal existence' and gain happiness from the perfection of skills. The means to do so is to constantly develop the utmost human capacity of reason, from generation to generation, bestowing each with ever more refined technology: hammer, steam-engine, electric motor, computer, artificial intelligence. To Kant, this teleological concept of (reason in) history is entelechic; he presumes (as many of his contemporaries did) a development for the better. To later thinkers, however, such as Hannah Arendt in her 1968 *Men in Dark Times*, the idealism of the enlightenment looks like 'reckless optimism in the light of present realities', i.e. the achieved capacity of mankind to destroy itself with nuclear weapons.[24] As mentioned, since then the advances in human intelligence have brought many more powerful means to life that can end or suppress human life.

Maybe Kant's optimism is the result of a premature conclusion from the third proposition in his *Idea* (to gain happiness from the perfection of skills, i.e. unlimited research) to the eighth proposition (the philosophical chiliasm, i.e. perfection of humankind). There is a tension between theoretical reason (that drives us to explore and invent as much as we can) and practical reason (that should forbid certain inventions). It is a tension between the *homo faber* as 'compulsive executer of his capacity' and man's ,responsibility for distant contingencies' to use Jonas' words. It is a tension between the enthusiastic "We can!" and the cautious "Why?" and "To what end?" to refer to Nadin again. In the new Faustian deal, that Nadin speaks of, the devil is the computer or rather: artificial intelligence, with which we trade better judgment for fulfilled desires. The obvious risk of such a deal is the extinction of men or their being locked in or out by post-human intelligence as addressed in 2015 by Alex Garland's *Ex Machina* and as early as 1968 in Stanley Kubrick's *2001: A Space Odyssey* which renders Kant's generational relay race of ever better tools as result of ever better use of the human capacity of reason in a famous and alarming short cut.

However, the metaphor of Faust leaves room for hope. If we perceive the new Faustian deal in the spirit of Johann Wolfgang Goethe, it is open ended. For in Goethe's play the bargain between Faust and Mephisto is not a "service for soul"-trade but a bet. It is Faust who self-confidently dictates the rules of the bargain:[25]

> *If the swift moment I entreat:*
> *Tarry a while! You are so fair!*
> *Then forge the shackles to my feet,*
> *Then I will gladly perish there!*
> *Then let them toll the passing-bell,*
> *Then of your servitude be free,*
> *The clock may stop, its hands fall still,*
> *And time be over then for me!*

Since Faust, who finally turns into a restless and somewhat reckless entrepreneur, wins the bet and is saved, we may look calmly on the new deal. Even more so in light of another important detail in Goethe's *Faust*, Mephisto's ambivalent nature announced when he introduces himself to Faust:

> *[I am] Part of that force which would*
> *Do ever evil, and does ever good.*

Such ambiguity and contradiction has long attracted German thinkers, as for example the Christian mystic Jacob Böhme who, in the early 17th century, understood the Fall of Man, i.e. the use of reason, as an act of disobedience necessary for the evolution of the universe. Two centuries later the negative as precondition of the good, the clash of antithesis and thesis was called dialectic. Georg Wilhelm Friedrich Hegel, who was influenced by both Goethe and Böhme, considered contradictions and negations necessary elements for the advancement of humanity. Before him, Kant employed contradictions as the dynamic means of progress when, in the fourth proposition of his *Idea* for example, he discusses the 'unsocial sociability' of man that finally turns 'desire for honour, power or property' into 'a *moral* whole'. The negative is the vehicle for the implicit purpose of nature with which Kant substitutes God and which, in the ninth proposition, he also calls providence. In light of this concept of dialectic progress Mephisto's further self-description sounds harmless:

> *The spirit which eternally denies!*
> *And justly so; for all that which is wrought*
> *Deserves that it should come to naught*

However, the confidence that everything bad is finally good for us may be nothing more than the "reckless optimism" that Arendt detects in the Enlightenment's spirit of history and humanity's role in it. What if we can't count on that dialectic appeasement any longer after the advancement of a certain capacity for destruction? What if providence turns out to be exactly what Mephisto says: simply negation (rather than Hegel's double negation) with negative results for all of us? What if we really ‚should get rid of the last anthropic principle, which is life itself' – as Felinto paraphrases the Argentine philosopher Fabián Ludueña – and accept a ‚universe without a human observer' rather than assume ‚man is the final step in the development of life'? What if technology turns out to be less an act of liberation from the determinations of nature than an obsession, entertained by the 'purpose of nature,' humans can't help even if it finally kills them? What if the ride we undertake in that "car"

on the digital highway does not have, as a kind of "divine algorithm," a built-in emergency brake in case human reason turns
out to be devastating?

Despite learning from the past and despite predictive analytics: with regard to the future we are blind. We may, hearing the diligent workers around us, celebrate the arrival of a
better world, while in fact people are digging our grave, as it
happens to Goethe's Faust. After a symbolic dialogue with the
Sorge (which means *worry* but also *care* in German) whom he
dismisses and who punishes him with blindness, Faust mistakes
the Lemuren digging his grave on Mephisto's order for his workers building a dam to defy nature.[26] Is this our situation? Are
we, without worries and care, blind about the implications of our
actions? Are we facing an inhuman, adiaphorized society while
hoping big data and algorithmic regulation will make the world
a better place? Are we turning ourselves into objects of "panoptic" control by pursuing datafication and the ubiquity of smart
objects? Is the rise of the machine the end of men? To come back
to our philosophical references: Does Hegel's Absoluter Geist
(the single mind of all humanity that becomes self-aware and
free through the march of reason) reach its destiny in the form
of artificial intelligence? Is the Kantian capacity for reason fulfilled once human consciousness is passed on to machines? Or is
it rather overdone?

There are many questions to be raised in light of ongoing
technological development. Media literacy, without a doubt, is
important and has to move on from vocational "How"-questions
to critical "What for?"-questions, from "How can I use these
media?" to "What do they do to us?" It is important to understand media in their historical context and from an anthropological perspective. As the following interviews demonstrate,
in such endeavor not only contemporaries such as Nicolas Carr
and Sherry Turkle can be helpful and inspiring but even pre-dig-
ital ancestors such as the French Blaise Pascal and the Swiss
Max Picard. If the discussion aims at a philosophical treatment
rather than a phenomenological approach people tend to turn to
Gilbert Simondon, Manuel DeLanda and Vilém Flusser. As these

interviews show there are more techno-philosophers to be (re) discovered for the discussion needed – and as this introduction suggests, Goethe's *Faust* and Böhme's mysticism could, should, be part of it.

Notes

1. Perry Barlow: *Declaration of the Independence of Cyberspace* (1996) (http://homes.eff.org/~barlow/Declaration-Final.html)

2. Jon Katz (1997): "Birth of a Digital Nation", *Wired* 5.04, April 1997 (http://archive.wired.com/wired/archive/5.04/netizen_pr.html). Katz soon extend his essay into a book: *Media Rants. Postpolitics in the Digital Nation*, San Francisco: Hard-Wired 1997. The following quotes are from the essay at the given source online.

3. See the NET Mundial conferences, the EU court "right to be forgotten"-decision on May 13 in 2014, or the turn of advocacy groups to the Federal Trade Commission to ban Facebook's fric-tionless sharing project in 2011 (www.cnet.com/news/groups-ask-feds-to-ban-facebooks-frictionless-sharing). A case in point from this book is demonstrated by Johanna Drucker stating that, if she had a say about the issues of the Internet, she would "get the FCC to protect us against the domination by private enterprise and corporate interests" (p. ...).

4. "We are at war with our own products and with our overwhelm-ing technological skills", wrote Klaus Lenk in his article "The Challange of Cyberspatial Forms of Human Interaction to Territorial Governance and Policing", in: V. Brian Loader (ed.): *The Governance of Cyberspace*, London, New York: Routledge 1997, S. 126-135: 133.

5. Stephen Ramsey: "DH Types One and Two", Blog entry on May 3rd, 2013 (http://stephenramsay.us/2013/05/03/dh-one-and-two)

6. Alan Liu: "Where is Cultural Criticism in the Digital Humanities", in: Matthew K. Gold (ed.): *Debates in the Digital Humanities*, University of Minnesota Press 2012, 490-509. Liu defines cultural criticism as "both interpretive cultural studies and edgier cultural critique" (p. 491). Dave Parry ("The Digital Humanities or a Digital Humanism") addresses the conflict "between a digital humanism of computational technologies as adjectival modification of humanities research trumping a digi-tal humanities of humanities-based research into the digital" and concludes: "it seems to me that the dominant type of digital

humanism privileges the old at the expanse of the new" (in: ibid., 429-437: 434).

7. Tom Scheinfeldt: "Why Digital Humanities Is 'Nice'", in: Gold, Debates, 59-60: 59. The most digital humanists may engage in, Scheinfeldt notes, are methodological debates which are solved either empirically or pragmatically.

8. Tom Scheinfeldt: "Sunset for Ideology, Sunrise for Methodology?", in: Gold, Debates, 124-126: 125.

9. See the interview with Johanna Drucker in this book, p. ....

10. Liu, Cultural Criticism, ibid., 494.

11. For the second type see Ramsey's blogpost (footnote 5), for the third wave see David M. Berry: "The Computational Turn: Thinking About the Digital Humanities", in: *Culture Machine* Vol. 12 (2011), p. 4 (www.culturemachine.net/index.php/cm/issue/view/23).

12. Jennifer R. Whitson: "Gaming the Quantified Self", in: *Surveillance and Society*, Vol. 11, Nr. 1-2 (2013), 163-176: 173.

13. See Umberto Eco's essay "Towards a Semiological Guerrilla Warfare" (1967) and the concept of *détournement* by the Situationist International.

14. Stanley Aronowitz: „Looking Out: The Impact of Computers on the Lives of Professionals", in: Myron C. Tuman (ed.): *Literacy Online. The Promise (and Peril) of Reading and Writing with Computers*, Pittsburgh 1992, 119–137: 133.

15. Victoria Wanga, John V. Tuckera, Kevin Haines: „Phatic technologies in modern society", in: *Technology in Society*, Vol. 33, No. 1 (2012), 84-93.

16. Matt Richtel: *A Silicon Valley School That Doesn't Compute*, The New York Times, October 22, 2011 (www.nytimes.com/2011/10/23/technology/at-waldorf-school-in-silicon-valley-technology-can-wait.html?_r=0); Nick Bilton: Steve Jobs Was a Low-Tech Parent, The New York Times, September 10, 2014 (www.nytimes.com/2014/09/11/fashion/steve-jobs-apple-was-a-low-tech-parent.html)

17. George P. Landow: "Hypertext as Collage Writing", in: Peter Lunefeld (ed.): *The Digital Dialectic. New Essays on New Media.* Cambridge, MA, und London: MIT Press 1999, 150-170: 156.

18. Deborah M. Edwards, Lynda Hardman: "Lost in hyperspace: cognitive mapping and navigation in a hypertext environment",

in: Ray McAleese (ed.): *Hypertext: theory into practice*,
Edinburgh 1999, 90-105.

19. Hans Jonas. *The Imperative of Responsibility*. Chicago:
    University of Chicago Press 1984, 26. Originally published in
    German in 1979.

20. Ibid., 9, 142, 9.

21. Evgeny Morozov: "The Real Privacy Problem" in: *MIT
    Technology Review* (October 22, 2013); www.technologyreview.
    com/featuredstory/520426/the-real-privacy-problem

22. While "data pollution" here refers to the cultural 'pollution'
    Morozov addressed, there is no question that digital media also
    cause real environmental pollution as for example Jussi Parikka
    strikingly demonstrates in his 2014 study *The Anthrobscene*.

23. Mark Zuckerberg and Priscilla Chan: *A letter to our daugh-
    ter*, December 1, 2015 - https://www.facebook.com/notes/
    mark-zuckerberg/a-letter-to-our-daughter/10153375081581634

24. Hannah Arendt: *Men in Dark Times*, San Diego 1968, 84.

25. Johann Wolfgang von Goethe: Faust I, translated by Walter
    Arndt, Norton Critical Edition, New York, London 1976, 41
    (verse1699ff.). The following quotes ibid. 33, verse 1335f.
    and 1338-1340.

26. Ibid., 289-294.

At the intersection of computational methods and the traditional humanities

Johanna Drucker

Johanna Drucker has a reputation as both a book artist as well as a pioneer of what has become known as Digital Humanities. She is well known for her studies on visual poetics and experimental typography (*The Visible Word* 1994, *Figuring the Word* 1998) but also for her investigations of visual forms of knowledge production (*Graphesis* 2014), digital aesthetics and speculative computing (*SpecLab* 2008) and *Digital_Humanities* (2012, co-authored). She has worked as a Professor in Art History (Columbia, Yale, & SUNY) and Media Studies (University of Virginia) and since 2008 is the inaugural Breslauer Professor of Bibliographical Studies in the Department of Information Studies at UCLA.

Johanna welcomes governmental regulation on the internet against 'neoliberal entrepreneurialism,' rejects new grand narratives 'reconfigured by the pseudo-authority of computation' and considers the sociality of contemporary existence an obstacle for 'interior life,' innovation, and zoophilia. She compares

Digital Humanities with the 'cook in the kitchen' and Digital Media Studies with the 'restaurant critic,' sees the platform and tool development in the Humanities as a professional, not academic track, she calls for a visual epistemology in times of Screen culture and diagrammatic knowledge production and she explains how to contaminate the world of quantitative and disambiguating underpinnings with the virtues of relativism and multi-perspectivism.

Prelude

Roberto Simanowski: What is your favored neologism of digital media culture and why?

Johanna Drucker: I'm drawn to neologisms that serve as both nouns and verbs–tweet, google, email–because they indicate a blurring of action and object in a way that embodies the fluidly unstable transience of digital media. But I also like geek, geekify, geek-out, and digerati (along with their offspring, the digeratini) used as self-identification.

RS: If you could go back in history of new media and digital culture in order to prevent something from happening or somebody from doing something, what or who would it be?

JD: I'd legislate against the violence being done to net neutrality and get the FCC to protect us against the domination by private enterprise and corporate interests. This will be the end of access to academic, scholarly, and independent thought online.

RS: What comes to mind if you hear "Digital Media Studies"?

JD: Digital Media Studies uses tools such as critical theory, cultural studies, media archaeology, bibliographical, textual, and visual studies, and a host of highly focused approaches to software, platforms, interface, networks and other technical aspects of networked environments to expose their workings. It is almost entirely a critical practice except when explicitly linked to making.

RS: If you were a minister of education, what would you do about media literacy?

JD: I'd insist that all elementary school kids learn to create and critique data sets, know some basic statistics, learn database structure, interface design, and know how to analyze search engines, be able to do some scripting/programming, and be taught how to do data wrangling and introductory digital media studies. Skill in reading texts and images for their arguments as well as their content remains essential, but across the full spectrum of media formats.

Politics and Government

RS: Web 2.0 culture seems to have tamed and commodified the wild, anarchistic Internet of the 1990s when people played with identity in IRCs and MUDs and built their own websites in idiosyncratic ways. Today, clarity and transparency are the dominating values, and for obvious reasons, since only true and honest information are valid data in the context of commerce. This shift has also changed the role of the government. While in the 1990s Internet pioneers such as John Perry Barlow declared the independence of Cyberspace from the governments of the old world, now it seems people hope for governments to intervene in the taking-over and commercialization of the Internet by huge corporations such as Google and Facebook. Thus, web activists calling for the government to pass laws to protect privacy online, and politicians suggesting expiration dates for data on social networks appear to be activist in a battle for the rights of the individual. Have tables turned to that extent? Are we, once rejecting old government, now appealing to it for help?

JD: The Internet began as a government research project, through linked cables connecting major research universities and facilities that had defense contracts. So the Net and the Web began under government jurisdiction. Concerns about regulation cut across a range of issues –protections and violations of privacy are only part of the larger landscape. The overarching disaster of our lifetime is deregulation of all aspects of social life, the demonization of taxation, extreme income inequity, and undermining of the social contract as conceived by the 18th century polymaths who designed the Constitution of the United States.

The non-standard approaches to interface that were part of CD-Rom era electronic literature, arts, and design, like those of first generation web sites, were less constrained by convention than today's menu-drive and side-bar organized ones, and innovation does seem to have stymied in the rush to fixity, to the conventional screen display. But the design issue is separate from the ideology of individualism (mythic, in my opinion) and the kind of libertarianism that lurks under the rhetoric of certain activist movements. I'm not an anarchist. Quite the contrary, I think cultures are about negotiation of and through limits on what can and can't be tolerated, allowed, condemned. I'm far more afraid of deregulation, the end of internet neutrality, and the intersection of rhetorical assertions that combine neoliberal entrepreneurialism, with its pseudo-individualism and pro-corporate ideology, and the inequities that intensify with disbalances of economic power. I'll take government regulation over that any time, and that does not have to mean compromises to protected rights and liberties such as free speech and privacy.

Do most Internet users actually know what their rights and responsibilities are as citizens, let alone how the laws of the Interstate Commerce Commission, the Federal Communications Commission, Department of Justice, and other agencies actually regulate the Web? I doubt it. Like many people, they want the government out of their lives when it comes to taxes, accountability and responsibility but they want it in their lives to fix roads, maintain services like police and fire, and come to their aid in a major disaster—or keep the internet "there" for them. Children and adolescents have the same relationship to their parents. We have to get beyond models of government as dysfunctional family relationships and see that we are the regulating and responsible parties. No other grownups are going to appear. The internet may have begun as a government research project, but service providers are for-profit businesses and we depend on their cables, routers, servers, and infrastructure.

RS: I like very much your analogy about kids and parents. A companion and counterpart to responsibility is the entrepreneurialism you mention which makes me think of the young, energetic, and very excited startups as portrayed in the *Silicon Valley* TV series. It's a specific mixture of technophile, profit seeking and changing-the-world intent; and it is problematic in all three regards. The German philosopher Hans Jonas, in his 1979 book *The Imperative of Responsibility: In Search of an Ethics for the Technological Age*, notes that the fatality of man lies in the 'triumph of *homo faber*' that makes him into 'the compulsive executer of his capacity.' The blithe excitement about social media, cloud computing and data mining we are encountering today seems to illustrate Jonas' apprehension: 'If nothing succeeds like success, nothing also entraps like success.' The inventive entrepreneurs in Silicon Valley and elsewhere may see data mining as the great adventure of our times in which they involve themselves as in former times courageous businessmen did as they embarked in dangerous voyages. The difference: today's explorers take the entire mankind on board in their search for assets – not to make them all millionaires but to become millionaires at their expense. Petty concerns for privacy or cultural sustainability are only in the way of such spirit of discovery, just as the aged couple Philemon and Baucis in Goethe's play *Faust* stood in the way of modern business practices when they refused to give up their land for industrialization. To justify the "death" of those who stand in the way of "progress," an important part of the IT-industry business is the management of moods. The public has to be convinced of the entrepreneurs' good intentions: namely that their goal is to develop better products and to offer improved customer care. My analogies exaggerate, I admit. However, I really wonder whether we not only need more regulations of social life, as you indicate, but also against the spirit of homo faber that mercilessly changes the world regardless of any negotiations of and through limits.

JD: OMG, I have friends in SF who report with horror the overheard conversations of the opportunistic "entrepreneurs" who are seeking any way to create a new niche in the data stream (an app, a service, a new social media mode, a filter, anything). This is similar to the way advertisers dissected bodies into "zones" to which they targeted hygiene products, and of course in the data world, the zones can be sliced infinitely, to any granularity. Data derivatives replicate endlessly, without limit. Ethics? Can they be monetized?

RS: I absolutely agree, while for some time and to some people its gift economy imperative let the Internet appear as the last resort of communism, it in fact has become a playground of coveting and ruthless neo-liberalism. In this process even an important public good such as knowledge has been centralized in the hands of a private company such as Google. On the other hand, would the US government or the European Union ever have been able to carry out something like Google's book project? Should –and could– they run a search engine free of advertisement and with an algorithm visible to all who care?

JD: The Digital Public Library initiative, started as a visionary project by Robert Darnton, and now headed by Dan Cohen, is a perfect antidote to the problems posed by having Google control so much intellectual content as well as create so many data derivatives. Though DPLA will not deal its information, and seems to have no plans to monetize user profiles and patterns, it does offer a first and hopefully successful move towards a networked cultural heritage and access. Scientific and social-science data should also be part of this kind of repository. Private enterprise should be subject to regulation, scrutiny, and control, of course. But anyone who thought the internet was a gift economy is blind to the ways ease of consumption conceals the complexities (labor, costs, infrastructure) of production. To support digitally networked cultural heritage in any way that will carry forward more than a generation is going to require a public-private partnership at the scale of Carnegie Libraries in the early part of the 20th century. That was a hugely transformative undertaking, endowed by industrialist-turned-philanthropist Andrew Carnegie, but it coincided with tax funded support for public education, universal literacy, a public library system, and other initiatives. A few nationally funded projects show how transformative the commitment to infrastructure can be. Australia introduced a national broadband initiative, has a vital national library and cultural heritage/preservation programs, and its archivists have been at the forefront of international discussions about the rights of diverse communities. This is all far from Google and private interests. I think we need to reconcile various mythologies that have no real bearing on contemporary issues with the reality of actual possible futures—I know it sounds shockingly un-fun, but regulation, governance, shared responsibility and accountability, taxation, distribution of wealth, caps on income and profits, all these things are essential if education, information, power distribution, and sustainable futures are going to be made possible in any realm, including digital and traditional literacy. I'm a realist, not an idealist, and escalating inequities in every area of the culture need to be recalibrated.

Algorithm and Censorship

RS: The numbers of views, likes, comments and the Klout Score – as measure of one's influence in social media– indicate the social extension of the technical paradigm of digital media: counting. The quantification of evaluation only seems to fulfill the cultural logic of computation, the dichotomy of like/dislike even to mirror the binary of its operational system. The desired effect of counting is comparison and ranking, i.e. the end of postmodern ambiguity and relativism. Does the trust in numbers in digital media bring about the technological solution to a philosophical problem? A Hollywood-like shift from the melancholia of the end of grand narratives and truth to the excitement of who or what wins the competition?

JD: Pretty pathetic as an image of our times, this return to the Roman Forum, thumbs up, thumbs down, court of public opinion and gladiatorial combat. Nishant Shah is eloquent on this topic, and has mustered vivid examples of the ways web-driven vigilantism and swarm-mob behavior can mete out injustice without any control transferring socially mediated behavior into real world violence. As for counting as a metric, a measure of all things, it has to be balanced with statistical understanding, analytic tools from the quantitative domain, as well as with the tools of critical theory. A number is always relative, and even the first lesson in statistics—of median, mean, and mode—immediately calls attention to the *relative* value of a quantity. Combine this basic work in statistics with fundamentals in critical theory – a number is meaningful only in a scale, all scales are human-derived, based on some perceptual framework within a domain of knowledge or experience (body temperature, cycles of a day, a human lifespan, the speed of light, absolute or not, has value because it signifies a certain limit of what we imagine to be possible).

The grand narratives are all there, still, but being reconfigured by the pseudo-authority of computation, that set of mechanical exercises that passes itself off as irrefutable logic, as if it were not subject, like all logics, to a higher order of rhetoric. All statements of supposed fact are arguments about the belief system within which they gain their authority. That is simply Ideology 101, along with the other basic tenets of ideology: the more something appears to be natural, the more it is cultural; one has only to ask in whose interests it is for this "naturalness" to appear to be so to begin to unpack the power structures by which it is operating. Go back to the formulation about computational method and number and apply these basic tenets and suddenly the machinations of bureaucratic and managed culture appear unmasked, their grounds of authority revealed.

RS: No doubt that numbers too are not innocent. As book titles teach us: *"Raw Data" is an Oxymoron* (ed. Gitelman, MIT Press 2013). However, somehow the new technology (and its statistical mode) seems to promise the solution to an old political problem: to know and count the opinion of people. In fact, statistics may be considered the ideal advocate of democracy insofar as numbers avert the distortion of communication. Any utterance beyond a vote, any comment beyond a like or dislike, is a form of manipulation of the opinion, belief, feeling of others. Habermas celebrates this communicative action as discourse ethics, Rousseau, in his *Contrat Social*, considers debates and discussion as counter intuitive to democracy, since it aims at overcoming differences by rhetoric power if not political and economic power over media. We may not be able to say whether the numerical rationality is superior to the communicative. But we may agree that statistics allows for a shift from a kind of synthetic-discursive exclusion to syndetic-additive inclusion.

JD: Indeed, the relative virtue of quantitative reasoning is, well, just that--relative. I'm contrarian enough to suggest that statistical processes *are* discursive. Numbers seem discrete, referential, and delimiting, but that does not make their authority absolute. Their value is subject to cultural conditions even if they pretend otherwise. I'm reminded of the peculiar delusion that F.T. Marinetti entertained in thinking that mathematical symbols–the plus and minus sign–should replace syntactic terms because they were more precise. But of course, they are not, they are reductive, but thus, often, ambiguous, hence the paradox. Language need not be referential, but numbers, because they represent quantities, always are—even if the value of the referent may be ambiguous. For instance, what does "one" mean—it depends on the system of metrics within which it is operating, right? Modernism's struggles with syntax of all kinds (literary, musical, visual) was an attempt to open the possibility spaces of non-representational aesthetics, or at least, open forms of discourse.

RS: The personal and cultural cost of personalization in digital media is the loss of chance encounters, the preclusion of the unfamiliar, the removal of diversity and of what we are not (yet). The algorithm is the censor people more or less approve of and even desire. This becomes problematic once people are addressed not as consumers but as citizens expected to be open to others instead of cocooning in their bubble. Hence, personalization, driven by economic force, is political. Are the actual policy makers in the digital media age those who program ego-loops, inadvertently undermining the foundation of a democratic society?

JD: These questions hark back to earlier eras, degrees of collusion between desire-producing apparatuses and the subjects interpellated into their workings. What difference does it make whether we are discussing theater, flickering shadows in the cave, or the current screens? Human beings are addicted to the Symbolic, and the illusion it gives them of being somehow connected to the Other. The screens are just that, and I think we are in the era of the Grand Object A, rather than the Petit. The transactional object, the mechanism of illusion, the point of reference to which we are cathected in our Imaginary relations to the Real, has assumed gigantic proportions. Most people would give up food before they would give up their cell phones or internet connections, even though they are really only connected to a device. No self, only its fictive illusion within constructs of subjectivity, can be confirmed in such transactions. "Self" in this construction (now or in antiquity, from paleo-consciousness to the present) is a kind of specificity, a location, a unique address and identifier—not completely fictional, but rarely as "different" as imagined. Cocooning? Citizenship? Some incentive for participation will have to appear if the broad mass of people are going to see themselves as stakeholders. In our generation, the slogan "the personal is political" was used as a rallying cry, but now the difficulty is in convincing most younger voters that the "political can be personal" in any sense. And given recent Supreme Court decisions in the US that allow private interests to determine policy to an unprecedented degree, this is understandable. When money is speech, government works in the private interest and individuals as well as communities are disenfranchised. The connections between individual illusions/delusions, the pursuit of lifestyle over knowledge or experience, and the political sphere are complicated, and also have to meet the realities of motivation and activism.

RS: Facebook portrays the sharing of as much personal information as possible as the precondition for a better world. While the economic interests behind this data worship are undoubted and certainly need to be addressed, the question remains as to why younger generations don't seem to care about privacy but establish, using Facebook millionfold day-to-day, radical transparency as the new foundation of our culture. Is the data-exhibitionism of digital natives the contemporary version to the sexual revolution of the 1960s?

JD: I love the phrase "data worship" but I don't see the parallel with 1960s sexual revolutionary activity. We were given permission and we took it. We lived uninhibited lives without fear—remember this was pre-AIDS, and in the most permissive use of contraception. I don't use Facebook, though I have an account, it lies dormant. I like interior life, and private life, though I advise all my students to live their lives as if they are public, that way they will never have a problem. If I were to run for public office, my private life would be a field day for the news media—I/we did everything, with whomever and whatever we wanted. I once lived with a cat who wanted to have sexual relations with me. At a certain point in my conditioned resistance to his advances, I had to ask myself what my problem was with his desires? I did not give in, in the end, but it did make me think about the proscriptions in place. I was raised by a Calvinist in a Jewish household, so showing anything to anyone or being the least bit conspicuous or desirous of attention was simply not permitted. American culture is built on these kinds of deep prohibitions. I don't believe in mortifying the flesh. In a full life, one lives erotically in all dimensions of the daily encounter with the world—not screwing everything that comes along (though that's just fine by me too, if that's what someone wants to do), but living a sensually aware and fully ecstatic state of being. If only we could sustain that kind of intensity in our relation to the world. But would you want to live that way in public? What difference does it make? Notions of privacy, propriety, decorum, are all historically and culturally set. Eros is a state of body-mind. So much is shut down, put away, prohibited and circumscribed within human experience. Why?

RS: Your words first of all remind of what two older Germans said about the value of privacy. The sociologist Georg Simmel declared a century ago: 'The secret is one of man's greatest achievements'; the writer Peter Handke admitted three decades ago: 'I live off of what the others don't know about me'. Secondly, one wonders what will be the consequences if we all live our lives in the public eye. There is the hope that if all the skeletons in the closet (and the cats under the blanket) are known, nobody will cast the first stone and what had been considered sinful will finally turn out to be a social habit. However, there is also the fear that life in the age of transparency and search engines will rather be as two younger Americans suggest: think of Marc Zuckerberg's nothing-to-hide-nothing-to-fear declaration and Eric Schmidt's warning 'If you have something that you don't want anyone to know, maybe you shouldn't be doing it in the first place.' What is your bet?

JD: I guess I think there is a difference between what can be known and what should be shown. The problem with too much exposure is aesthetic as much as moral—the banality of it makes so much information uninteresting, generic. Ask students to do a drawing of a chair and a coat and they all do something interesting, highly revealing, very personal. Ask them to show you their diaries/sketchbooks—they are shockingly similar. If every frog around the pond is speaking at night, who will listen? Time and attention, as we know, are the valuable commodities of our times. Competition for these will only grow. How many Karl Ove Knausgaard accounts do we need? How many Jenny Cams?

Art and Aesthetics

RS: Nobody today speaks of *digital* art. Does this mean that digital art has ceased to exist or does it mean all art is digital?

JD: Gosh, no, not all art is digital! Lots of fine works of sculpture, painting, installation work, performance, drawing, and musical arts exist that have nothing to do with digital production. Just that the stigma of the "digital" went away so we can just think about the works as art—are they interesting, engaging, successful. We don't talk about oil paint art or instrumental art, so why emphasize a medium or technique?

RS: Well, if a medium has a message this message may also affect how we produce and perceive art. I would hold that computation, transformation, participation, and craftsmanship are some central aspects specific for the aesthetic of art born in digital media.

JD: Oh yes, I completely agree that there is a specificity to the ways digital production engages with conceptual, material, and aesthetic dimensions of production. But only some digital work is reflecting specifically on those aspects of process. I don't analyze every poem in terms of its use of typography, because many are so conventionally composed and laid out that the poet was clearly working within an already absorbed set of instructions for composition, not working with composition as a material aspect of their work. I think aesthetic is always about *how* something is made and thought, so in that sense, again, I agree. I just don't think every artist is reflecting on these issues in and as their production.

RS: People have said that art in or of digital media must be political even if its intentions are to be utterly formalistic. If art is based on technology the focus on form draws attention to how technology works and this is already an act of reflection or education. From this perspective, one would assume that digital literature is literature that addresses the politics of digital technology. What is your experience in this regard?

JD: All art is ideological, but that is different from saying it is political. All works engage with value systems and their operation, all artistic expressions are arguments for their forms (every novel is an argument about what a novel should/could be). Claims for the "political" are usually made for the most dull and didactic art, not work that actually makes for change or effects any structural transformation of power or process. The ideas that exposing the medium, calling attention to its machinations, showing how something makes meaning or effect—these are all features of modernist belief in epistemological defamiliarization. All fine and good, but the tediousness of didactic work plays into the worst neo-Liberalist affirmations, as the work of Claire Bishop, among others, makes very strikingly clear. Who are we kidding? The tasks of reworking the ideologies that have come to prevail since the Reagan-Thatcher era are daunting. Technology is neither a cause nor an effect, but a historically coincident formation that works on certain faultlines, exaggerating tendencies and taking advantage of affordances. But technologies have to be adopted by receptive cultural conditions and ecologies. As to the politics of digital technology, that goes right back to the points I made above, about the way ideology works to conceal its workings.

RS: I agree with your favoring of the epistemological defamiliarization over didactic ambitions; as Adorno states in his essay on commitment and art: "If art is to live on, it must elevate social criticisms to the level of form, de-emphasizing social content accordingly". I would add, with Claire Bishop, that, on the other hand, even self-reflective art – such as the 'cozy situation' of a cooking-performance by Rirkrit Tiravanija – may actually pave the way for (neo-liberalist) affirmation. As for literature based on digital technology, academics have considered the option and need to navigate through a multi-linear hypertext as the replacement of the passive by the "active reader" thus implicitly praising mechanical activity over cerebral. Today electronic books and appropriate apps allow for "social reading": bookmarks and notes can be shared with other readers of the same text and conversation can start immediately. The words used to distinguish the new reading habits from the old claim a positive connotation. What could be wrong with being *interactive* and *social*? Why, our grandchildren may wonder once, would anybody want to withdraw a book from the others instead of sharing the reading experience, as it was common until the 18th Century? There are different ways of looking at the end of the cultural technique of immersive reading. What is your perspective?

JD: The distinction between active and passive reading modes does not depend on technology any more than 'chose your own adventure' type fiction depended on digital media. Torah reading is always active, situated within conversation and discussion.

What is passive about that? The entire experience of the text is based on interpretation in a community. Some reading you want to do on your own. Social reading is useful for some things, but do we have to share everything? Technology that allows multiple readers to access a text simultaneously does not require shared commentary or conversation. As for combinatoric work or stories with variable endings, they were structured into the children's amusements known as *harlequinades* in the 19th century, and written into print based works, such as the exemplary Julio Cortázar work, *Hopscotch*, first published in 1963, twenty years before the wonderful *The Policeman's Beard is Half Constructed* (1984) was written by Racter, a program.

But the question of access is of course different from either interactive reception or combinatoric or hyperlinked composition. The reality that multiple copies of a work can be accessed simultaneously is great, but along with this privilege, we have to be vigilant about not losing the privileges that went with buying books—such as the right to circulate an individual copy after first sale and so on. Uniqueness doesn't always cancel circulation—the *Mona Lisa* exists in a single, unique canvas, but the original has been seen by many more people than most works created as artists' books in the spirit of the so-called "democratic multiple." Of course the whole mechanical reproduction and aura argument is relevant here too. DaVinci's portrait is a mass culture icon through its reproduction.

My point is simply that many claims for works, values, innovation, or advantages turn out to be more complicated—even contradictory—than at first glance. As for immersive reading, it is only one among many modes, but what computational techniques allow are certain processing skills that aggregate and synthesize results from corpora that are too large to go through using traditional reading modes. They point toward the places to do the close reading, as needed. The range of reading experiences may broaden, but reading as an experience remains, for now. Whether the alphabetic code will disappear as the central mode of linguistic transmission (it undergirds the internet) is another question altogether.

Media Literacy

RS: Many observers of digital culture announce the shift from deep attention to hyper attention. The French philosopher Bernard Stiegler even speaks of a threat to social and cultural development caused by the destruction of young people's ability to develop deep and critical attention to the world around them. Is this academic nightmare justified? Or is this just another reiteration of a well-known lamentation about the terrifying ramifications of all new media?

JD: I tend to agree with Bernard Stiegler, though I would add that the single most shocking feature of the way people, young ones in particular, are living their lives is that they have no interior life and no apparent need or use for it. They live entirely social existences, always connected and in an exchange, no matter how banal, about the ongoing events of daily life. Reflection, meditation, imaginative musing, these are all missing, jettisoned, discarded and disregarded. Innovation, change, invention–these have always come from individuals who broke the mold, thought differently, pulled ideas into being in form and expression. Too much sociality leads to dull normativity.

RS: The birth of conventionalism out of the spirit of participation; this is a strong statement that many of the young will not be happy to hear. But lets drive your point even further. My thesis would be: People live entirely social lives for in the age of individualism life is too big to be absorbed alone. In (post)modern society where past and future have become unreliable concepts every moment takes on an intensity that is hard to bear. One lives in the here and now and permanently feels unequipped for an appropriate reaction. Without a rich interior life, without a reflection, meditation, and imaginative musing experiences – be it Venice, Grand Canyon, Da Vinci's *Mona Lisa* or the sudden rainbow – become indigestible bits we don't know what to do with: except posting them. The unquestioned imperative of sharing is the new way to live up to important and trivial moments alike. It forwards the moment experienced to others who will "solve it" with a number of likes. Sharing is a way to mask the horror vacui. If Blaise Pascal once, in the 17th century, stated: "all the unhappiness of men arises from one single fact, that they cannot stay quietly in their own chamber" we may add today: people cannot only not be alone in an empty room they are also unable to cope by themselves with the events they encounter.

JD: Yes, well, there it is. I spend so much of my life alone and solitude is as important to me as water and air, it is the medium in which I breathe, that I am an anomaly. I have a horror of constant contact, of being used up, absorbed, taken out of the being-ness *in* life as lived. I so prefer to watch times of day shift to watching any programmed entertainment. I'm not much of a sharer, though I like real conversation, dialogue, and enjoy consuming the endless spectacle of daily life in its direct and mediated range of poignancies and follies. The horror of the real is the cruelty of the world, of human beings to each other, which is unspeakable. Mediation is the assurance that we are not the suffering ones, because they are the enunciated subjects. Hideous indeed. What glass do we think we are on the other side of? I wonder.

RS: Digital Humanities are a keyword in the current discussion about the present and future of the Humanities. It has many facets and, as the discussion suggests, at least a dark and a bright side. However, there seems to be very different notions of what digital humanities actually are. Some reduce it to digitized corpora or to the use of networks for communication, others include digital media studies. What is your perspective?

JD: I characterize Digital Humanities as work at the intersection of computational methods and the traditional humanities. The production of digitized corpora was and is one of the outcomes of this intersection. My standard line is to say that Digital Humanities is the cook in the kitchen and that Digital Media Studies is the restaurant critic. As far as I am concerned, you have to know how to do things and make things in order to be able to think arguments into being as works in any medium, analogue or digital. I would extend this by noting that much of my work in the last ten years has been part of an overarching argument that humanities *methods* as well as humanities

content—that the humanistic approach to knowledge is fundamentally interpretative, observer-dependent, situated culturally and historically, necessarily partial, constrained by circumstances, tolerant of ambiguity.

This puts my approach at odds with computational techniques and approaches to knowledge that imagine user independent approaches, repeatable results, universal and absolute
objects produced by empirical inquiry. I don't include classroom
technology, online learning, or critical media studies in Digital
Humanities, though these are closely related fields and each is of
value. Digital Humanities has become too obsessed with definition, and is at risk of becoming a service field without intellectual
content or problems. I think Andrew Prescott has pointed this
out as well, asking where are the intellectual contributions of
Digital Humanities now that we are almost two decades into the
field? I keep insisting that until a project in Digital Humanities
has produced work that has to be cited by its home discipline—
American History, Classics, Romantic Poetry, etc.—for its *argument* (not just as a resource)—we cannot claim that DH has really
contributed anything to scholarship.

RS: If you don't include critical media studies in Digital
Humanities, I as a media theorist who considers the critical
discussion of the cultural implications of new technologies as a
central part of media literacy hope there will be room and funding for such digital media studies besides the trendy Digital
Humanities. I am afraid the focus on the making and managing
of information could eventually override the traditional characteristic of humanities to question knowledge. For many graduates in the humanities the promised land meanwhile seems to
be what has been discussed as Alternative Academic Careers
for Humanities Scholars. I have the feeling this direction further promotes the shift from critical media studies to affirmative
media management.

JD: The #AltAc discussion has indeed introduced confusions as
well. In some ways, #AltAc is a sideways step into the work that
librarians and information professionals have done for years. But

it brings the design and development of platforms and project technology in the humanities into the equation. How else would we have tools like Zotero, or Neatline, or Omeka if we didn't have humanist-technologists committed to their development? But suggesting it is an alternative *academic* track sends the wrong message to the public and to administrators—it is a *professional* one, I think. The research done in an #AltAc mode is not discipline specific. The distinction is important because substantive, discipline-specific humanities research needs support. If you are working all year in an admin position, especially if you are also teaching, the research you do may be in platform and tool development but you don't have the time, hours in the day, to become an expert in the Romantic fragment and poetics, or the interpretation of the eco-political impact of the Norman conquest, or the construction of celebrity in 18th century French culture.

They are different kinds of work. I'm happy to work with my colleagues in the Library. They are dedicated professionals, but they are not "alt" anything, they are people whose work is premised on a subject specialization and on expertise in professional areas. These are essential skills. Most #AltAc advocates are not trained information professionals, they are in administrative positions trying to catch up with what MLIS programs teach, while trying to develop humanities-oriented services and platforms. That is a specific kind of research in the professional arena. Either path is consuming. Domain-specific research takes a lifetime of accumulated knowledge and dedication, continued attention to developments in the field, among peers, and it produces new knowledge. It cannot be done around the edges of full-time administrative work. Research into platforms, protocols, data management, design—these are also legitimate, but they belong to the information domain, not the humanities. Creating the impression that humanities research can be done on "one's own time" around the edges of full-time work plays right into the current diminishment of respect for the humanities. This is not in the interest of Digital Humanities or anyone else. We need Digital Humanities professionals, not diminished academics.

RS: Against the 'default position that the humanities are in "crisis",' in the 2012 book *Digital_Humanities* you and your coauthors Anne Burdick, Peter Lunefeld, Todd Presner, and Jeffrey Schnapp portray the computational turn in Humanities as an opportunity of bringing the 'values, representational and interpretative practices, meaning-making strategies, complexities, and ambiguities of being human into every realm of experience and knowledge of the world.' As one of those values, you suggest 'thinking beyond received positions and claims to absolute authority' supporting 'a genuine multiverse in which no single point of view can claim the center.' How do you bring relativism and multi-perspectivism into a world of quantifying methods and algorithmic analysis? What obstacles do you see?

JD: A simple demonstration to show the multiverse is to imagine a faceted interface that allows us to see a collection of artifacts from a variety of perspectives. Consider an online museum displayed through a set of filters that organize and select objects according to different criteria: the knowledge of an original collector, a scheme of standard metadata from a western perspective, in accord with a classification scheme from an indigenous community, and so on. Each structuring organization offers a different argument, different set of hierarchies and values in its presentation. The quantitative or disambiguating underpinnings don't have to determine what happens at the level of display, and the parallax of comparative views into data or organizations structured into data take apart the singularity that is the usual perspective of a monograph. Imagine a view into a spatial representation of Rome—show it to me as Augustus saw it, as Michaelangelo saw it, as Mussolini saw it—think about the spatialization of power and its connection to point of view, daily routines, routes, events. The city stops being a given. It stops being a singularity, and turns into a multiplicity of perspectives, each of which is experiential.

For more than a decade, I've been working on using digital techniques for modelling temporalities, and that work has investigated highly subjective models of experiential time, referential time (from documents), relative time, and other modes that can't be expressed in timelines borrowed from the empirical sciences. Most recently I've been working on the graphical expression of irreconcilable chronologies in the history of writing and the alphabet, particularly in the late 18th century, just on the cusp of geological reckoning with the ages of the world, its formation, and evolution. This is a time when biblical chronologies and Olympiads were the two stable reference systems for any historical event, but historical records and actual chronologies also existed. Prehistory was a mystery, unfathomable, though controversies reigned about whether people existed before Adam. This is half a century before geological discoveries and evolution upset the entire belief system. When you think that within a hundred years, theories of the birth of the universe, big bang, galaxy formation, and the understanding of the millions of years through which the earth and its species formed would all be articulated, it is mind-boggling. So how do we model these knowledge systems, show their distinctions and differences, not as errors, but as rhetorics, as argument structures?

These are tasks well-suited to the mutable conditions of display within a digital environment, I think, though we will have to let go of the attachment to easy, reductive eye-candy that has been the stuff of information visualizations as they have been inherited from the natural sciences and brought into the digital humanities. The intellectual and epistemological problems in using visualizations are many, beginning with a fundamental fallacy about representation—that an image can "be" in a relation of equivalence or identity with that which it claims to represent. Many other fallacies follow from this, but we went through decades of deconstruction and post-structuralism and seem to have forgotten all of the lessons we learned as we (humanists) rush to uncritical engagement with methods from other fields. When you realize that language has many modalities—interrogative and conditional, for instance—but that images are almost always declarative, you begin to see the problems of representation inherent in information visualizations. They are statements, representations (i.e. highly complex constructions and mediations) that offer themselves as presentation (self-evident statements). This is an error of epistemology, not an error of judgment or method.

RS: The unlearning of deconstruction and post-modernism, this is what I meant above when portraying the quantitative turn as the epistemological happy end that overcomes the relativism and ambiguity of postmodernism. As for the difference between language and images you point out, the book also states that Digital Humanities 'necessarily partakes and contributes to the "screen culture" of the 21ST century' – which you already stated in your project *Wittgenstein's Gallery* in which you take qualities specific to images and see how they could work in texts, and vice versa. *Digital_Humanities* admits to the tension between the visual and the textual, but doesn't accept an either/or approach nor the subordination of the one to the other. However, as you just stated it, the visual and the textual are two very different systems of signification and communication. To quote yourself at a symposium on Digital Humanities in Hong Kong in 2014: a word doesn't cast a shadow and an image can't be conjugated. You have extensively worked on the visual of the textual, as it were. How do you see the collaboration of both in this context? What role should visual studies or rather the study of visual communication play in Digital Humanities?

JD: I was at a dinner party this year with a very senior and rightfully esteemed scholar of visuality, an equally senior literary critic, and a younger poet who suggested that images and texts are 'now the same', because they both appeared on the screen display as pixels. I was appalled by the stupidity of this remark. Might as well say that images and texts printed in ink on newsprint are the same order of thing because they are produced in the same medium. Text and image are processed in different parts of our brains and by different means. More than 50% of primate cerebral cortex activity is given to visual experience, and this is dramatic by contrast to that of other animals. What is striking to me is that we do not have a field called visual epistemology, no dedicated discipline.

Visual studies was its own thing, a rejection of art history's hegemonic attachment to high art, an attempt to expand the social and cultural parameters of what was allowed to be looked at and how. But visual studies, perversely, was little concerned with visuality, and very concerned with politics, social practices, economics, ideology and so on. This left visual epistemology undeveloped. We do not have a good language for critical discussion of graphics, or of graphical principles of organization and argument. What, for instance, is the difference between hierarchy and proximity in terms of the creation of meaningful spatialized relationships in graphic design? Huge. But do we teach these principles? Communicate them? And yet, now, in the world of screen-based communication exchange and continual transactions, the need for critical engagement with the workings of graphical form could not be greater. My new book, *Graphesis: Visual Forms of Knowledge Production*, which was just published by Harvard University Press, is an attempt to outline the foundations of a broad-based approach grounded in the history of graphical knowledge and its practice. Sadly (perversely), for a book about visual forms of knowledge, it is badly designed, on poor paper, and dismally printed, with images that are way too small and a layout that has none of the exquisite elegance that Emily McVarish brought to our *Graphic Design History: A Critical Guide*. But so be it. The content of the book, will, I hope still be of some use in the larger conversation.

RS: The poet you meet over dinner should have known better since poetry, though it works with images, does so in language. What he or she should have brought up is that the word in digital culture is in decay, since new technologies more and more shift communication from the linguistic to the visual mode. Take an app such as Snapchat which, through the promised ephemeral character of its images, invites users to document rather than describe. No need to voice how one is doing if one can send a snapshot of sitting in front of the TV legs on the table beer in hand. It is faster and it requires less cognitive effort. The exciting aspect of such form of communication is its increased ambiguity and semantic surplus: It is up to the perceiver what specific aspect of the photograph she responds to with an image that again says more than thousand words and hence leaves it to the perceiver to what of those 'words' she wants to respond. So, if Digital Humanities moves to visual forms of knowledge production this may be the academic equivalent to the development in digital culture.

JD: Absolutely! Hence my call for visual epistemology as an essential and emerging field. In what does knowledge consist when it is encoded in visual, graphical, diagrammatic, schematic, and other forms we process through vision? I do not believe, along with the rest of my other poet friends, that we remediate all visual experience into language. Visuality is a primary mode of perception, representation, mediation, processing, and cognition. For years, every time I went to an art history theory conference, the conversation turned to the question of how to develop a visual mode of criticality—enacted in and through visual means. Look at Robert Frank and the sequencing of the *The Americans*. Juxtaposition is a critical move, one that operates across a divide that prevents closure into singularity. This can happen within an image. Winslow Homer's amazing painting of confederate soldiers as prisoners is a masterwork of juxtaposition and difference operating within visual codes. You never exhaust the looking and comparing and the way the differentiation and specificity of each individual is produced by and across these rifts.

RS: UCLA is one of the rather few universities that has a Digital Humanities center. What is your experience in this center regarding student expectations and faculty collaboration?

JD: Just to be clear, the Center for Digital Humanities does not offer any degrees, graduate or undergraduate, it is a research and teaching support unit, and actually does more of the latter than the former. Our research infrastructure is as fragile as anyone else's, I think. But we did mount an undergraduate minor and a graduate certificate as an interdisciplinary effort across schools and departments. We are thinking about a Master's Degree that would be a stand-alone two-year degree with a subject specialization or a three-year combination with MLIS. This is all fluid, and we may look at other options as well, but we are trying to think about how to best prepare our students for jobs in private and public enterprises, cultural institutions, media and business, academic and non-academic positions.

The needs for data wrangling and production, critical understanding of databases, analysis, visualization, data mining in text and image, mapping, network analysis, and the techniques of digital publishing are all pressing. My goal is to provide students with the skills they need to work in digital, networked environments while also having an understanding of history, theory, culture, and some humanistic discipline in which they have a passion and feel like a stakeholder. If you love something and want it to be valued, understood, passed on to a broad public now and for generations to come, that makes your motivation very different than if you are only trying to perform a task efficiently. The students have been terrific, and they are living evidence of the viability of our approach. In our first group of graduating minors, the reports on how their classes got them jobs, next steps, an edge for graduate school or for work in some governmental, non-governmental, or other sector have been legion. It's been gratifying. We'll have to see how the graduates do, but they are an enthusiastic bunch.

Getting an in-depth specialization in Digital Humanities while learning the general landscape of tools and possibilities is important as well. We need someone who can teach coding. You can do a lot without knowing any Java Script, for instance, but being able to write code is a crucial skill for digital work. I would argue that structured data is the primary feature of digital platforms, and manipulating data comes after that, but knowing how to read code, understand how it works, how its syntax and specialized vocabulary function, provides real insight. I won't swap it for literature, for poetry, or for art, but I will allow that it is its own form of writing, an expression whose rules and features are integral to our culture's operations. But like so many things, I distinguish between having a reading knowledge and a working skills—even if I can read code and understand how it works, I'm not going to get good enough to make it make sense for me to be my own programmer. Life is too short. I drive a car without having built one, use paints without creating my own pigments, print with lead type without have designed a set of punches or cast my own fonts. I think it is important to distinguish between what you need to know and what you need to do individualy, what your skills and strengths are, and where you are in the ecosystem. I'm a better coach and mentor than practitioner in many arts, and that seems appropriate. I can think things that I don't believe others do, and that is my contribution. Contrarian thought. It's my niche.

Reading back through my answers, I realize I sound cranky, critical, and a bit despairing about the state of world and the fate of the humanities. But I actually believe that the only way we can change the course on which we are currently is to engage with those values and methods that are central to humanistic thought and to incorporate the interpretative rhetorics of the humanities into the work we do, not just the analysis of work done. Humanistic methods, with their emphasis on situatedness of knowledge, of the partial and incomplete understanding of the world and its workings, and a commitment to imaginative and speculative thought, may open possibility spaces as yet not manifest within our current sphere of understanding. These are very early days for Digital Humanities, but my hope is that as the future unfolds, it will be the humanistic dimensions that gain more traction in the field—not just as content, but as methods of knowledge, analysis, and argument.

Of Capta, vectoralists, reading and the Googlization of the university

John Cayley

John Cayley is a pioneering practitioner and theorist of digital language arts, a poet and a translator specializing in Chinese poetics. He won the
Electronic Literature Organization's 2001 Award for
Poetry while still in the UK, and is now a Professor
of Literary Arts at Brown University, directing its
MFA program in Digital Language Arts. His work
has explored ambient poetics, writing in immersive
audiovisuality, and aestheticized vectors of reading
(thereadersproject.org), with theoretical essays on
code and temporality in textual practice, and 'writing to be found' with/against proprietary statistical
models of language. *The Listeners* (2015) is a critical
aesthetic engagement with transactive synthetic language, representing a shift in his work toward language art for an aural as much as a visual readership.
For John Cayley's writing in networked and programmable media see programmatology.shadoof.net.

John Cayley positions 'capta' against 'data', reveals vectoralization as algorithmic determination within a new socioeconomic architecture, bemoans the blackmail of 'terms of service' as well as the infantile misunderstanding of what it is to be a social human by Mark Zuckerberg and the serfdom of narcissistic selves to the data-greedy service providers. He underlines the dumbness and deception of statistics and algorithmic agency, wonders when the vectoralist class of big software will, eventually, be 'too big to fail,' speculates about unrealized artworks with Google Translate, rejects "social reading" and fears Digital Humanities.

Prelude

Roberto Simanowski: What is your favored neologism of digital media culture and why?

John Cayley: I don't seem to have a favorite that comes to mind although 'codework' and 'codebending' surfaced as I mused. These are terms for new and hybrid practices that require lexical focus as we strive to understand or reimagine them. Years ago I suggested that 'programmaton' should replace 'computer' in English. This did not catch on. New words must become good words, otherwise they will not survive.

RS: If you could go back in history of new media and digital culture in order to prevent something from happening or somebody from doing something, what or who would it be?

JC: I would certainly have done what I could to prevent the rise of proprietary, (so-called) social media. I would try to isolate and prevent certain mechanisms that log and accumulate and process the transactions of human beings such that their social and transactional identities are constrained by capta-driven computational processes in the service, primarily, of commerce.

RS: Capta-Driven? You refer to Johanna Drucker's differentiation between given and taken data?

JC: My use of capta does come, in the first instance, from Drucker's reintroduction of the term. I've commented on my use of it in an essay.[1] 'Data' has become a very common term. It's been prevalent for decades, especially since the advent of the database, as indicating, I suppose, the raw material of research. I think that there should be more of a debate about what is and is not data. Etymologically, data means 'that which is *given*' as evidence of the world. However, the tools we use to take what the world gives may overdetermine the material evidence that we are able to gather. Arguably, the computational regime is overdetermined in a number of respects. It can only accept and process—as putative data—those things that can be represented in terms of discrete symbolic elements. It will tend to favor the quantitive accumulation and analysis of these things, this so-called 'data.' Drucker makes the same sort of argument and following her, I prefer to use capta, for what has been 'taken,' when referring to the raw material collected and processed by networked services or indeed by the regime of computation in general. In her article, Drucker suggests that the conventional and uncritical use of 'data' implies a "fundamental prejudice" subjecting humanistic interpretation to relatively naive statisti-cal applications, and skewing the game "in favor of a belief that data is intrinsically quantitative—self-evident, value neutral, and observer-independent."[2] If we call what we collect and analyze 'capta' rather than 'data' then at least we signal our awareness of the likely prejudice and open a door that allows critical interpre-tation to reinvigorate our debates and concerns. The distinction is fundamentally important and it is remarkable to consider that this seems to be the first time that it has been clarified for the era of Digital Humanities.

RS: So the term 'capta' indicates that digital data or rather all data is not just given, raw, unprocessed material, but material taken from somewhere within a specific method and frame-work. Surprising and alarming if the Humanities should not be aware of this issue after all the debates in their disciplines about whether or not there are facts before interpretation. We will return to Digital Humanities. First let me ask this: If you were a minister of education, what would you do about media literacy?

JC: I would ensure that the media infrastructure of educational institutions was commensurate with the most advanced, proven media infrastructures deployed by major corporations in the technology sector. I would seek to introduce legislation that required corporations to supply digital media infrastructure to educational institutions as a condition of their continued operation.

Politics and Government

RS: While in the 1990s Internet pioneers such as John Perry Barlow declared the independence of Cyberspace from the governments of the old world, now it seems people hope for governments to intervene in the taking-over and commercialization of the Internet by huge corporations such as Google and Facebook. Thus, web activists calling for the government to pass laws to protect privacy online, and politicians suggesting expiration dates for data on social networks appear to be activist in a battle for the rights of the individual. Have tables turned to that extent? Are we, once rejecting old government, now appealing to it for help?

JC: When exactly did we, collectively, reject old government? I do not think it is a matter of turning back. Governments have continued to exist as complex conglomerations of institutions to which we consent—more or less, and *pace* all manner of negotiation and struggle—in the matter of the administration and regulation of our sociopolitical lives. The world of the network has seen the rise of new and alternative institutions. These emerged and are now powerful in, as you say, an environment that was surprisingly unregulated. New institutions now affect and corral and enclose (vectoralize, in Mackenzie Wark's terms) significant aspects of our lives as humans, for huge marginal profit. They have done this unwittingly and irresponsibly with our unwitting and irresponsible consent—*default* consent to their 'terms of service.' Our past institutions of value-preservation and governance were equally unwitting and irresponsible in this process. What happens now is that we pause, take stock, and try to see more clearly how the institutions of the past and those of the future might interrelate more responsibly and help to redefine, as individuals and societies, what we believe that we want to be and do and own. Otherwise, we will simply become, by unregulated, data-driven, statistical *force majeure*, what the algorithms of the new institutions determine that we want.

RS: You refer to Mackenzie Wark's notion of vectoralists in his *A Hacker Manifesto.* Can you say more concerning your perspective on the relationship between vectoralization, algorithm and capta?

JC: Mackenzie Wark proposes that, historically, there is a new productive and at least potentially progressive class of hackers, and a new corresponding exploitative class: the vectoralists. I find his proposals useful. Briefly, and with apologies to Wark, the hackers compose/produce algorithms that reveal vectors: vectoral potentials in the swelling currents of informational, data=capta transactions. Hackers may maintain an agnostic position concerning the significance or value of the data=capta that their algorithms bring into new relations with human order or, for that matter, human disorder. However the vectoralists of 'big software' discover where and how to exploit certain, profitable vectors of attention and transaction, and then acquire control over both these vectors themselves and the productive labor of those hackers that create them. They build these algorithms into a new socioeconomic architecture, which I now call big software. They own this architecture and profit from the use of the services it provides. They seek to enclose the commons of digital transactions within their architectures and systems, the vectors of which they carefully control.

As I say, the hackers are, in principle, agnostic about data=capta. If data=capta better represented what is given by the world, they would continue to hack with this better material. Vectoralists care even less about whether they are dealing with data or capta because their motivation is simply to seek profit from whatever transactions have been vectoralized. As a function of recent historical and technological developments, there is simply so much capta now and for the time being, that we are likely to be held within its artificial, computational biases for many years, perhaps until it is too late for us either to reject the representation of our transactional lives by capta, or to insist that computation comes to grip with some of the true data that we should be able to give, or to withhold.

RS: It is interesting that vectorialists such as Google side with web activists opposing the government's attempts to constrain the free use of data online on behalf of intellectual property rights as seen from SOPA, PIPA, and ACTA. It appears to be the case that never before has a new medium generated such ambivalent responses to central issues of law and rights—their enforcement and preservation, the potential for freedom and radical change.

JC: It is not necessarily ambivalence or contradiction that characterizes the responses of activists and critics. For example, since it is raised here, existing custom and law associated with intellectual property is irremediably flawed and quite unable to comprehend or regulate a significant proportion of digitally mediated transactional and cultural practices. More and more of these practices—the writing and reading that is conventionally regulated by copyright law—are so much altered by digital mediation and digital affordances that our fundamental expectations and potentialities are changed beyond easy recognition and beyond assimilation by existing custom and law. Moreover, our creative and discursive practices are now inextricably intertwined with their network mediation—the internet and its services—and so the questions and conflicts—those of adversarial law—surrounding institutions of copyright and intellectual property have shifted from who creates and owns what, to who controls the most privileged and profitable tools for creation and who controls the most privileged and profitable means of dissemination.

RS: This shift is, I think, very well illustrated by Google when it advocates the liberty of information against newspapers that demand some payment for using their lead paragraph in news. google. The newspapers have a point—since here the profit goes to whoever disseminates the content that others provide—but they have no chance if they want to be listed by Google. Which brings me to the next question. In his book *The Googlization of Everything (And Why We Should Worry)*, Siva Vaidhyanathan speaks of Google's 'infrastructural imperialism' and calls for the public initiative of a 'Human Knowledge Project' as 'global information ecosystem.' Aware of the utopian nature of his vision, Vaidhyanathan adds that Google has been crowding out imagination of alternatives, not the least of which by its reputation for building systems that are open and customizable – so far. Should we mistrust the positive record and worry? Would the U.S. government or the European Union ever have been able to carry out something like Google's book project? Should –and could– they run a search engine free of advertisement and with an algorithm visible to all who care?

JC: Given the variety and scope and general applicability of network services such as Google's, Amazon's, Facebook's, it is, frankly shocking that existing national and international institutions—those traditionally engaged with all the activities that we consider most valuable and essential to human life, such as research, knowledge production, education, governance, social interaction, the planning and organization of everyday life, reading and writing, retail logistics—have not been able to effectively resist or, perhaps, co-opt or even, effectively, tax in kind (for a more equitable redistribution of cultural benefits) the activities of the new vectoralist institutions. Why shouldn't governments get themselves involved on our behalf? Probably for the same reason that governments can no longer control their banks and can no longer make their banks work for their citizens. Perhaps the vectoralist corporations are now also—culturally—'too big to fail?'

What is clear is that inequalities in the distribution of power over the vectors of transaction and attention—commercial but especially cultural—are simply too great. This power was acquired far too quickly by naive and untried corporate entities that still appear sometimes to be naive and untried, although they are perhaps now simply brazen and unregulated. This power is consolidated by agreements—literal, habitual, and all-but-unconsidered by the network 'users,' ourselves, who enter into them—to 'terms of service' that are not mutual and which will only reinforce and increase the disparities between 'server' and 'client.' And this power is consolidated by the inadequacies of existing custom and law since huge marginal profit has allowed the new corporations to acquire, on a grand scale, conventionally licensed intellectual property along, inevitably, with the interest and means to conserve this property through existing—and in my opinion, inappropriate—legal mechanisms, mechanisms that are incommensurate with the culture and commerce of networks, clouds, big data, big software.

RS: As for another vectoralist corporation: What comes to mind when you hear the name Mark Zuckerberg?

JC: A shy, but arrogant and infantile misunderstanding of what it is to be a social human. A consent to mechanistic services that are dedicated to simplistic conceptions of humanity while arrogantly extending these conceptions to every possible human engagement with privacy, self-expression, desire, and so forth. Complete denial of the fact that proprietary social media is fundamentally the theft and enclosure of transactional personal information. Complete denial of lived experience, even in terms of empirical data, and instead the substitution of an implicit claim that what social media collects as so-called 'data' reveals the world as it is or should be; whereas social media conceals, more effectively than ever and from more people than ever, how the world—as power and profit and violence—actually is. Shock, that such a sad individual has been recast as a commercial and sometime (im)moral exemplar.

Algorithm and Censorship

RS: To move from the person to the platform: The focus on numbers of views, likes, comments in social media and many other websites indicates the quantitative turn that our society takes. The desired effect of counting is comparison and ranking, i.e. the end of postmodern ambiguity and relativism. Does the trust in numbers in digital media bring about the technological solution to a philosophical problem? A Hollywood-like shift from the melancholia of the end of grand narratives and truth to the excitement of who or what wins the competition?

JC: Remember those postwar decades—a period taking us up into at least the mid 1990s—when there was a widely prevalent popular suspicion of statistics? Especially of both government-gathered and marketing statistics? How could (dumb) statistics ever reflect the richness and nuance of human life? But now we have big data, and analytics, and these will allow self-professed 'IBM'ers' (apparently personable, active individuals of a certain vision) to 'build a smarter planet.' In fact, all we really have is more statistics: several orders of magnitude more statistics. 'Data' is a misnomer. Philosophically and also in terms of empirical science per se, 'data' should be understood as what is given to us by our (full, phenomenological or empirical) experience of the world. However the records of big data are simply records of (see above) capta, the captured and abducted records of transactions with—merely—that portion of human life that is capable of being assimilated by the current regime of computation: no more, no less, and certainly not enough to express the fullness of what we are.

In what follows, I'm sort of adapting and paraphrasing from the essay I've cited above. The ability to store, digitally, and analyze, algorithmically, overwhelming quantities of data has rendered it 'big' in combination with the near ubiquity of portable and mobile devices, fully networked and capable of collecting, transmitting, and so allowing the aggregation of both data and meta-data gathered from an ever-increasing proportion of human movements and actions: from transactional, communicative exchanges of all kinds. These may be representations of any-thing—from the highly significant and valuable (finance, trade, marketing, politics, ...) to the everyday and commonplace (social-izing, shopping, fooling around ...). Personal analysis of all but a minuscule part of this data would be humanly impossible and so, at the cost of commensurate, individual human attention, algorithmic agencies promise to predict trends and visualize patterns from what has been collected with unprecedented sta-tistical accuracy and previously inconceivable power. The ques-tion of what this data represents—what exactly it gives us of the world—remains little-examined. Because the cost of collection is so low and because the methods of collection are now inciden-tal and habitual, the tangentially-related profits—derived chiefly from the reconfiguration of advertising—are massive, and far from exhausted.

It is not only that we seem to have given ourselves and our (self-)evaluation over to 'counting' but we are refusing, any lon-ger (as we once, arguably, did) to acknowledge that the motiva-tion for this is not our common or collective benefit, whatever the service providers may claim.

RS: Your answer clearly indicates your skepticism and even anger at the role statistics and big data play in current society. Such is the appeal of numbers that the expression "data love" has been coined to describe society's immature infatuation with digitization and datafication. In the end, this love is narcissistic. Given the fact that Internet companies use data and algorithms to customize the website they show us, the ads they send us, and the information they give us, one metaphor to describe the digi-tal media age may be narcissism. In digital media studies such customization is translated to "daily me" (in Cass Sunstein's book *Republic.com*) or "you-loop" (in Eli Pariser's *Filter Bubble*). The fate of Narcissus is well known. The personal and cultural cost of personalization in digital media is the loss of chance encoun-ters, the preclusion of the unfamiliar, the removal of diversity and of what we are not (yet). The algorithm is, you just pointed it out, the censor people more or less approve of and even desire.

This becomes problematic once people are addressed not as consumers but as citizens expected to be open to others instead of cocooning in their bubble. Hence, personalization, driven by economic force, is political. Are, hence, the actual policy makers in the digital media age those who program ego-loops, inadvertently undermining the foundation of a democratic society? Or is the alert regarding personalization hyperbolic and rather the clandestine update and comeback of the claim of critical theory that cultural industry impedes citizens' release from their self-incurred tutelage?

JC: The apparatus into which we stare is something far worse – in terms of psycho(social)analytic structures shall we say – than the pools or mirrors of Narcissus. We are in the grips of what Talan Memmott calls the narcissystem, a syndrome he creatively delineated long before a billion of us began to do so much more than simply gaze longingly at our reflections. The pool and the mirror have the benefit of a certain objectivity: they reflect only what they see. The waves of reflective feedback into which we gaze now are waves of images that we construct ourselves.

In the early history of the internet the fashion was to project ourselves as the kind of hopeful, fictive, 'transitional' monsters that theorists such as Sherry Turkle once tried to convince us were pyschosocially or even politically progressive. Cyberutopianism reckoned without the unconscious, and more specifically without the blind and venal desire that drive majorities, as many as a billion willing persons. In our current situation, questionably progressive experimentation – for which read monstrous, hopeful self-delusion – has given way to a mass acquiescence: a cyber(pseudo)activism that 'logs in' – agreeing to terms – as its no longer over-hopeful, transactionally authenticated self and then strains to construct a plausible, attractive, *like*able image which it can gaze upon and consider together with all its other equally – if marginally distinctive – *like*able (friendly) selves. The newness of this situation is merely the *accessibility* of the (big) 'data' of self-(re)presentation. This appears to be accessible to all, and so it is – so long as 'access' means the reflective feedback of narcissistically lovable, *like*able self-image(s), as naively shared imaginaries.

However the fact that *effective* access to the data – its aggregation for the manipulation and delivery of attention (to advertisement) and (instant commercial) transaction – is in the hands of a small number of private corporations, demonstrates that a familiar systemic mass neurosis – the narcissism here and now stimulating this response – is in thrall, in service, in serfdom to the service providers: the vectoralist class of big software. If the 'culture industry' was a set of negotiable institutions, sometimes subject to the critique of critical theory, then the more pressing threat - for us currently - is the media-driven, default predominance of network systems, pandering to mass psychology in a post-natural, unholy alliance.

RS: From this speech and from your more academic writings such as 'Terms of Reference & Vectoralist Transgressions" I take it that you consider search engines, for example, to be an aspect of social media.

JC: Any reply hinges on an understanding of 'social media.' This term is currently applied to network services that allow digitized (and thus prejudicially grammatized) transactions that are, without question, nonetheless within the purview of social human interactions. But to claim that these media are in any way definitive or constitutive of (all) human social experience is, clearly, a profound misdirection, one that the popularity of the term tends to encourage. Networked media are used for social transactions but they co-opt social activity and engagement selectively, according to the development of technological affordances and, now also according to the (specific moral and explicitly commercial) motivations of the service providers (their leaders and executives).

If our understanding of 'social media' includes network services that seek to capture the data of social interaction and reflect it back to human users, then, yes: Google has always been 'social media.' From the moment Google collected the data implicit in search terms that had been entered over time and adjusted its services accordingly, it was 'social media.' If we reserve 'social media' for those services that seek to identify and normalize human social agents and then capture the data from those transactions that they subsequently choose to mediate via the services in question, then Google still qualifies, but does so from the moment that it required or suggested or presupposed (note that it does now often presuppose coherent human identity without any need for explicit login) its services as subsequent to the login or identification of a human agent engaged with its services. This I date, loosely, from the introduction of Gmail in 2004 and, at least since the advent of Google+, a constrained, digitized and computationally implicated enclosure of the 'social' – as in the generally understood sense of 'social media' – is quite clearly inalienable to Google and all of its networked services, including and perhaps especially search, since search is such a vitally important aspect of network interaction.

RS: To go even further in evaluating Google's net-service, Google—and other search engines, although Google is the predominant exemplar—is accused of manipulating the way that the Internet is presented to us by way of its PageRank. The objection is twofold: on the one hand, one may question the ranking's statistical and algorithmic foundations, i.e the popularity and accessibility of a searched phrase is likely to be ranked above its complexity or intellectual challenge. This objection, one may say, does not so much address any pitfalls of Google's process as those of democracy itself where everybody has an equal say regardless of her intellectual or political resources. On the other hand, one wonders to what extent Google really does follow a questionable paradigm of "datocracy". Although, the actual criteria of Google's ranking are unknown, we do know from Google Instant Search results that a pure law of numbers is being submitted to some degree of censorship. To give an example: While it is certainly believable that 'amazon' pops up if we type an 'a,' we might be surprise to be offered 'porsche' and 'portugal' for 'por.' Does Google modify the way the Internet looks to give us a more moral view of how it represents us to ourselves?

JC: The simple answer to this question is: yes. You state the position quite clearly and the evidence is available to all of us. Our problem is the characterization of the new institutions – and of Google as exemplary of vectoralist big software. These institutions do what others preceding them have always done. They respond to human needs and desires and propose how best (and most profitably) these might be accommodated in terms of persistent sociopolitical and socioeconomic practices – precisely: institutions. The problem is the unprecedented accumulation of cultural as well as economic power in institutions that are: young, and proprietary, and, as a function of the latter condition, *enclosed* – black boxes to the vast majority of their 'users.' Our problem is the relatively unexamined properties and methods of these institutions. They are new and they are doing much that is new and much that is, apparently: beneficial, interesting, exciting. But this is no excuse, no reason for us not to give these new policy makers serious (re)consideration, before, that is ... they are 'too big to fail.'

RS: More on Google: What about its "shared endorsement" proposal to deploy user ratings and photos in ads to make advertisement more social.

JC: Again, in my 'Terms of Reference', I discuss, as highly problematic, what I see as the appropriation of material *that is proper to human users* and its automatic, algorithmic incorporation into advertisement. Habitual and unthinking agreement as to 'terms of use' or 'terms of service' are what make this possible. However, I do not believe that human users, yet, have any real understanding of what they are handing over and giving up. "Shared endorsement" is simply a euphemistic gloss for what is going on, for what has been going on ever since search results and webmail pages began to show us advertisements that are composed, in real time, from the actual words – material that belongs to us, in a real sense – that we have used to form a search or to write an email. The way that language is inscribed in computation – such that is it is immediately assimilable in terms of discrete lexical symbols and thus immediately subject to algorithm – also makes this easily possible for big software. But I see this, literally, as the theft of something that is proper to myself, and its appropriation, by regular processes (not even by other humans, directly) into advertising of which I am very likely to disapprove and which may actually offend me. "… This is material / Appropriation of cultural interiority to venal desire, / Wrongly subjecting and reforming you-and-I / Within a false enclosure of precisely that which / Should never be enclosed: the openness of all / That we inscribe."[3] As Google and the other social network services move on to *algorithmically* appropriate our images and our opinions for their revenue-generating advertisers, I hope that there may be a greater outcry and a better awareness of what is happening. Oddly, ordinary humans seem to be far more sensitive to the robot-theft of their "image" as compared to any robot-theft of their words.

RS: To come back to the other vectoralist corporation that portraits itself as a neo-moralist institution, Facebook declares the sharing of as much personal information as possible as the precondition for a better world. In October 2013 Facebook made headlines by allowing teenagers to share content not only with friends and friends of their friends but everybody on Facebook. While Facebook Inc. explains this move as giving teenagers – and especially the socially active among them such as musicians and humanitarian activists– the same access to the broader audience that they have on blogs and Twitter, we all know that it first and foremost allows the aggregators and advertisers access to impressionable young consumers. The economic interests behind this data worship are undoubted and certainly need to be addressed – as you do, pointing to the collection of commercial transactions and data aggregation. However, the question remains as to why younger generations don't seem to care about privacy but establish, using Facebook millionfold day-to-day, radical transparency as the new foundation of our culture. Siva Vaidhyanathans, in a talk at Stanford University (on May 16, 2011) about his book *The Googlization of Everything (And Why We Should Worry)*, calls for a "dignity movement" that needs to address that having a certain level of anonymity and "breathing room" is part of both being human and being social. Would such movement be more than the helpless response of digital immigrants to their kids and grandchildren whose data-exhibitionism only carries their own public display of affection since the sexual revolution of the 1960s in a paradoxical way to the extreme?

JC: As already indicated above, when we debate these issues—privacy, personal secrecy, the contrary socialized 'openness' that networked media provide for activities that we previously considered to be difficult or dangerous or undesirable to communicate—we are not doing so in the abstract, or in a true public, or in a genuine agora, where access to the events and effects (the capta or data) is equally distributed or is distributed according to locality and local custom as defined by the affordances of the human body, prosthetically enhanced or otherwise. The events and effects of the so-called sexual revolution were accessible to its participants and to those reporting on behalf of broadcast, one-to-many media. Behaviors altered; times changed; opinions changed; markets, politics, and culture evolved in response. The behaviors and opinions, events and effects, as generated by authenticated individuals within Facebook's network make all of these events and effects—in their digitally inscribed form as big data—immediately accessible to a system of aggregation and analysis that is now explicitly geared to the service of a commercially implicated mission. If I am open about a behavior, or desire, or opinion, that is one problem for me; if this data is immediately and automatically appropriated, that is another problem, but it is more of a problem for society than it is for me. I have already made the moral effort to be open. Perhaps I feel I have done something good or at least true. Why should I go on to worry that what I have done might be bad for others. It is surely bad for all of us that only Facebook and one or two other huge corporations 'know' statistically and immediately what appears—commercially? politically? psychosexually?—to be 'best' for all of us.

Art and Aesthetics

RS: Nobody today speaks of digital art. Does this mean that digital art has ceased to exist or does it mean all art is digital?

JC: Except in the special case of what might be called computational art or computational aesthetics, the digital is not media specific. In other words, digitization and digitally enhanced—programmable, networked—media can be and are applied to any traditional or new medium; and broadly across all artistic practices. The tendency, over time, has been to discover that a huge proportion of contemporary practices rely on digital media. So yes: it's effectively all digital. Then let's just call it art. I recently redesignated the rubric under which I work within a university Department of Literary Arts (Creative Writing). I now work in Digital Language Arts. 'Digital' conveys a strategic emphasis: the academy still needs to promote an engagement with digital media. However the arts that we practice are arts of language, *basta*. Some of us, but not all, do also practice electronic literature proper which, following the analogy of electronic music, entangles literature with computation and with a large measure of technicity.

RS: People have said that art in or of digital media must be political even if its intentions are to be utterly formalistic. If art is based on technology the focus on form draws attention to how technology works and this is already an act of reflection or education. From this perspective, one would assume that digital or electronic literature is literature that addresses the politics of digital technology. In your work, you are making use of digital technology in various ways. How political is your aesthetic use of technology?

JC: At an earlier point in my life and career as a digital language artist I often characterized myself, unapologetically, as a poetic formalist. In poetic practice, at this time (before the turn of the millennium), there did not seem to me to be sufficient formalist engagement and so I was content to pursue this variety of aesthetic practice because I preferred it and, in a sense—somewhat pretentiously—as a corrective. Is this political? I am still concerned that artists engaged with language as their medium should have a better understanding of this medium as such, and I do not think that this is an easy study when language is at issue. Does this incline me to formalism?

The rise of digital media is historical, unprecedented. But it is difficult to say exactly what about the digital is specific and unalloyed with other historical developments. Recently, I have begun to think that, in the era since the war, following on the development and proliferation of stored-program Turing machines, humanity has been, historically, presented with a whole new domain of symbolic practice, precisely that of programmable and networked media (my own long-standing phrase for what others have called 'new' or 'digital media'). Events and effects in this new domain are changing, fundamentally, what we are and how we act. Those of us who began, early on, historically, to work in this domain did have the opportunity to produce work that may already have had important sociopolitical and socioeconomic consequences. To have been a digital practitioner is, at the least, to have been politically active, but we do not yet understand the consequences of, especially, our earlier actions, or, for that matter, our present engagements. I would hope that my other answers, above, to your earlier questions demonstrate that I have—quite recently—discovered a number of ways in which my present work is highly political.

RS: They certainly do; and your work together with Daniel Howe *How It Is in Common Tongues*[4] is an exciting example of a formalistic and political approach: It assembles Beckett's *How It Is* by searching online for the longest possible phrases from the Beckett text in contexts that are *not* associated with Beckett. Using the mechanisms of search engines in order to find the words of an authorized text where they are still, if only momentarily, associating freely the work addresses questions of ownership and copyright. An example also of how Google changes writing and turns, as a means of art, into a subject of political consideration. *How It Is in Common Tongues* is a work that obviously addresses some of the issues you raised above such as vectoralization and capta. Apart from the work you have done, what art project would you like to have initiated, if you could go back in time?

JC: I would have chosen or composed, carefully, a short literary text in English and a somehow corresponding short literary text in French. I would then have offered these texts, every week or fortnight or month to Google Translate, from its inception, and faithfully recorded and time-stamped the results. I am undertaking a similar exercise with Apple's Siri. When I remember, I dictate, alternately, one of two idiomatic English text messages to Siri every week. The results are interesting and I may publish them one day. Are either of these aesthetic projects? I believe that my lost opportunity (as opposed to the texts for Siri) would be far more amenable to aestheticization.

RS: The marriage of literature and digital media goes back to offline hyperfiction written in Storyspace and sold on floppy disc allowing the reader to navigate on her own behalf within the links offered. Some academics considered this trace of interaction as the replacement of the passive by the "active reader" thus implicitly praising mechanical activity over cerebral. Today electronic books and appropriate apps allow for "social reading": bookmarks and notes can be shared with other readers of the same text and conversation can start immediately. The words used to distinguish the new reading habits from the old claim a positive connotation. What could be wrong with being interactive and social? Why, our grandchildren may wonder once, would anybody want to withdraw with a book from the others instead of sharing the reading experience, as it was common until the 18th Century? There are different ways of looking at the end of the cultural technique of immersive reading. What is your perspective?

JC: I now read a great many ebooks (traditional texts transcribed for tablets). As soon as I can, I turn off their few and feeble 'media-progressive' affordances. I do not want to know how many of you underlined what. I do not want you to know what I underline. I do not want to 'interact' (i.e. transact) with any of you. I would not, in any case, be interacting with you. We would all, chiefly, collectively, if we agreed to do so, be offering some data=capta concerning our thoughts and opinions to the aggregators and vectoralists. Something inside me knows this. I turn off all the 'interactive' and 'social' functionalities. I read and drink my wine and muse. When I am courageous enough, I interact with people whom I know, and I imagine making things, even things in programmable media, that are beautiful, including in terms of the new ways that they interrelate—symbolically, linguistically.

Media Literacy

RS: Many observers of digital culture announce and bemoan the shift from deep attention to hyper attention. Is the concern justified? Or does it just reiterate a well-known lamentation for the terrifying ramifications of all new media?

JC: There is no longer any doubt in my mind that the rise and proliferation of networked and programmable media has driven unprecedented and historical changes in the properties and methods of knowledge, knowledge production, and the archive. Access to books and works of reference will never be the same. The Library is becoming a collection of Data- or Knowledge Bases. Libraries and Archives are increasingly interlinked and open—even if the new institutions that provide this linking and openness are untried, unregulated and, themselves, closed. If reading can be understood as the set of widely various cultural practices that allow human beings to process symbolic—especially natural-language—inscriptions and performances, then reading must now be a very different set of such culture practices. Reading has changed. If reading has changed then the human subject has changed.

RS: Changed for the better or for the worse?

JC: It is a more difficult proposition to ascribe a value judgment to these changes. However, in so far as they are driven, predominantly, by forces whose motivation is not directly and intimately associated with the human experience of and engagement with knowledge production—with art and learning—then there is the possibility that the momentum of human culture as a whole is in the process of shifting, significantly if not radically, away from an inclination that more was aligned with, for example, "deep and critical attention to the world." My answers above contribute to this commentary, honing its dystopian melancholy. I do *not* believe, by the way, that a mission "to organize the world's information and make it universally accessible and useful" is in any way necessarily allied with a project of knowledge production and learning or artistic practice and endeavor.

RS: Part of this dystopian melancholy is probably the lack of the right decisions at the right time during the career of digital media. Before the Internet became available for private and commercial use it was administered by the university. Today one has the impression the university is no longer on top of development in this domain. How should academic institutions have responded to the upheaval of new media? How should they become more involved today?

JC: Universities must integrate digital infrastructure—including all the latest affordances of networked and programmable media—with academic infrastructure. They must build this infrastructure into their own institutions and ensure that it is governed by their academic mission and also that their academic missions are responsive to the integral digital infrastructure that they will have created. In concrete terms: universities should cease to have staff-only 'computing' or 'information technology' departments that are in any way considered to be (ancillary) 'services.' Instead they should recast these services as academic infrastructure and fold their governance into the same organizational structures that manage their faculties' teaching and research. Otherwise—and we already see this happening everywhere, not only in the terrible rise of the MOOC—differently motivated services outside the institutions of higher education will first offer themselves to universities and then, quite simply, fold their academic missions and identities into vectoral-ist network services.

Digital mediation is historically unprecedented in this respect at least: it presents itself as service or facility but it quickly goes on to establish itself as essential infrastructure. Because of this, it becomes remarkably determinative of practice and ideology while continuing to be managed and developed *as if* it was still a service. As a matter of fact, digital services are provided as free or low-cost commercial services. As such, they appear to be optional or elective although by now, surely, they have the same status as utilities in the developed world. Cutting off internet provision is like cutting off electricity or gas. The same syndrome plays out in the relationship between a univer-sity's management of its 'computing services' on the one hand and its academic and intellectual mission on the other. Before an institution like a university fully realizes and internalizes the fact that practices demanding of digital infrastructure will be constitutive of its academic mission, its computing services are willingly swallowed up by more 'cost-effective' and more inno-vative services provided from *outside* the institution. These, as infrastructure, may then go on to reconstitute the institution itself. 'Google' swallows computing services at precisely the his-torical moment when digital practices swallow knowledge cre-ation and dissemination. Hence 'Google' swallows the university, the library, the publisher.

RS: This prospect is darker than dystopian melancholia. And it may not yet be the end of these processes of ingestion. Think of the Googlization – not only regarding who controls the data but also how they are accessed and processed – of the Humanities, i.e. think of Digital Humanities. Some of us fear the same quan-titative turn in the Digital Humanities reinforcing what is tak-ing place in contemporary society, and finally infecting even those disciplines that are supposed to reflect and interpret society's development, turning Humanities into a sub-branch of Science. Others hold that "algorithmic criticism" doesn't aim at verifying and stabilizing meaning through the replacement of interpretation by counting. On the contrary, "algorithmic criticism" and "distant reading" may offer new insights in the way knowledge or data respectively is organized and open up new opportunities for close reading and interpretation. What do you fear or hope from Digital Humanities and how do you see their relationship to Digital Media Studies?

JC: See our discussion of art above. Drop the 'digital' from 'Digital Humanities.' But, by all means, do use every digital and networked instrument and affordance to further any kind of research that could be seen as a contribution to the project of the Humanities as such. If insights and statements can be made on the back of algorithmic criticism or distant reading, they are no less insights and statements for all that—provided the methodologies are sound.

When the cart drags the horse, when digital instruments are valued for 'seeing' only what and whatever they happen to 'see,' then we do have a problem, the problem of capta. I recall attending a fascinating conference presentation of 'distant reading,' in the course of which we were offered visualizations based on 'data' from Amazon's recommendation engine as if this was untainted, empirical evidence for some aspect of the sociology of literature. Amazon's engine is a complex system of software processes, transacting in a limited and continually changing manner with human readers of literature. Not only is it complex, the details of its operations are secret, proprietary, and, clearly, commercially directed. To suggest that we should consider data records generated by this complex system as unqualified evidence of the human culture of reading: this is fundamentally flawed scholarship. The strange circumstance is that we do not—yet—seem to perceive it as such: as flawed and requiring qualification. The conference paper was very well received. We seem to believe that systems like Amazon's are already a part of the given, empirical world. On the contrary, software may have become 'big' but the whole point of software is surely that we can change it to an extent that we cannot change many other material conditions of our world. None of us should treat it as given; most especially and emphatically not Digital Humanists.

RS: At the end of his 2011 book *Reading Machines. Toward an alorithmic criticism*, Stephen Ramsay states: 'algorithmic criticism looks forward not to the widespread acknowledgement of its utility but to the day when „algorithmic criticism" seems as odd term as „library based criticism." For by then we will have understood computer based criticism to be what it has always been: human-based criticism with computers'. It is telling and frightening that even a critic of the quantitative turn in the Humanities fails to see the difference between a library and an algorithm, the first being a location presenting books as such; the second being a method that presents a statistical reading of books. If even critical observers are blind to the medium and its message, how optimistic shall we be?

JC: I agree with you and I have the fear. The library is an institution that we have built and worked both within and against over time. Algorithms are also, at least initially, composed and created by human beings, but they proliferate and change very quickly in response to many kinds of human and, perhaps, their own, 'needs' and 'desires,' without anything like the same inculturated understanding of history—of the library, for example. Moreover, algorithms can be owned and controlled by, essentially, corporations that are privately, commercially motivated, driven by vectors and vectoralists who may not share our values, whoever we may be or may desire to become.

Notes

1. Cayley, John. 'Terms of Reference & Vectoralist Transgressions: Situating Certain Literary Transactions over Networked Services.' *Amodern 2* (2013): <http://amodern.net>

2. See Johanna Drucker, 'Humanities Approaches to Graphical Display,' *Digital Humanities Quarterly* 5.1 (2011), online: (?).

3. Cayley, John. 'Pentameters toward the Dissolution of Certain *Vectoralist* Relations.' *Amodern* 2 (2013): <http://amodern.net>.

4. http://elmcip.net/node/5194

Mediascape, antropotechnics, culture of presence, and the flight from God

Erick Felinto

Erick Felinto is a professor for media theory at the State University of Rio de Janeiro and author of several books and articles on cyberculture, media theory and cinema. He was actively involved in the production of the Flusseriana (a dictionary of Vilém Flusser's concepts, edited and published by the ZKM and the University of the Arts, Berlin), as a collaborator and translator and is currently working on a book on the notion of 'Philosophical Fiction' in Vilém Flusser. He is the organizer of the conference series *The Secret Life of Objects* which explores the transformation within the Humanities and the ecology of media.

Erick Felinto addresses the growing digital illiteracy compared to times before graphical user interface and calls, with Vilém Flusser, the hacker the actual educational ideal of our time. He discusses the enthusiasm and misconceptions in early net culture discourse, sees 'speculative futurism' and 'theoretical fictions' as the discursive strategy of tomorrow, considers technology as an 'uncanny form of life' and inevitable correction to the dictate of nature, explains the different concepts of posthumanism, and questions that (human) life is necessarily the ultimate goal of the cosmos. He explores the dialectic of silence and phatic communication in new media in the context of a general shift from the 'culture of meaning' to a 'culture of presence' and the exhaustion of the interpretative paradigm in the Humanities.

Prelude

Roberto Simanowski: What is your favored neologism of digital media culture and why?

Erick Felinto: I'm not a big fan of neologisms, but if I had to choose one it would probably be "mediascape". I like the term for two reasons. First, it translates our complex and intricate media scenario as just one large structure of interconnected technologies, notwithstanding the specific differences between each medium and its audiences. And if there's some truth to Friedrich Kittler's dictum that 'the general digitization of channels and information erases the differences among individual media,' then this neologism is more relevant and useful now than ever before. Second, I find the convergence between the notions of media and landscape very interesting, because it characterizes our current situation in terms of a specific "mood" or "ambience". It's impossible to live "outside" of media, because media is everywhere and endows every event of our daily lives with a specific mediatic quality. For me, the metaphor of an electronic or digital landscape conveys the singular feeling of living in a time where social relations and even the culture are constantly being filtered through the lenses of several media devices. A Brazilian theoretician, Muniz Sodré, talks about a fourth "bios", or mode of existence, following the previous three coined by Aristotle. Now we experience the "mediatic bios" as a new form of life complementing (and overpowering) the other ones: *bios theotikos* (contemplative life), *bios politikos* (political life) and *bios apolaustikos* (sensual life). I think this kind of approach is also interesting because it collapses the radical separation between nature and culture or nature and technology that modernity strived to establish.

RS: What comes to mind if you hear "Digital Media Studies"?

EF: I don't like the expression very much, because it suggests that we should study digital media apart from other kinds of media. The field of digital studies suffers from memory loss, treating the past as if it were only a preamble to the marvels of the digital world. Yes, there are several particularities to digital media that need to be taken into account, however, I believe we can better understand these particularities by comparing them with previous technological paradigms. That's why I prefer the term "media studies" as a more inclusive label, which also doesn't imply a radical break with the past or any kind of special status granted to the present situation. That's also the reason why I believe the rise of media archaeology (the works of Wolfgang Ernst, Knut Ebeling and Jussi Parikka, for instance, come to mind) represents one of the most exciting events in the recent history of media theory. According to Parikka, media archaeology 'sees media culture as sedimented and layered, a fold of time and materiality where the past might be suddenly discovered anew, and the new technologies grow obsolete increasingly fast.' In that sense, I specially like Siegfried Zielinski's idea of seeking the new in the old instead of the other way around. A critical appraisal of our current mediascape demands an examination of the past in order to ascertain which interesting paths and potentialities have been left underdeveloped or abandoned.

RS: If you were a minister of education, what would you do about media literacy?

EF: I'd certainly do everything in my power to make media literacy mandatory at the level of high school education, with a special focus on programming languages. Two of my favorite media theorists, Friedrich Kittler and Vilém Flusser, strongly believed in the importance of computer literacy for future generations.

Politics and Government

RS: Today, web activists are calling for the government and governmental institutions such as the European Union to pass laws to protect privacy and net neutrality, while in earlier times Internet pioneers such as John Perry Barlow declared the independence of Cyberspace from the governments of the old world. Do those governments that 'do not know our culture, our ethics, or the unwritten codes that already provide our society more order than could be obtained by any of your impositions' as Barlow stated turn out to be our last hope in the battle for the rights of the individual and the freedom of the Internet?

EF: Yes, there seems to be a significant shift regarding the role of government within digital culture. It's not so much that activists now see governments as allies in their fight for Internet freedom, but rather the idea that it's preferable to side with (some) governments rather than with large private corporations such as Google. However, the situation might be slightly different for every country. The Brazilian case is very interesting, since our Congress is now working precisely on a special draft bill (Marco Civil da Internet) intended to guarantee civil rights in the use of the Internet and regulate the behavior of service providers. The bill states that Internet access is a prerequisite for the exercise of civic rights. It was developed collaboratively by means of public consultation and its main goal is to assure the principle of net neutrality. Some people even say that the bill represents a chance for Brazil to take international leadership in the fight for a freer net, by adopting a political position that is directly oppositional to conservative initiatives such as ACTA (the Anti-Counterfeit Trade Agreement, which was rejected by the European Parliament in 2012).

RS: This sounds as if the Brazilian parliament is much more prepared to discuss the political and cultural implications of digital media than politicians in other countries who mostly have no clear concept about the matter of new media and leave it to journalists, academics and net-activists. Who is behind the discussion in Brazil?

EF: Well, not really. Several specialists in digital technology and Internet culture participated in the process. Debates and public hearings around specific issues (for instance, on the privacy rights of internet users) were organized and people from different sectors and walks of live had the opportunity to voice their concerns and offer suggestions. However, as democratic and comprehensive as this process may sound, the results so far have been somewhat disappointing. Some of the main problems have to do with the definitions of intellectual property and fair use, which are still fairly conservative. Sérgio Amadeu Silveira, a professor and Internet researcher who participated in the elaboration of the bill, believes that the most conservative aspects of the draft are a result of the powerful lobby exerted by the telecommunication and copyright industries. The bill was passed in April, 2014, but many people believe it still needs some improvements . There's a very heated and fruitful debate going on in Brazil regarding topics such as open software and copyright. Some academics are still working together with the government (or at least some of its more progressive sectors) in order to pass new legislation that proves to be adequate and relevant for the context of digital culture.

It's interesting to note that Brazilian President Dilma Roussef had requested the Congress to prioritize the bill's vote right after the allegations of espionage by the NSA came to light. The government believes that the creation of data centers for companies like Google or Facebook in Brazil can prevent the transmission of private information to foreign agencies, so they tried to include this provision in the bill, I'm not sure if they succeeded, since I still didn't have the time to read its whole text In any case, I don't think this is realistic and I doubt it would be enough to stop the NSA (or any other foreign agency, for that matter) from spying on us. The situation is highly complex today because there seems to be a mixed perception about the role of government in digital culture. On the one hand, it can embody the "dark side of the digital" (to evoke the title of a symposium organized by Richard Grusin at the UWM in May 2013) when it monitors social networks in order to prevent the organization of protests

– as has been recently happening in Brazil – and control people's access to information. On the other hand, it can be an ally in the fight for a better Internet when it regulates the obligations of service providers to its customers and tries to guarantee net neutrality, which is supposedly one of the main principles of the above mentioned "Marco Civil".

But there might also be another factor at work in this shift in the perception of the government. More and more people have access to the Internet, but are digitally illiterate. In fact, most people don't want to go through the trouble of learning code or software languages and we don't have special programs to teach them that. Back in the heroic times of the Internet, when we still didn't have perfected GUIs (graphical user interface), one needed to have at least some minimal training in digital literacy. Hackers were the main "dwellers" of the digital territories. As Gabriela Coleman states in her 2013 book *Coding Freedom*, while the Internet's architecture in the 1980's was open, practically speaking it 'operated under a lock' with the keys available only to a select number of hackers and engineers. Today the situation is quite different and the development of effective GUIs is partly to blame for this. People just want to punch keys and see things happening. Perhaps we should pay more heed to Kittler's arguments in essays such as *There is no Software*. Interfaces can be a way of shielding us from the complexity of the hardware and the creative unpredictability of noise. Trial and noise have been all but abolished in the extremely closed and copyrighted software systems that we use in our machines. Hackers still experiment, code and break things, but regular people ask for guidance. As the big companies become increasingly untrustworthy, there is no alternative but to turn to the government (the lesser of two evils).

RS: What you describe – punching keys with no idea about code – points to a central aspect of nowadays cultural habits: people want immediate gratification and they want it with as little effort as possible. This is true not only for our interaction with technology but also for our relationship to knowledge given that we hardly read through books or essays any longer until we understand but rather ask the search machine to give us the answer right away. We will come back to the issue of complexity and thinking later. For here we may note the rule of thumb that effort and understanding relate to each other in inverse proportion. In this perspective and in regard to understanding new media the hacker – in the broader sense of the term – seems to be the actual educational ideal of our time.

EF: I believe so. Hackers display some traits that are fundamental for a creative and active participation in digital culture. They're often self-taught and always question the stability of systems or the arbitrariness of protocols. Of course, most governments have gone to great lengths to make sure that hackers appear as irresponsible and dangerous in the eyes of the general public. However, there are some situations where activists and governments can be allies. Our most progressive former minister of culture, Gilberto Gil, once said: 'I'm a hacker, a minister-hacker' (something that would be unthinkable, say, in the United States). In a time when big corporations are increasingly colonizing cyberspace, we need to imbue people with the hacker ethics of freedom, creativity and experimentation. In a short article published in Switzerland in 1990, Vilém Flusser drew an interesting argument concerning the reunification of Germany. For him, more interesting than the process of *Wiedervereinigung* (reunification), which would ultimately serve the purpose of establishing other frontiers (Germans and non-Germans), was the digital revolution being set in motion at the time by hackers all over the world. According to him, hackers were the living proof of the foolishness of setting borders and the creative power of the gray zones. Flusser was a very radical critic of fixed identities, of rigid frontiers, of authorship and ownership. Yes, this may sound romantic and unrealistic, but I think it's precisely this kind of romanticism that we need in an age when the market seems to be invading every living space.

RS: Let me pick up Flusser's romanticism and his critic of fixed identity in the context of digital media. In contrast to more pessimistic media theorists such as Jean Baudrillard and Paul Virilio, Flusser predicted a telematic utopia of unrestricted and democratic global communication. And indeed, the early Internet seemed to meet Flusser's advocacy of noise and fluid identity developed in his autobiography *Bodenlos* (Groundless, 1992) and his book *Von der Freiheit des Migranten* (The Freedom of the Migrant, 1994; English 2003). However, with the critical turn in Digital Media Studies in the last 10 years, the notion of the Internet as an "identity workshop", as Sherry Turkle described it, or the new public sphere for free political discourse has been widely abandoned (cf. Morosov's *Net Dellusion*, Turkle's *Alone Together*, Lovink's *Networks Without a Cause*, Pariser's *Filter Bubble*). Do you see a place for Flusser's optimism today?

EF: It is true that Flusser was at times excessively optimistic about the potentialities of the "telematic society" (the term with which he named the socio-cultural formation we used to define as "cyberculture" until recently). However, this enthusiasm was not uncommon in the theoretical discourses on net culture in the early 1980s and 1990s. He was also somewhat simplistic when he confronted mass culture with digital culture, although always in a very poetic manner. He liked animal metaphors and compared the public in the mass media environment to a worm (*ein riesiger Wurm*), which kept digesting, excreting and consuming the same content again and again while believing it was receiving new information. For him, the opposition between mass media and digital media was very clear. The first represented a societal model composed of apathetic, passive people, incapable of creating anything new, while the second stood for interactivity and a playful engagement with the culture. For Flusser, freedom was synonym with the capacity to play with our technological apparatuses and try to find ways to circumvent their inscribed programs.

RS: Playing with the technological apparatuses reinforces the idea of the hacker. The passive/active opposition, however, that was also used and mis-conceptualized in the hypertext discourse of the 1990s, certainly needs to be revisited in light of more and more hyperactive readers less and less able to absorb complex information.

EF: Nowadays we understand that mass media and digital media can't be so neatly separated and the theological-utopic faith in the liberating powers of the digital sounds a bit naïve (except maybe for a handful of authors such as Pierre Lévy). However, none of these traits disqualifies Flusser as an extraordinary thinker and a precursor to contemporary media theory. I strongly believe that Flusser can be aligned, at least partially, with the research program that has been termed recently as "German media theory". His cybernetic vision of the culture, the centrality of media (and, most importantly, of the *materiality* of media) in his worldview and his archaeological approach to the pair society/technology situate him in an epistemological space that is not very distant from the speculations of a Friedrich Kittler or a Siegfried Zielinski. In fact, Kittler was an admirer of Flusser and invited him for a professorship in Bochum a few months before his death in 1991. In the preface to *Kommunikologie weiter denken*, the book that transcribes Flusser's lectures in Bochum, Kittler dubs him a "prophet" and a "founder hero" of contemporary media theory.

RS: A "prophet" and "founder hero" of media theory similar to Marshal McLuhan? And similar "non-academic", "metaphoric" and "sloppy" as McLuhan has been criticized in German introductions to media theory?

EF: The trope of the prophet, also ascribed to thinkers such as McLuhan (a major influence on Flusser's thought), lead to the very peculiar situation of a scholar who was frequently mentioned, often described as a pioneer, but very scarcely studied in depth. For many people, Flusser was someone who wrote about important topics and stated some interesting things, but was ultimately a dilettante, lacking the seriousness of a full-fledged university professor. In Germany, he was often compared to McLuhan, although not always in a good way. I also believe he tackled with several aspects of the contemporary discussion on posthumanism (another trademark of "German media theory"), notwithstanding the fact that he was, in many ways, a traditional humanist at heart – but this kind of contradiction may likewise be found in Nortbert Wiener, the father of Cybernetics. His obsession with animal metaphors and tropes is evocative of the contemporary wave of media studies that dissolve the borders between biology and technology or nature and culture, such as Jussi Parikka's *Insect Media* (2010) or Sebastian Vehlken's *Zootechnologien* (2012).

For instance, Flusser's *Vampyroteuthis Infernalis* (2011), recently translated into English (there's actually translations of the versions Flusser wrote in Portuguese and German), is an extraordinary philosophical essay on our technological condition. But what strikes me as extremely original is how he approaches the problem by means of a very peculiar allegory. He defines his essay as a "philosophical fiction", where the main character is the strange marine creature (an octopus) named in the book's title. The character works as a sort of twisted mirror-image of man, while at the same time offering Flusser the opportunity to relativize categories that are traditionally referred exclusively to man, such as "art" and "culture". *Vampyroteuthis Infernalis* is a speculation on the possible future outcomes of the technological revolution, and, albeit essentially optimistic, Flusser does not exclude the possibility that these news technologies end up promoting new forms of totalitarianism and control.

RS: What form of totalitarianism?

EF: Well, if the *Vampyroteuthis* indeed works as an allegory of technology and the foundational relationship between man and technics, then it should always be structured between the poles of reason and emotion, calculation and imagination. When Flusser discusses the emergence of this strange octopus, he claims that we can only have a meaningful encounter with it by balancing the cold gaze of science and technology with poetry and intuition (this refers to the Portuguese manuscript, the German version is a bit different, which makes things more interesting and complex). Vampyroteuthis is a scientific entity – in fact, an actually existing being, assigned by Biology to the class of the *cephalopoda* –, but also the stuff of legend and imagination. This kind of dualism lies at the core of Flusser's thinking and is never solved. It can be translated into more philosophical terms in the central conflicting forces of Cybernetics and Heideggerian phenomenology, both powerful sources of Flusser's reasoning. As Flusser himself puts it, in order to be effective, his fable of the wondrous marine creature has to be '"fictitious science", that is, the overcoming of scientific objectivity in the service of a concretely human knowledge'.

RS: This reminds me of Hans Jonas who in his 1979 book *Das Prinzip Verantwortung. Versuch einer Ethik für die technologische Zivilisation* (The Imperative of Responsibility: In Search of an Ethics for the Technological Age) demands an 'imaginative casuistic' about the possible consequences of current developments. In 2012, Geert Lovink in his book *Networks Without A Cause: A Critique of Social Media* proposed a similar method for Internet Studies coining it 'speculative futurism'.

EF: I think Lovink's proposition is indeed very close to the heart of Flusser's project. When Lovink writes that 'Humanities should do more than describe the times we're living in' and defends the need 'to celebrate singular modes of expression,' he is summoning cultural theorists to speculate about the present and the future with the full extent of their imagination. This move requires expressive strategies that appropriate the possibilities of non-academic modes of discourse, such as fiction and poetry. To be sure, Flusser was not the first advocate of this intellectual strategy, which has some respectable historical antecedents, neither the last thinker who resorted to it. In fact, I believe theoretical fictions of this kind will become increasingly popular as a discursive device in the years to come. Let's compare, for instance, the flusserian technique of the "philosophical fiction" with the strategy adopted by Manuel de Landa in his *War in the Age of Intelligent Machines* (1991), published only four years after the *Vampyroteuthis* (1987). De Landa performs an extraordinary *de-centering* of the human gaze by placing an intelligent war-machine as the narrator of his book. What would a work of history look like if a robot instead of a human being had written it? In such a work, human beings would be nothing more than 'pieces of a larger military-industrial machine: a war machine', in other words, only part of a larger (organic-mechanic) assemblage. De Landa's book is equivalent to a philosophical fiction – or an exercise in "speculative futurism", if you will – that narrates the past from the point of view of a future sentient, non-human being. His robot historian is a machinic version of the organic Vampyroteuthis: they represent the position of an imagined "other" through which we can acquire an innovative perspective on ourselves. In *Kant in the Land of Extraterrestrials*, without ever mentioning Flusser, Peter Szendy terms the use of radical imagination in philosophical discourses as "philosofiction" and quotes Derrida's statement that 'all philosopher's have made fiction a keystone of their discourse'. For Szendy (and also for Flusser), philosofiction is a discursive strategy that works 'as both an opening and a limit – as an imaginary access to the other, but without experience of the other'.

We're now simply taking this idea to its farthest consequences. It's interesting that Lovink talks so much about "speculation" in his book, because I'd go so far as to suggest that we've been experiencing a "speculative renaissance" in the last twenty years or so, not only in philosophy (the young philosophical movement called "speculative realism" comes to mind), but in all fields of the Humanities. Steven Shaviro, in his book *Connected, or what it means to live in the network society* (2003), has stated that it is only by writing cultural theory as science fiction that one can hope to be 'as radical as reality itself'. In Flusser, however, imaginative speculation is to be a trademark not only of theoretical writing, but also of all our dealings with technology. Science and technology that are not associated with imagination and intuition can easily turn into the complete rationalization of life. Therefore, the apocalyptical vision of an administered society is a very real possibility for Flusser, with technologies being used for the control of populations and the suppression of all attempts to disrupt the status quo (and nothing can be more disruptive than imagination).

There's a beautiful passage in *Kommunikologie weiter denken* where Flusser frames the dilemma between order and freedom in theological terms. Like Walter Benjamin, Flusser appropriates and secularizes theological notions in order to discuss profane topics, such as art and technology. Freedom is only possible because the world has holes (*Löcher*) in it. The fact that God is an imperfect designer (or "programmer", as Flusser puts it), like the demiurge of the gnostics, allows for the existence of extraordinary events. Flusser plays here with the double meaning of the German word *Wunder*: "wonder" and "miracle" at the same time. Freedom is connected to wonder, our capacity to marvel and engage in an imaginative relationship with the world. This engagement is itself a source of wonder and miracles. There are holes we can exploit, and the decision to exploit them is tantamount to committing a "sin" (*Sünde*). Then comes the most striking statement, when Flusser explicitly affirms that freedom *is* technology, in fact, *the* "real freedom" (*die eigentliche Freiheit*), and he criticizes the disdain of most French and German intellectuals for technology (especially Heidegger). What technology offers us, when dully combined with imagination and art, is a way of predicting and preempting the future. Technics is thus the possibility of driving the outcome of a situation into a direction other than that dictated by nature. Therefore, the real danger lies not in technology itself, but rather in its isolation from the realms of art and creativity.

RS: To me, the opposite seems to be the case once we look closer and in a more specific manner at the issue: Freedom is not enhanced but reduced by information technology for it fills all the holes that allow extraordinary or uncontrolled events. For example, if Big Data mining produces reliable information about all kinds of if-then-correlations, it doesn't require much imagination to see the government, the health department, insurance companies and credit institutes asking people to refrain from behavior with unwanted *then*-consequences. Such demand is unlikely as long as the consequences of certain *ifs* are not discovered or certain. However, knowledge obliges. The flipside of conducting measuring is taking measures – its looming concepts are *predictive analytics* and *algorithmic regulation*. Hence, don't we, in the context of the information and control society, face the paradoxical equation that knowledge and freedom relate to each other in inverse proportion?

EF: Well, Flusser understands the technological gesture as an act of freedom against the determinations of nature. When man starts altering his natural habitat – for instance, by transforming a branch into a stick –, he is already engaged in the technological enterprise. Flusser was well aware of Heidegger's criticism of (modern) technology as a form of "enframing" (*Gestell*) and calculation of the world. He certainly sees the danger in a use of technology that seeks only to control and predict. And I know this sounds paradoxical, since I used precisely words like "predict" and "preempt" in my previous answer, but I think that Flusser had a very particular idea regarding these "preemptive" powers of technology. For him, it is not so much about controlling our fate or becoming, as it is about the opening up of new possibilities not already programmed in our natural state. Although he used words like "preempt" (*vorwegnehmen*), his expression of choice was "suppose" (*annehmen*). In fact, in a book that bears precisely this verb as its title, *Angenommen* (2000) ("suppose that...") he contrasts his way of thinking with that of the futurologist, since he is interested in improbabilities rather than in probabilities, the latter being the subject matter of the futurologist – and this is precisely why his imaginative scenarios and suppositions never cease to acknowledge the fundamental role of otherness. This relationship to the "other" – understood both as our fellow human being and as the emblem of an ever-open field of possibilities – is central to Flusser's thought.

I see some interesting connections between Flusser's proposals and R.L. Rutsky's notion of *high techné* (coined through a very interesting dialogue with Heidegger) as a form of relationship to technology that is not external to man, but rather constitutive of the human being in his entwinement with art, technique and otherness. As Rutsky himself puts it, the change we need to effect in our dealings with technology must be a 'mutational process that cannot be rationally predicted or controlled; it can only be imagined, figured, through a techno-cultural process that is at once science-fictional and aesthetic'. Technology is thus characterized as endowed with agency, as if it were an uncanny form of life that continually unsettles and challenges (in an "aesthetic" manner) the position of the human subject. The future envisioned by this change is, again, essentially *posthuman*, not of course in the sense of securing the boundaries of the subject through the use of prostheses or a cyborg body, but rather of destabilizing it, of acknowledging the 'otherness that is part of us', as Rutsky put it. This sounds very Flusserian to me.

RS: If, with Flusser, we understand technology as an act of freedom against the determinations of nature and if, with Rutsky and many others, we look at human relationship to technology as constitutive of their beings, allowing them, as you say, to go in a direction other than that dictated by nature, we may also remember Immanuel Kant's notion about the 'purpose in nature' as discusses in his 1784 essay *Idea for a Universal History with a Cosmopolitan Purpose*. Kant considers the 'purpose in nature' that man go 'beyond the mechanical ordering of his animal existence' and gain happiness from the perfection of skills. The means to do so is to constantly develop the utmost human capacity of reason, from generation to generation, bestowing each with ever more refined technology: hammer, steam-engine, electric motor, computer, artificial intelligence. To Kant this endeavor will be a walk 'from barbarism to culture' and finally, despite all conflicts and contradictions on the way, make the world a better place, as the slogan reads today. Needless to say, that Kant's idealism has been rejected, especially in light of the fact that the advance of human intelligence has brought many powerful means to life that can end or suppress human life: from nuclear weapon to self-learning artificial intelligence.

In this context I find the analogy of technology as art very interesting if applied to Kant's 'philosophical chiliasm'. Can we think of technology as something challenging and unsettling the common view, including the view on technological progress, in the way we expect from art? Does technology propose a different perspective in a rather ambiguous way, as we experience with art, or does it rather establish, unambiguously and eventually inevitably, a new way of seeing and doing things? In my view there is a central difference between art and technology: while the message of art eventually is the difference of being, the message of technology is "just" a different way of being – a 'change of scale or pace or pattern that it introduces into human affairs' as McLuhan describes the '"message" of any medium or technology'. This inevitable, rather than possible, change is what I have in mind when I asked to what extent the statistical perspectives Big Data mining enforces limits the freedom of being different. I guess we will have to wait and see how the "governmental data mining" and "governmental predictions", as portrayed for example in Tal Zarsky's publications or in *Changing Behaviours: On the Rise of the Psychological State* (2013) by Rhys Jones, Jessic Pykett and Mark Whitehead, eventually affect human behavior.

EF: It's interesting to note, since I repeatedly mentioned Flusser's romanticism, that Kant's notion of 'natural purpose' served as an inspiration for the romantic organic concept of nature. So Kant and the romantics are not as distant as they might appear initially. For Flusser, however, technology should offer us a bridge between the powers of reason and the capabilities of imagination. We must engage with technologies that make us dream (about the future, for instance). He was not interested in a form of knowledge devoted to the regulation of life (as in predictive analytics or algorithmic regulation), but sought instead to promote a creative, artistic relationship to technology as a very peculiar form of knowledge, which approaches truth and reality through their opposing side (*Gegenseite*), as it were, via art and philosophical fictions. Of course, we can always ask whether this creative, libertarian form of relationship with technology will prevail over its uses as an instrument for the measurement (and control) of the world. Perhaps Flusser let his romantic vision of new media get the best of him.

Anyway, to properly answer the initial question on Flusser's optimism, unlike Agamben, for whom technology is part of the mechanisms that keeps us under control and incapable of achieving a more authentically human (and animal and posthuman) condition, Flusser believes in the libertarian potentialities of the technical image and the artistic and playful nature of new media. To be sure, Flusser's vision is utopian (and messianic, like Agamben's), but it's a utopia we should always strive to materialize. In any case, I believe his optimism is better than the brand of technological pessimism that is characteristic, for instance, of much French theory produced in the last 40 years.

RS: We already discussed Flusser's belief in the libertarian potentialities of new media with respect to Big Data Mining. Now you point out his optimism and utopianism regarding technology and the posthuman. Let me press you on this a bit more. In his book *Vom Subjekt zum Projekt. Menschwerdung* (From Subject to Project. Becoming Human, 1994), Flusser moves his idea of the constant reinvention of the Self and the steady departure from what is home and custom (in German *Wohnung* and *Gewohnheit*) from the context of migration to the framework of technology. However, one of the pejorative keywords about new media – not only since Eli Pariser's *Filter Bubble* or Cass Sunstein's *Republic. com* but already in Andrew Shapiro's *Control Revolution* (1999) – has been "daily me" or "you-loop" signifying the customization and personalization of what one encounters on the Internet. This personalization, which many people more or less approve of and even desire, has been addressed as the preclusion of the unfamiliar, the removal of diversity and of what we are not (yet). If the statistical logic of the algorithm so easily and powerful overrides the cultural concept of otherness, what role will technology play in the project of posthumanism?

EF: There are several ways of understanding the term and the concept of "posthumanism". For instance, in his *The Souls of Cyberfolk* (2005), Thomas Foster discusses what he considers to be two radically different forms of posthumanism. On the one hand, there's the brand of posthumanism that was developed in cyberpunk literature, which was essentially progressive and libertarian. Cyberpunk didn't see technology as something external, but rather as pervasive and intimate. It also dismissed or at least complicated the reductionism of dualities like utopian/dystopian and male/female. On the other hand, there's also a kind of posthumanism that can serve politically conservative agendas. Movements like the World Transhumanist Association or Extropianism, according to Foster, align themselves with an ideal of "self-realization" that is pro-market and individualistic. Also, it's always possible to discuss posthumanism in concrete, down to earth and shortsighted terms or choose to approach it in a more abstract, philosophical manner. While the first option treats posthumanism mostly as an effect of material technologies (particularly digital and genetic technologies) on the traditional makeup of the human body and mind, the second one takes a more complex instance, treating contemporary technologies as just one specific and visible manifestation of a much older and often invisible force.

The latter is Argentine philosopher Fabián Ludueña's perspective in his brilliant work *La Comunidad de los Espectros* (2010). Ludueña employs the term "antropotechnics" to define 'all the techniques by means of which the communities of the human species and the individuals that compose them act upon their own animal nature with the intent to guide, expand, modify or domesticate their biological substrate, aiming at what philosophy at first and later the biological sciences have grown accustomed to call "man".' Religion is, of course, one of our most fundamental forms of antropotechnics, one devoted to the *spectralization* of man (what really matters is the spirit, not the body). In that sense, the contemporary biotechnological revolution would be nothing more than a radical secularization of the ancient Christian eschatology. While several thinkers now claim the need of a reckoning with the animality that all anthropotechnics tried to expel from the human sphere, Ludueña, in his book *Para além do princípio antrópico: por uma filosofia do outside* (2012) attempts to go even further. For him, we should get rid of the last anthropic principle, which is life itself. It is incumbent

upon us to develop a philosophy capable of thinking or specu-
lating about the objectivity of the universe without a human
observer. Life is not necessarily the ultimate goal of a cosmos
that is composed mostly of inorganic matter, no less than man is
the final step in the development of life. In other words, why busy
ourselves with a phenomenon that is so marginal and exceptional as life, 'if not because man still conserves in life a desire
to explain himself?' Ludueña's project is closely related to some
other interesting contemporary philosophical enterprises that
tackle with issues of posthumanism, such as Eugene Thacker's *In
The Dust of this Planet* (2011).

In this context, to embrace the posthuman means to develop
new ways of philosophizing – for instance, by elaborating a 'philosophy of the outside, of death and the specter,' as Ludueña proposes. Perhaps it's possible to reframe the question by resorting
to three different kinds (or degrees) of posthumanism. The first
kind corresponds roughly to the one Foster attributes to movements such as Extropianism. Rather than being an authentic
posthumanism, it's a sort of super-humanism, since its main goal
is to extend the dominion of the human race to the whole cosmos
and augment certain human traits by means of technology (life-
expectancy, powers of reasoning etc.). The second kind invites us
to reconnect with the animal and deconstruct the anthropocentric principle that has guided western thought since its inception
(but which, according to Ludueña, still clings to the "anthropic
principle"). Finally, there is a kind of extreme or radical posthumanism, in which not only man, but also the very idea of life, as
a privileged entity, needs to be overcome. All this philosophical
preamble seemed necessary, because although posthumanism
may strike us as a very recent problem, it can also be framed as
a millennia-old topic that underscored the whole history of philosophy and that's still fundamental for all coming philosophy.

Now, which kind of posthumanism should we ascribe to
Flusser? With his fascination for animals and his criticism of
anthropocentrism, he was probably closer to the second type,
but with the particularity of a belief in technology as the tool for
tapping into the unrealized potentialities of the animal. In the

German version of the *Vampyroteuthis*, Flusser not only speculates about how the telematic society shall be able to modify our
psychic structure, dissolving the boundaries of the "I-capsule"
(*Ich-Kapsel*), but also hints at a possible posthuman future when
man will be able to modify his genetic composition in order to
realize all possibilities dormant in the primordial cells. We can
certainly question the accuracy of Flusser's first prediction,
since new media and social networks have not accomplished
the desired openness to the other, the disintegration of the
"I-capsule", as you mentioned in the question (at least not yet...).

However, the second speculation remains open to debate.
This speculation is further developed in "Arte Viva" (*Living Art*),
an unpublished text written in Portuguese in which Flusser
approaches what he considers to be two major concurrent and
also converging technocultural revolutions: Telematics and
Biotechnology. For him, the latter represents the possibility of
recuperating the ancient notion of "ars vivendi" (*the art of living*). Whereas the revolution of telematics promises the programmability of our lives, the other one (Biotechnology) promises the
programmability *of all life*. Why should we be stuck in our current biological configuration? Why, for instance, can't we design
brains that are completely spherical (like the octopus') instead of
semi-spherical? What kind of new thoughts and forms of action
could emerge from such a reconfiguration of the brain and the
body? Genetic manipulation will be the ultimate form of art,
since it will operate on our own bodies rather than on any external objects. In the future, if we manage to combine the organic
with the inorganic, we will create 'organisms that will replace
the inanimate machines with 'living' artificial intelligences (no
longer composed of silica, but rather of nerve fibers).' In order to
be "transcendentally creative" – in other words, in order to introduce novelty and noise into a system – Biotechnology will need
to insert new materials (like silica) in the genetic code of living
beings. The hybrid beings originating from these processes will
then give rise to new forms of thought that we are currently incapable of contemplating. In sum, the issue of posthumanism (in
Flusser or in general) is so complex and multifaceted that we've

just begun to scratch its surface, and the place of technology within this topic still needs to be more thoroughly investigated.

Media Literacy

RS: In his 1948 book *Die Welt des Schweigens* (The World of Silence), Swiss cultural philosopher Max Picard portrays silence not as absence of noise but as the context of consciousness. In the silence of nature, man is confronted with the before creation/after finitude and consequently his own mortality. Today with the ubiquity of mobile technology we escape silence even in the remotest corners of the earth. Against the background of Picard and others who called for moments of contemplation in a life increasingly accelerated by new media (think of Kracauer's essays *Those Who Wait* and *Boredom*), how do you see the philosophical implications of digital technology?

EF: I didn't expect to see Max Picard's name mentioned in an interview about digital media, but it's an interesting question. He was a very accomplished writer in his lifetime, having been praised by personalities like Rainer Maria Rilke and Herman Hesse. Today, however, he is all but forgotten and any mention of traditionalist thinkers like Picard may sound old-fashioned, although I believe there are some interesting similarities between his philosophy of language and Walter Benjamin's. *Die Welt des Schweigens* is a very beautiful essay on man's original relationship to silence, which for Picard is also the realm of divine transcendence. The fact that we now live in a world of noise and babbling is a symptom of our metaphysical and cultural decay, according to Picard. Chief among the causes for this decay is technology, especially media technology. I think we need to read Picard in the context of the *Kulturkritik* (cultural critique) that was a distinctive trait, in the early and mid-20th century, of the literature devoted to the analysis of the social changes brought about by the modernization of life – mainly in the German-speaking world.

The main problem for Picard was the acceleration of time, which lead mankind to a continual state of flight, ultimately, a

flight from God (*Die Flucht vor Gott* is another essay by Picard).
To be sure, the flight from God is not something particular to our
age, but the problem now is that there's no longer an objective
world of faith. Whereas in the past man could individually make
the decision of fleeing from the world of faith, we now experience the opposite situation: it is necessary that each individual
continually decide to embrace the world of faith and stop fleeing.
Therefore, this state of flight became the existential trademark
of our times. Of course, modern media are definitely to blame
for this change. Picard believed that cinema, for instance, was
the perfect medium to effect the flight from God (and from ourselves). For me, Picard is a thinker who had brilliant intuitions,
but who must be taken with a grain of salt, to say the least. It
must be said, however, that Picard was not in favor of a simple
Luddite solution. Destroying the technologies that now extend
all around the globe would only make the situation worse.
Nonetheless, I believe that we could in fact use a little bit more of
silence and contemplation in the midst of our always technologically agitated and busy lives.

RS: I bring up Picard because I consider his take on silence
and God essential in order to understand certain aspects of new
media. Let me elaborate on this. Picard notes in his book that
there is more silence in a human being than she can spend in
a life time. This rather poetic utterance, that Rilke certainly
would have subscribed to, seems to conflict Blaise Pascal's
famous statement: 'all the unhappiness of men arises from one
single fact, that they cannot stay quietly in their own chamber.'
Alone, Pascal believes, man 'feels his nothingness, his forlorn-
ness, his insufficiency, his dependence, his weakness, his empti-
ness.' His being prone to death, Pascal explains, haunts every
human, 'so that if he be without what is called diversion, he is
unhappy.' However, for Pascal the solution was not escaping the
quiet chamber, i.e. silence, but listening to God. This is the link
to Picard: the flight from God prompts the flight from silence.
The link to new media is what Picard calls noise (Wortgeräusch):
the constant sound of words that do not originate from silence
and do not return to silence but exist in their own right without

the urge to mean anything. The linguistic term for this is *phatic communication* the popular definition *small talk* – its field of practice are networks and applications such as *Facebook* or *WhatsApp*. Despite Picard's appeal, permanent communication for communication's sake has become the ruling principle of contemporary culture, a kind of placebo conversation referring to nothing other than itself. The aim of this kind of conversation is to avoid the moment that, like Pascal's quiet chamber or Picard's silence, would leave one alone with oneself. What may sound like cultural pessimism – and certainly would to Pascal and Picard – can also be seen as a way to ensure the continuation of the project of modernity. Because the return to God – or any other Grand Narrative that give our life transcendental asylum – would only confirm what Nietzsche once suspected: that the greatness of our deed, to have killed God, is too great for us. Accordingly, Gianni Vattimo notes in his book *Religion* (1996), edited together with Jacques Derrida: 'To react to the problematic and chaotic character of the late-modern world with a return to God as the metaphysical foundation means, in Nietzsche's terms, to refuse the challenge of the over(hu)man(ity).' In this perspective, the *phatic communication* – the noise Picard despises – prevents us from seceding the project of modernity by celebrating an eternal recurrence of the same in the constant worship of steadfast presence. Hence, *Facebook*, *WhatsApp*, *Instagram*, *Snapchat* and similar places keeping the carousel of communication alive allow us to feel happy without the danger of silence and the answers silence may offer. New media is – as metaphysics of aimlessness – not the problem but the solution of modern life.

EF: This is a very intelligent way of framing Picard's question within the context of new media. I believe we are experiencing a major social and cultural transformation that is intimately connected to the way we use communication media. Instead of focusing on the production of information and meaning, we're moving towards a culture of entertainment. We want to experience sensations, to have fun, to be excited. If silence is becoming impossible, meaning also seems to be in short supply theses days. Perhaps your question can be reframed in these terms: small talk is an expression of our need to be continuously entertained and avoid the need of serious talk. This shift can also be expressed, as Hans Ulrich Gumbrecht suggests in his book *Production of Presence* (2004), in the transition from a "culture of meaning" to a "culture of presence". In other words, the cultural practices connected with the body, materiality and sensation are given precedence over the ones connected with (immaterial) meaning and interpretation. Of course, from the point of view of a cultural pessimist, this is certainly disastrous. The Frankfurtian philosopher Cristoph Türcke, for example, defines our contemporary need for excitation as an addiction in his book *The Excited Society* (*Erregte Gesellschaft*, 2002). Evidently, since God is no longer a viable intellectual solution, we need to replace him with something else. Türcke incites us to step on the break and fight the endless procession of audiovisual excitation with a focus on moments of sedimentation and tranquility. We have to create social "islands" of concentration and art should be our most important weapon in this battle. But I don't think we need to isolate ourselves from the surrounding media environment in order to do that. Sometimes, as Gumbrecht argues, this is possible precisely through media (a film, for instance). In this sense, Gumbrecht's idea of being "quiet for a moment" amidst the noise of our technological engagements sounds very compelling to me.

RS: Interesting that you bring in Gumbrecht's "culture of presence" that indeed can be understood as the philosophical supplement or rather precursor of the technological development we are experiencing. In my interview with David Golumbia I considered Gumbrecht's aesthetics of presence as an affirmation of the "That" without the question for the "Why". His desire to be in sync with the "things of the world" also relieves us from the obligation to better ourselves and the world around us – which Gumbrecht considers the obsession of the Frankfurt School and the *Kulturkritik* it represents. It is obvious how far this perspective has moved art from its role as estrangement and negation

of the status quo as Adorno, Türcke's reference point, conceptualized art.

EF: My problem with the present situation is not so much the
rise of entertainment or the decay of meaning. After all, we have
been interpreting phenomena for at least the last two millennia.
It's about time we started experiencing more intense relationships with our bodies and the materiality of our surroundings.
The problem is the colonization of all domains of life by entertainment. It's almost like we had the obligation to be entertained
(and worse, to be "happy"). Well, I want the right to be sad, I
want to be able to find more spaces of silence within the tor-
rent of images and excitation the media continually offers. In
his study on Picard, Christian Fink asks whether thinkers like
him can still be relevant, especially in the context of the so-
called "medial turn" and new paradigms of research such as the
"materialities of communication", which compels us to focus on
the non-significant and material aspects of the communication
processes rather than on its meaningful contents. I'd say "yes",
I believe that *Kulturkritik* can still play an important role in the
current situation. If nothing else, at least to keep at bay the
sometimes excessive hype surrounding new media.

On the other hand, I understand how Gumbrecht's idea of
being in sync with the things of the world might be read as an
abandonment of the critical enterprise (as it traditionally implies
a form of distancing towards the world). However, one must not
forget that Gumbrecht's goal was never simply to dismiss the
importance of the hermeneutic tradition and its achievements.
He makes it clear, time and again, that his project runs parallel to this enterprise and strives to counterbalance the overpowering force of interpretation in the Humanities. Additionally,
although I still find valuable lessons in the tradition of critical
thinking, I agree with Gumbrecht's diagnostic about the loss of
belief in a "world-reference" and the epistemic crisis we've been
facing since the nineteenth century. This crisis makes the traditional position of the critic as a distanced observer untenable
nowadays. My interest in recent philosophical movements like

"Object-Oriented Philosophy" or theoretical paradigms such as the "New Materialisms" comes from a belief that they reflect a certain *Zeitgeist* that is proper of our current experience of the world. Yes, after having said so much about the world – to the point that no linguistic reference to reality still seems viable – we need to go back to the things themselves (but certainly not in the Husserlian sense of this expression!).

Gumbrecht himself acknowledges the possible accusations directed at a theoretical program that has no 'immediate ethical or even "political" orientation,' but he remains convinced that the main task of theory and teaching today is to point to instances of complexity rather than prescribing how they should be understood. By means of this attitude, he also notes how close some of our academic endeavors can be to actual artistic practices – and I like this idea very much. I still believe in the powers of criticism, but we've been doing it for a long time and there seems to be a sense of exhaustion in the Humanities regarding interpretative practices. Art is another way of bettering ourselves and the world around us (or so I believe it). Being in sync with the world – which can't, by no means, be a permanent situation – doesn't mean necessarily to be in harmony with it and doesn't preclude me from engaging with critical activity from time to time.

RS: I am on Gumbrecht's side to the extent that the hermeneutic approach to art or any artifact of culture should not impoverish and deplete what we experience 'in order to set up a shadow world of "meanings"', as Susan Sontag notes in her essay *Against Interpretation* to which Gumbrecht alludes in his essay *A Farewell to Interpretation*. Sontag's essay addresses the 'hypertrophy of the intellect at the expense of energy and sensual capability' as an escape from the challenging and unsettling nature of art we discussed above. She famously ends her essay with the notion: 'In place of a hermeneutics we need an erotics of art.' Gumbrecht's embrace of reality seems to be the realisation of such erotics. However, in the afterword *Thirty Years Later* to the anniversary issue of her essay collection *Against Interpretation* (2001), Sontag distances herself from her original attack on interpretation given the ongoing shift from symbolic concerns to intensities of direct sensual stimulation in contemporary culture. At the end of the century, giving up the search for meaning has turned out to be a much more efficient and popular strategy for escaping the experience of crisis – that she expects art to present – than the fixation of meaning. This is especially the case if interpretation does not aim at stabilizing meaning but is attributed with the 'nihilistic vocation' to 'reveal the world as a conflict of interpretations' as Gianni Vattimo states in *Beyond Interpretation: The Meaning of Hermeneutics for Philosophy* (1994). Contemporary theory conceptualizes the hermeneutic endeavour as conveying complexity and different, conflicting perspectives rather than a prescription of how to understand things. I wonder how practical Gumbrecht's "culture of presence" is to archive this aim, if the encounter of different perspectives onto the things of the world is replaces by the idea of being in sync with them. This may reflects a certain *Zeitgeist* – as does the intention of Object-Oriented Philosophy to overcome the Kantian and postmodern 'correlationism' – but this *Zeitgeist* strikes me as an escape from the epistemic aporia that (post) modernity has passed on to us. Hence, I agree that the 'epistemic crisis,' as you put, makes 'the traditional position of the critic as a distanced observer untenable,' however, I hold that it makes the position of a critical critic even more indispensable. And I agree with Gumbrecht to the extent that his project of a "culture of presence" is indeed meant as a supplement but not replacement of the "culture of meaning".

To come back to the first part of your statement, I also agree that the problem is not the occasional shift from the paradigm of meaning to the intensity of the moment but the ideal of idle hyperactivity. In this respect, Sherrry Turkle, in her book *Alone Together* (2012), regrets that we flee from every possible "downtime" into the business of our "can't wait" online conversations and states: 'But if we are always on, we may deny ourselves the rewards of solitude.' Such sentence hardly makes sense to younger people today if William Deresiewicz is right with his observation in his Chronicle of Higher Education essay *The End of Solitude* (2009): 'Young people today seem to have no desire for solitude, have never heard of it, can't imagine why it would be worth having.' Deresiewicz conclusion is alarming: 'But no real excellence, personal or social, artistic, philosophical, scientific or moral, can arise without solitude.' In the same tone of culture pessimism Nicholas Carr, in his 2008 article *Is Google making us stupid?* and later in his 2011 book *The Shallows – What the Internet is Doing to Our Brains*, discusses the consequences of online media for literacy. From Carr's perspective, multitasking and power browsing make people unlearn deep reading and consequently deep thinking. The shift from deep attention to hyper attention has been announced and bemoaned by many intellectuals of whom Cristoph Türcke with his *Erregte Gesellschaft* is one example of them in the tradition of the Frankfurt School. Another is the French philosopher Bernard Stiegler who speaks of a threat to social and cultural development caused by the destruction of young people's ability to develop deep and critical attention to the world around them. Is there a real threat or is this just another reiteration of a well-known lamentation about the terrifying ramifications of all new media?

EF: I try to steer clear of this kind of assessment, because even the titles of these books operate according to the same logic they supposedly criticize. *Is Google making us stupid?* or Andrew Keen's *The Cult of the Amateur: How Today's Internet is Killing our Culture* (2007) sound to me like rather sensational and biased titles. It's precisely the kind of titles that are fashioned in order to sell books and generate hype. The analyses are often simplistic and one-sided. Stiegler is, of course, much more sophisticated, but I think we have to read him with a caveat. With works such as his or philosopher Barbara Cassin's book *Google-moi* (2007), we usually have the impression of hearing, over and over, the traditional complaints of the old European intellectuals against the ill effects of the (mainly US-dominated) media culture. Perhaps the main problem is the historical tendency to the monopolization of the human senses by one particular form of media in detriment of others. The insistent myth of progress sees history as a linear development, in which new media are destined to inevitably replace and banish old technologies. In the current market-driven system, the past is a place we never should wish to return to. In other words, why can't we play with the possibilities of new media, while at the same time navigating through several other (more traditional) forms of cultural experience, such as literature, for instance? That's why Siegfried Zielinki's plea for the heterogeneity of the arts and media sounds so relevant nowadays. We need to keep moving forward, but always with an eye in the past, in order to escape the historical prison of technological progress.

RS: Change of subject to a somehow related issue: Digital Humanities seem to be the new buzzword in the Humanities. What do you think about it and how do you see its relationship to Digital Media Studies?

EF: I'm all for the development of new investigative strategies in the Humanities, as well as for the promotion of productive dialogues between hard and soft sciences. However (and perhaps because I don't like buzzwords), I'm not so enthusiastic about Digital Humanities. It's not that I see anything intrinsically wrong about it. It's rather a question of taste and affinity. It's just something I am not so interested in pursuing, specially when there are so many other interesting things going on in the Humanities right now. My only fear regarding Digital Humanities is that it becomes a new form of methodological totalitarianism. I'm a little concerned with the grandiose rhetoric that can be found in some books on Digital Humanities. It's surprising that only a handful of people in Brazil have heard about Digital Humanities, because it perfectly fits the philosophy and guiding principles of the governmental agencies that fund research. It's supposed to be collaborative and it apparently can give the Humanities a more scientific outlook. A few years ago I remember hearing the constant criticism from funding agencies that researchers were writing too many "essays" in Brazil. What they meant is that we needed to do more grounded research and incorporate more empirical data in our assessments. Although I acknowledge the importance of all these precepts, including the notion of collaborative research, I fear they might become the only socially sanctioned guidelines for research in the Humanities. If we manage to avoid privileging research paradigms and methods on the basis of *how scientific they look*, then there's nothing to fear. On the contrary, Digital Humanities can become a valuable asset in the theoretical toolbox of the Human Sciences, although some concern has been raised, for example, about its disregard for issues of race and gender.

As for its relationship to Digital Media Studies, I like the idea of inclusive and diverse fields of research – and that's why I prefer the term "media studies" over "digital media studies", like I stated in a previous answer. Depending on how we use Digital Humanities it can even help bridging the gap between the analogical and the digital worlds. What we need is the multiplication of possibilities, not their reduction to one or two dominating paradigms. I think that the best works in Digital Humanities are aware of the dangers I mentioned here and are ready to react to them. A good example would be the volume *Digital_Humanities* by Anne Burdick, Johanna Drucker, Peter Lunenfeld, Todd Presner, and Jeffrey Schnapp (2012), which acknowledges the need of diversity by stating from the start that this new research program should be 'an extension of traditional knowledge skills and methods, not a replacement for them.'

Computerization always promotes centralization even as it promotes decentralization

David Golumbia

David Golumbia teaches in the English Department and the Media, Art, and Text PhD program at Virginia Commonwealth University. He is the author of *The Cultural Logic of Computation* (2009) and many articles on digital culture, language, and literary studies and theory. He maintains the digital studies blog *uncomputing.org* and edits *The b2 Review*: Digital Studies magazine for the *boundary 2* editorial collective. His *The Politics of Bitcoin: Software as Right-Wing Extremism* is forthcoming in 2016 from the University of Minnesota Press, and he is currently working on the book *Cyberlibertarianism: The False Promise of Digital Freedom*.

David Golumbia presents four reasons why he considers "hacker" groups such as Anonymous right-wing activism, states that in the regime of computation today the mathematical rationalism of Leibnitz has prevailed Voltaire's critical rationalism, and proposes a FDA for computer technology. He doesn't see the Internet as Habermasian "public sphere," considers Digital Humanities a 'perfect cyberlibertarian construct,' bemoans the capitulation of universities to new media corporations, and calls for a balance of both modes of thinking, the hedgehog and the fox, in the digital age.

Prelude

Roberto Simanowski: What is your favored neologism of digital media culture and why?

David Golumbia: My least favorite digital neologism is "hacker." The word has so many meanings, and yet it is routinely used as if its meaning was unambiguous. Wikipedia has dozens of pages devoted to the word, and yet many authors, including scholars of the topic, write as if these ambiguities are epiphenomenal or unimportant. Thus the two most common meanings of the word— "someone who breaks into computer systems," on the one hand, is by far the most widely-understood across society, and "skilled, possibly self-taught, computer user" on the other, is favored to some extent within digital circles—are in certain ways in conflict with each other and in certain ways overlap. They do not need to be seen as "the same word." Yet so much writing about "hackers" somehow assumes that these meanings (and others) must be examined together because they have been lumped by someone or other under a single label. Today, "hackers" are bizarrely celebrated as both libertarian and leftist political agitators, "outsiders" who "get the system" better than the rest of us do, and consummate insiders. My view is that this terminological blurring has served to destabilize Left politics, by assimilating a great deal of what would otherwise be resistant political energy to the supposedly "political" cause of hackers, whose politics are at the same time beyond specification and "beyond" Left-Right politics.

RS: Could we then, in allusion to Geert Lovink's book title and complaint *Networks Without a Cause*, speak of hacktivism or rather hackerism without a cause?

DG: In my mind, much of what is celebrated as "political activism" by "hacker" groups such as Anonymous is more easily parsed as right-wing than as left-wing activism, but because it gets labeled "hacker" people are hesitant to read the actual politics for what they are.

RS: Why do you see this as right-wing activism?

DG: I consider it right-wing for four reasons: first, because the issues on which it focuses are usually ones on the agenda of the far right (the dissolution of the state, the celebration of individual freedoms over social equality, and a diminished focus on the dangers of concentrated capital); second, because to the degree that hackers declare overt politics, they are usually those of right libertarianism; third, because its culture is so retrograde with respect to Left issues, such as gender and racial equality; fourth, because it celebrates power, both at the individual and personal level, and often celebrates its exercise without any discussion of how power functions in our society. These last two both mitigate, for me, the partially leftist appearance of the anti-rape and anti-pedophilia campaigns sometimes engaged in by Anonymous and others. This is made more bizarre by the fact that the term "hacker" was first popularized in the "skilled computer user" meaning and that among the most famous hackers were Bill Gates, Paul Allen, Steve Jobs, and Steve Wozniak. "Hacking" is supposed to be counter-cultural and resistant to capital, say some on the Left, but many tech business leaders today call themselves hackers; not only does Mark Zuckerberg call himself a hacker, but Facebook makes "hacking" a prime skill for its job candidates, and all its technical employees are encouraged to think of themselves as "hackers."

I have begun some work in which I try to disambiguate the "technical" definitions of "hacker" from its actual deployment in social discourse, and my tentative conclusion is that "hacker" means something like 'identified with and desirous of power, and eager to see oneself and have others see oneself as possessing more power than others do.' That isn't what I see as a welcome political formation. I don't think the criticism I am making here is quite the same topic about which Lovink is writing in *Networks Without a Cause*, as his subject there is what Evgeny Morozov and others have called "slacktivism," or the belief that one is causing or contributing significantly to political change by communicating over social media. At least in those cases, the causes to which one is committed are often clear, even if the results of one's actions are not always clear at all. With "hacking," I am concerned about something closer to effective action that takes on a cloak of Left-oriented social justice and equity concerns, but in fact tends much more clearly to serve Right-oriented interests; I see this concern as the reason Barbrook and Cameron, Borsook, and Winner identified the notion of "cyberlibertarianism," about which I've written a fair amount recently in terms of its impact on Left political goals.

RS: If you could go back in history of new media and digital culture in order to prevent something from happening or somebody from doing something, what or who would it be?

DG: I can't help but find it very interesting to imagine what the Internet would be like today if in 1991 the Commercial Internet Exchange (CIX) had not been established and the High Performance Computing Act had not been passed, and the Internet remained generally off-limits for commercial usage. I think we would today have a wonderfully useful set of tools some of whose problems would not exist or would be substantially mitigated, and I think we would have much less techno-utopianism: especially the suggestion that if we just let capital do what it wants and get out of the way, all of our problems will be solved.

Politics and Government

RS: Speaking of the internet's commercialization, while in the 1990s Internet pioneers such as John Perry Barlow declared the independence of Cyberspace from the governments of the old world, now it seems people hope for governments to intervene in the taking-over of the Internet by huge corporations such as Google and Facebook.

DG: I always saw the rejection of government as unwelcome and part of a general pro-corporate and often explicitly libertarian rejection of core values of democratic governance. Government is and has been the only effective guarantor of egalitarian values that I know of in our world. Libertarians attack this principle specifically; their pro-business philosophy targets places where democratic processes, up to and including rulings of the US Supreme Court, suggest that Constitutional principles require regulatory and statutory guarantees of equality. I am not sure I see yet a robust enough recognition that a rejection of government is itself a rejection of almost the entirety of democracy in any coherent form in which it's been articulated, and that the result of rejecting it can only be massive concentrations of power and capital.

RS: Given the different perspective on the role of the government in society in the US and in, say, Germany one wonders how the Internet would have developed if it had been invented in Europe.

DG: I know much more about the US than about the European context, but my impression is that Europe would have been much more cautious about the commercialization of the Internet, which I think would have been a much better way to run the experiment. Some European countries often have robust rules about the "right to representation" or the notion that individuals "own" any or all data about themselves, and having built out the Internet with that as a foundation would, to my mind, have been preferable.

RS: While for some time and to some people its gift economy imperative let the Internet appear as the last resort of communism, it meanwhile has become a playground of neo-liberalism even centralizing an important public good such as knowledge in the hands of a private company such as Google. In his book *The Googlization of Everything (And Why We Should Worry)*, Siva Vaidhyanathan speaks of Google's "infrastructural imperialism" and calls for the public initiative of a "Human Knowledge Project" as "global information ecosystem". Aware of the utopian nature of his vision, Vaidhyanathan adds that Google has been crowding out any imagination of alternatives, and achieving this not least—and ironically—by virtue of its reputation for building systems that are open and customizable -- so far. Should we mistrust the positive record and worry? Would the US government or the European Union ever have been able to carry out something like Google's book project? Should -and could- they run a search engine free of advertisement and with an algorithm visible to all who care?

DG: We should worry, and though I agree with Vaidhyanathan in many ways, there are some ways in which I think the critique needs to go deeper. The Internet was never a bastion of communism, not without a kind of thoroughgoing establishment of foundations which it never had, and certainly not once the restrictions on commercial use were lifted. At some level I think some kind of public accountability for central mechanisms like search is absolutely imperative, though what forms these can take are not at all clear to me, since exposing parts of the search algorithm almost necessarily makes gaming search engines that much easier, and gaming seems to me a significant problem already. Computerization is always going to promote centralization even as it promotes decentralization—often in one and the same motion. Advocates of decentralization are often almost completely blind to this, directly suggesting that single central platforms such as Facebook, Wikipedia, Twitter and Google "decentralize" as if this somehow disables the centralization they so obviously entail.

This is therefore a set of problems created in no small part by the promulgation of ubiquitous computing itself. At this level I am not sure that having Google search be "owned" by the public or a private corporation makes that much of a difference, although the arguments for it being a public resources (as advanced by legal scholars such as Frank Pasquale and others) I find persuasive, and the existence of governmental communications systems in the past, despite right-wing attacks on them, is compelling evidence that governments can run such systems not just efficiently but also with respect for the equality interests inherent in such systems (that is, the US Postal Service, under constant attack from Republicans, not only works well, but provides services at low cost to populations to whom the provision of services is not economically advantageous).

Centralization is one problem, and I believe we need a much more robust and thoughtful critique of the tendency toward centralization itself: that regardless of its benefits, its drawbacks are more serious than most commentators want to admit. Wikipedia, in my opinion, which in many ways resembles the Human Knowledge Project, is of great concern to me precisely because it intends to be and has partly succeeded at being *the* single site for the totality of human knowledge, and I think there are compelling reasons to suggest that the very idea of a single site for the totality of human knowledge is itself politically suspect, despite its benefits. This is an abstract-level concern, like my concern with Google, that does not have much to do with the actual character of particular Wikipedia pages or the results of particular Google searches, but with a question more like that of monopolies and antitrust. In the heyday of antitrust jurisprudence in the US, it was widely-acknowledged that monopolies of various sorts over any part of the market were inherently unwelcome. Today, under the influence of highly interested parties who themselves want the advantages of concentrated economic power, that thinking has been almost entirely cast aside, and I think it is today needed more than ever, or at least as much as it was in the days of Standard Oil.

Algorithm and Censorship

RS: The numbers of views, likes, comments and the Klout Score –as measure of one's influence in social media– indicate the social extension of the technical paradigm of digital media: counting. The quantification of evaluation only seems to fulfill the "cultural logic of computation" as the title of your 2009 book reads that addresses the aspiration in politics and economics to organize human and social experience via computational processes. The desired effect of counting is comparison and ranking which allows for determining normality and detecting deviance with the effect of predicting, controlling and disciplining human action. However, the effort to measure and classify dates back to at least the Enlightenment and is part of a modern understanding of nature and society. Is computationalism hence nothing more than the continuation of the epistemic logic of modernity by new means after the intermission of postmodern ambiguity and relativism? Where do you see the problem of this concept?

DG: You write: 'the effort to measure and classify dates back to at least the Enlightenment.' That's true. The point of my book is not to deny the effectiveness or importance of quantification; it is to dispute the view that its methods are the only ones that apply to the human sphere. As I briefly discuss at one point in the book, with the Enlightenment comes both the view, most usefully and tellingly associated with Leibniz, that human reason is entirely a function of what we call in a narrow sense rationality—that is, the view that everything in the mind, or everything important in society, can be reduced to mathematical formulae and logical syllogisms. Against this, we have what is sometimes thought of as the "critical rationalism" of Voltaire, a more expansive version of rationalism that recognizes that there are aspects to reason outside of calculation, which in Voltaire's case might include phenomena like irony, skepticism, and a certain humility about the potential of human beings to grasp the totality of experience.

More recently, Derrida encourages us to use the term "reason" in place of this more expansive notion of "rationality," pointing out how frequently in contemporary discourse and across many languages we use the word "reasonable" to mean something different from "rational." I argue in my book that the regime of computation today encourages the narrow view of rationality—that human reason is *all* calculation—and that is discourages the broader view, that reason includes other principles and practices in addition to calculation and logic. I believe some versions of "modernity" tilt toward one, and some tilt toward the other. Projects to quantify the social—including Klout scores, the quantified self, and many other aspects of social and predictive media—advertise the notion that calculation is everything. I think we have very serious reasons, even from Enlightenment and modernist thinkers, to believe this is wrong, and that historically, regimes that have bought into this view have typically not been favorable to a politics of egalitarianism and concerns with broad issues of social equality. My hope is that the pendulum is swinging very far toward the calculation pole, but that eventually it will swing back toward the broader view of rationality, recognizing that there are dangers and fallacies inherent in any attempt to thoroughly quantify the social.

RS: The notion that quantification undermines egalitarianism seems paradoxical, since one could argue numbers, by nature, symbolize equality. Think, for example, of the one head-one vote rule today in contrast to previous restrictions on the base of certain qualities: possession, education, gender, ethnos. What is your concern?

DG: I just don't agree that 'numbers by nature symbolize equality' and I'm not sure how or why one would assert that. Numbers are abstract objects that can symbolize and enforce inequality every bit as much as equality. The one person-one vote rule is a numerical system designed to ensure equality; the one-property owner-one vote rule that the US had in its early days was a numerical system that ensured inequality (as was the "3/5 compromise" under which slaves counted as less than other members of the population for purposes of democratic representation). Further, the reduction to calculation, which is what I talk about—the view that everything can and should be reduced to numbers, particularly when it comes to the social world—has historically been associated much more with Right than with Left political systems, as I discuss at length in my book.

RS: Your book seems to confirm the technological determinism explored, for example, in Alexander Galloway's *Protocol. How Control Exists after Decentralization* (2006) and shares his call for resistance which itself is repeating the call to resist the tyranny of transparency by fog and interference proposed in Tiqqun's "The Cybernetic Hypothesis" (2001) and before by

Deleuze in his discussion with Antonio Negri „Control and Becoming". How do you see today the option to undermine computation and cybernetics as the central means of unlimited rationalization of all human activity in contemporary society?

DG: I take "technological determinism" to be the view that the form of a given technology inherently, and to a large extent regardless of human intervention, shapes society. Using that definition, I would disagree strongly that my book, Galloway's, and the other works you mention endorse technological determinism—quite the opposite in fact. While I think Galloway and I would agree that certain technologies tend to come with implicit politics, these have often been formed by the developers of the technology, and are always or almost always subject to the social matrices in which those technologies are embedded, and the technologies themselves are largely shaped by those social matrices. I agree with Galloway's suggestions about the "tyranny of transparency." To me the way to resist that is to put politics and social good above other values, and then to test via democratic means whether technological systems themselves conform to those values. When they don't, even if they are fun, attractive, addictive, or even very useful, it seems to me we have an obligation as a society to consider limiting or even rejecting those technologies. Otherwise the deterministic factors become all about the market—what can be sold to us, using the most advanced technical means possible to determine what we are least able to resist. That is a tyranny of the market that is antithetical to democracy. I believe we have built a technical system that solicits and captures far too much information about us, and that the only solutions to the enormous problems that it causes are to scale the system itself back, however contrary to received wisdom that may sound. Further, the fact that we are generally prohibited even from considering any such scaling-back of technology as long as a small enough group of people wish to purchase it—witness here the controversy over attempts to regulate or perhaps prevent the distribution of Google Glass, and the extremely arrogant insistence on the part of Google itself and many early adopters that only they have the right to decide whether the technology is acceptable, even if it has detrimental effects on many other people.

RS: Google Glass may be a good example of what I mean by technological determinism and why I am skeptical regarding the prospect of human interventions. You are completely right, Google Glass, as much as Facebook and other new communication technologies, has been formed by developers who more or less represent certain social practices or desires. Given the age of many programmers and their longing to be the next teenage millionaire by coming up with the right app, one wonders to what extent they fulfill social desire and to what extent they produce it. However, my notion of technological determinism alludes to McLuhan's notion that first we shape technology and then technology shapes us. Hans Jonas, in his book *The Imperative of Responsibility: In Search of an Ethics for the Technological Age*, basically repeats this assumption, stating that human power over nature has become self-acting and has turned man into a "compulsive executer of his capacity". Isn't the development of Facebook (its imperative of radical transparency) and the invention of Google Glass (its aim to have the computer and Internet as handy as possible) the inevitable expansion and consequence of what has been created before? To put it this way: When does the cultural logic of computation turn into the logic of technology itself with the result that technology is no longer caused by culture but rather determines it?

DG: Technologies, especially once they are released, absolutely do exert shaping powers on society. Where I part ways is on the question of "inevitability." It is not inevitable that the democratic citizenry should or will accept Google Glass; it was not inevitable that we accepted nuclear power (and we could have accepted it much more than we have); it was not inevitable that the Internet would be commercialized; it is not inevitable that Facebook (at least in something like its current form) is legal, not least for the reasons you mentioned earlier regarding European law, which differs from US law in some important respects regarding the kinds of representations found on Facebook. Television itself was structured by a range of legal and engineering decisions which could have been handled differently. McLuhan is an extremely gnomic thinker, as he not just admits but openly embraces, and it's not always clear how to take some of his statements—even in "the medium is the message," it's not clear which aspects of "the medium" count as "the medium" and which don't. One of the main targets of libertarians in the US is the Food and Drug Administration (FDA), which they believe "impedes innovation." I think the history of the FDA is very clear, and that we have been well-served by having a democratically-empowered body of experts and citizens determine whether or not a particular drug is more harmful than beneficial. Computer technologies are now openly advertised as having life-altering effects as extreme as, or even more extreme than, some drugs. The notion that such powerful technologies must be allowed to proliferate subject only to the "regulation" of the market only fits into libertarian ideas of democracy, and I think and hope that we will reach a point where we understand that democratic constraints on technology are not merely welcome but necessary. Another area where this exact issue is raised is drones. Right now, in the US, FAA and other regulations prohibit most kinds of drone use (other than in military operation). There is nothing inevitable about the question of whether these laws change, and if they don't change, the future will be very different than if, as techno-libertarians demand, the laws are removed and drone operators are just allowed to do as they like.[1] And I do think, following the FDA model, that it is critically important to have democratic regulation of at least some technologies prior to their release, as well as some kind of democratic review of technologies after they have been released. I do not think it is out of the question, for example, that the EU and/or the US will, eventually, prohibit certain parts of the functionality today associated with Facebook.

RS: A FDA for digital media seems to be as reasonable as the FDA is. In Germany there is discussion whether one should create a ministry of the Internet. Of course, there would, especially in the US, be much objection against any regulations. And sure enough there would be references to John Stuart Mill's Essay *On Liberty* and warnings against any kind of 'nanny statecraft' that claims to know better what is good for its citizens – who themselves may find Google Glass just cool and convenient but a bit pricey. However, another 'message of the medium' – and request for the digital media FDA – is customization which causes the loss of chance encounters, the preclusion of the unfamiliar, the removal of diversity and of what we are not (yet). This becomes problematic once people are addressed not as consumers but as citizens expected to be open to others instead of cocooning in their bubble. Hence, personalization, driven by economic force, is political. Are the actual policy makers in the digital media age those who program ego-loops, inadvertently undermining the foundation of a democratic society?

DG: My short answer to your question is a resounding yes. This is a major concern of mine and other critical thinkers about the Internet. Rather than looking at the machine (at websites, Twitter streams, Facebook chats, etc.) to see evidence of "democratization," we should be looking at society itself to see the direction in which it is moving. There is some to my mind highly tendentious research suggesting that certain kinds of anti-authoritarian protest movements may be fueled by the introduction of Internet and mobile telephone communication (mostly in the "Arab Spring"), but this is very different from the question of how such technologies impact existing and deeply embedded democracies. If we look at the period from the early 1990s to the present day in the US, for example, this coincides with one of the most dramatic shifts to the political Right in our history. To be sure this shift started in the 1980s and included many forms of media such as television and radio, but it is absolutely clear that the introduction of the Internet did very little to stop that shift.

Further, it is startling how much the organizational materials of the political Right worldwide sound almost identical to that of the Left, in praising digital and mobile technology as enabling the realization of its political goals. This to me embodies one of the deep paradoxes in Internet evangelism: on the one hand, it says, print and other forms of information technology enabled or even created democracy; on the other, it says, these technologies were insufficient, and something new is needed that jettisons many of the affordances those older technologies had. At worst, one can imagine folks like Jeff Jarvis and Clay Shirky in 1776 saying to Benjamin Franklin, "if only you had the Internet, you'd be able to really have a democracy." This seems like a willful misreading of history to me, one that happens to converge with some very powerful commercial interests.

As your question suggests and as the work of scholars like Matthew Hindman implies, for many different reasons the Internet does not "force" individuals to engage with a wider array of political opinions and in many cases makes it very easy for individuals to do the opposite. Thus we have a new kind of centralization that is not itself regulated in the way that the public service provision of news by the much-derided "big three" television networks in the US of the 1960s and 70s were. There, the centralization was acknowledged and a variety of voluntary and legislative measures were taken to ensure these centralized services fed the public interest—and at that time we had a very robust and very interactive political dialogue in the US. Today, we have unacknowledged and entirely unregulated centralization, and among the most partisan, divisive, and uninformed political discourse in the US that we have ever seen, in part due to the utopian rhetoric that says Internet media is democratizing in a way no other media has been before.

RS: From a German point of view, I can confirm your perspectives with regard to Jürgen Habermas, whose 1962 book *The Structural Transformation of the Public Sphere: An Inquiry into a Category of Bourgeois Society* is often mistaken as a blueprint for the democratic sphere of the Internet. However, in his essay "Political Communication in Media Society: Does Democracy still have an Epistemic Dimension? The Impact of Normative Theory on Empirical Research" (in his 2008 book *Europe: The Faltering Project*), Habermas himself considers the asymmetric system of traditional mass media the better foundation for a deliberative, participatory democracy than the bidirectional Internet. The Internet, he concedes, undermines the old gate-keeping and allows everybody to participate in the discussion. However, the fragmented public sphere online obstructs an inclusive and rigorous debate of the cons and pros of a specific issue and thus does not foster a well informed political engagement.

DG: I agree with this very much. There is a great deal in Habermas that calls into question the easy adoption of his work to the Internet as if it is a realization of his "public sphere." Further, while I am no huge supporter of network television, I find the cribbed accounts of political discourse under the "big three" to be highly contrary to history, both in terms of individual behavior and overall politics. People in general were *more* informed in the 1960s and 1970s than they are today; they were less tolerant of absolutely crazy, fact-resistant political interventions; politics was more productive. I'm not saying this was caused by the networks (although having 3 sites of information about which everyone conversed excitedly may not have been such a bad thing, and is "participatory" and "interactive" in many important senses that Jarvis, Shirky, Jenkins and others dismiss far too quickly), but that the idea that the Internet "democratizes" political discourse seems contravened by the fact that political discourse has become notably less rich, less interactive, more divided, and less productive than it was under earlier media regimes.

RS: Early 2016 one may even ask to what extent it is the distraction and dispersion of the audience on the Internet that allows a person with the discourse quality of Donald Trump to become a presidential candidate.

Art and Aesthetics

RS: People have said that art in or of digital media must be political even if its intentions are to be utterly formalistic. If art is based on technology the focus on form draws attention to how technology works and this is already an act of reflection or education. From this perspective, one would assume that digital art and literature are art and literature that address the politics of digital technology. What is your experience in this regard?

DG: I would never say art "must" be anything. "Art," whatever that is, serves many different purposes, including frequently, no particular purpose at all, other than "being." Art may be used or not used for any number of purposes, intended or not intended by its creators. What resonates for me in this question is the huge amount of digital art that takes as its subject the operation of digital technology itself. I think art can be successful if and when it addresses politics, though it certainly does not need to. Art that addresses digital politics, which at this point includes many ordinary novels and short stories as well as more overtly digital forms, can be as successful as any other art, however we define "success." But there is absolutely a considerable amount of digital art whose purpose appears to be mainly or entirely the demonstration of the capabilities of digital tools. This art strikes me as completely formalist, devoid of any overt politics, and usually lacking any emotional or aesthetic content with which audiences can connect. The inherent politics of such work seems to be to exalt the wonders of the digital world, and for the most part I don't find that a particularly promising direction for the arts to take—it almost functions as a kind of advertisement for Photoshop or for HTML 5 or whatever technology the work is created in, and it is rare that technology demos work, at least for me, in the same register that functions for me as aesthetic, no matter how broadly conceived. It is certainly the case that some of the best digital art (Jodi, Shulgin, Mark Napier, Pall Thayer, Rafael Rozendaal) reflects in various ways on the condition of the digital, but that rarely if ever appears to be its over-riding concern.

RS: To take your skepticism on just flexing the technical 'muscles' even further, one could say this kind of digital art carries out the shift from the culture of meaning to the culture of presence promoted, for example, in Hans Ulrich Gumbrecht's 2004 book *Production of Presence: What Meaning Cannot Convey.*

Though, Gumbrecht does not discuss new media, he considers the '"special effects" produced today by the most advanced communication technologies' as possibly 'instrumental in reawakening a desire for presence.' In this aesthetic theory for the 21st century desire for presence favors materiality and intensive moments over interpretation. The agreeable argument may be that one should not resist the physical and aesthetic pleasure of an artwork by reducing its energy, vitality, and expressiveness to a particular proposition, as Susan Sontag famously stated in her essay "Against Interpretation" in 1964. The problematic consequence, however, is the sheer affirmation of the That without the question for the Why let alone questioning the That. As Gumbrecht puts it fairly clearly, being in sync with the 'things of the world' relieves us of the obligation to better ourselves and the world around us. It is obvious how far this aesthetics has moved from Adorno's notion of art as estrangement and of thinking as negation of the status quo. I wonder to what extent the formalist version of digital art and the contemporary aesthetic theory more or less unconsciously collaborate to step beyond the critical perspective on society you address in your answers above.

DG: I quite like this line of thinking, and it resonates to me to some extent with my experiences in teaching; reading the most breathless of techno-utopians, one might imagine that today's "digital natives" would be almost uniformly enthusiastic about thoroughgoing computerization and the many digital gadgets and effects they live with. Instead—and with the notable exception of very computer-identified hacker and proto-hacker students—I find much the opposite. I find the students, as you suggest, hungry in an intuitive but often explicit sense for the kind of embodied, present experiences for which the digital is usually a mediation, impatient with the tools and their own absorption in them, impatient even with the emphasis on special effects in cinematic media. Though my students are a subset oriented toward literary study, there are many very digitally-fluent folks among them, and I am continually surprised and heartened by the number of them who are deeply skeptical about the wonders being continually sold to them, and who seem to have a fairly good grasp on certain aspects of human experience (the body, face-to-face socialization, relationships, issues of life and death) that writers like Jarvis and Shirky appear to want us to think are vanishing entirely. This also seems to me to connect to the ideas of David M. Berry and Bernhard Stiegler and others, that the plasticity of "human nature" itself to some extent guarantees a building and/or rebuilding of what they (somewhat mechanistically for my taste; like your other interviewee Mihai Nadin, I am a great admirer of the anti-mechanistic biological theories of Robert Rosen) call "long circuits."

Media Literacy

RS: What comes to mind if you hear "Digital Media Studies"? or "Digital Studies" or "Web Studies"?

DG: These are names for existing and valuable fields of academic study. I am concerned that they don't actually name usefully discrete areas of social practice, so that people who go to school now to do "digital media studies" may license themselves to omit huge amounts of cultural practice (chiefly, that which occurred before the mid-1990s, and that which does not occur on a screen), and that these omissions end up not just informing but even structuring the work done by such investigators. You can't understand human culture well by restricting yourself to such a narrow time period. That has been a problem for subfields of Media and Communication Studies to begin with, and a narrow focus on "digital media" threatens to be even worse.

RS: In your book and in your answers above you argue against techno-utopians praising the Internet as a road to more democracy and urge we need to notice and address the ethical, cultural and political costs of computing. What role do or should institutions of elementary and higher education play in this regard? Are Digital Humanities of help or – if replacing interpretation by algorithm, hermeneutics by statistics – rather part of the problem?

DG: The 2013 MLA-conference contained the panel "The Dark Side of the Digital Humanities" which is being followed up with a special issue of *differences* called "In the Shadow of the Digital Humanities," in which I have an essay called "Death of a Discipline." Part of what I argue in that essay is that Digital Humanities is a kind of perfect cyberlibertarian construct—on the one hand, it tells us, it is a method that says nothing about politics; on the other hand, it attracts and often promotes a very specific politics that is deeply at odds with other understandings of the humanities. One aspect of that politics is a resistance to teaching about the core political and politico-philosophical issue that ground any serious understanding of the nature of society and of civic organization. As such, while I am generally in favor of teaching about the "ethical, cultural, and political costs of computing," I consider it more urgent simply to return to teaching ethics, politics, and cultural politics in a much more thoroughgoing way. In too many ways the advent of the computer has enabled a turning-away from such matters throughout the educational system, in favor of a "skill-based" program that is largely a political front—a way of teaching one politics above all others, one that does not even admit the possibility of dissent. Too often the "ethical, cultural, and political costs of computing" are taught from a single, packaged perspective: that "hackers" and "Hacktivists" like Anonymous, Barrett Brown, Jacob Appelbaum, Aaron Swartz, Andrew Auernheimer, Julian Assange and others constitute a site of meaningful resistance to the social costs of computing. From my perspective, they are part of the orthodox view, a pre-scripted site of self-described resistance that is in fact much more continuous with than opposed to the concentration of power. Power is the topic that needs to be addressed throughout the educational system in a much more resistant way than it currently is; these hackers for the most part advocate the use and concentration of power (in their own persons and institutions rather than those they dislike), and political theories that attract me are those that inspire us to resist the accumulation of power in the first place, and its careful, ethical, and judicious use when its use is required.

RS: It has been argued – for example in Berry's 2011 *The Philosophy of Software* – the computational turn in the Humanities could convert the referential totality of human life into a computational 'knowing-that' and knowing how to transform subject matter through calculation and processing interventions. Does Digital Humanities foster the computationalism you address in your book and discussed above with respect to Leibnitz and Voltaire as representatives of two quite different views in the Enlightenment on human reason? Burdick, Drucker, Lunefeld, Presner, and Schnapp in their 2012 book *Digital_ Humanities* (which you have written about on your Uncomputing blog) see Digital Humanities as an ambassador of the Humanities bringing the 'values, representational and interpretative practices, meaning-making strategies, complexities, and ambiguities of being human into every realm of experience and knowledge of the world.' Does Voltaire still have a future after Leibnitz succeeded so fundamentally with his idea of algorithmic machines and formal logic? Or do we have to understand the computational turn as the rejection of Voltaire's irony and skepticism that has thrived for two or three decades in the name of postmodernism?

DG: In my book and in everything I write and say, I try to make clear that my intent is not to eradicate the Leibniz line of thinking, but to suggest that its prominence today makes the Voltaire line extremely hard to see, and that we desperately need both. Not just that, but Voltaire, Swift, and others show the profound danger in the univocal adoption of the Leibniz line—this is something we have known for hundreds if not thousands of years, and it's hard-won knowledge and wisdom, and the fact that we do seem on the verge of forgetting it today is part of what makes the digital revolution frightening. The two books you mention are interesting, because I see Berry as advocating a view that I cannot discount entirely—that a new version of the Voltairian critical reason will emerge as a part of and reaction to widespread computerization. I see this view also in the thought of Stiegler, and I hope it's correct and keep looking for evidence that it may be. On the other hand, the Burdick et al *Digital_Humanities* book strikes me as disheartening evidence in the other direction; I see it as asserting exactly that the Leibniz way of thinking overcomes and makes unnecessary the Voltaire line, and in this sense it comes close to arguing many times that the activities we associate with humanistic practice should be replaced by computation; one notes how rarely anything in that book can be construed as positive commentary on what it repeatedly slurs as "traditional" humanistic practice, including any kind of humanistic scholarship that does not celebrate the digital as utterly transformative.

RS: Since you mention Bernard Stiegler, in his 2008 article *Is Google making us stupid?* and later in his 2011 book *The Shallows – What the Internet is Doing to Our Brains*, Nicholas Carr discusses the consequences of online media for literacy. From Carr's perspective, multitasking and power browsing online make people unlearn deep reading with the effects being carried offline, and with the result that they also unlearn deep thinking. Stiegler certainly shares such perspective and even sees the destruction of young people's ability to develop deep and critical attention to the world around them as a threat to social and cultural development. What is your take on this?

DG: I take Carr's concerns very seriously. I find the reaction to it among the digerati to be too colored by one form or another of a quasi-religious faith in computerization. I think there is lots of empirical evidence to suggest that what Carr is worried about is actually taking place—that certain kinds of political and cultural discourse are, in fact, quite a bit "shallower" than they were for most of the recent and even less recent past. I find Stiegler's comments on Carr to be among the most important interventions in this discussion we have to date. In addition to discussing him occasionally in several recent works, Stiegler offered a seminar in 2012 on Plato, a fairly significant part of which was devoted to Carr; the first session is called "From Nicholas Carr to Plato."[2] If I understand correctly, in addition to and to some extent against Carr's analysis, Stiegler makes two points that seem absolutely vital. The first is, essentially, about temporality: that the time of the digital is a kind of perpetual "now," one that continually suggest a break with everything that has come before, and that this temporality interrupts "long circuits" that are somewhat akin to Carr's "deep thinking," but gain some specificity by being framed in temporal rather than spatial terms. The second is a point that I don't think anyone else has made, or at least has not made as clearly and as well: that even if we accept that digital media is having profoundly interruptive effects on human thinking (which I think Stiegler does, as does Carr, and I find it hard to disagree with this), we actually end up having a contradictory understanding of "the human" if we suggest that human beings will necessarily be unable to develop new "long circuits" that compensate for, and perhaps even extend, the capabilities that may be getting pushed aside at the moment. Rather than having faith in a deterministic technology that will itself "liberate" us from the problems it causes, and rather than dismissing the concerns of writers like Carr and Stiegler and Sherry Turkle and many others, this position allows us to imagine cultural and cognitive re-inscriptions of digital capabilities that recognize that some of what the digital currently pushes away may, in the longer run, be things we as a society do not want to abandon.

RS: This sounds as if the problem technology brings with it also containsentails the solution and will actually advance humanity by pushing to further advance develop its faculty of reason. To play the devils advocate(and to employ a different kind of dialectic), wouldn't it, rather than hoping that certain traditional human capabilities are not abandoned but re-inscribed, be exciting to see the loss as the actual win? In 2010 *Times*-Columnist Ben Macintyre compared the hyper-attentive, power-browsing disposition of the digerati with the fox in Isaiah Berlin's essay "The Hedgehog and The Fox" (1953) about the two modes of thinking. While the hedgehog, Berlin argues, 'relates everything to a single central vision, one system, less or more coherent,' the fox 'pursues many ends, often unrelated and even contradictory.' Berlin favors the fox, as does Macintyre who praises the Internet for turning all of us into foxes because to him – and to a certain extent also to Berlin – the hedgehog-thinking is totalitarian and fundamentalist. Could we appreciate the loss of deep read-ing from this perspective? As openness to different, even con-tradictory information and standpoints and as rejection of any new Grand Narrative; the prevalence of the database paradigm over narrative.

DG: This is a complex question that I've addressed a bit in other answers; I certainly hope that something like this is the case. But I'm discomfited by the portrayal of "narrative" or what I'll also call "interpretive" knowledge as "traditional" and there-fore the database as forward-looking or avant-garde, among other things. The current "fox" forms are ones promoted by commercial power, as a form of political power; they are forms that, whatever their tremendous power today, have been present in human society from its earliest days. No doubt, "fox" think-ing and "hedgehog" thinking each have their day; taken to the extreme, either one can and will be destructive. But in my life-time, I cannot remember moments when it seemed so possible, or when we saw so many argue, that one side or the other had been proven essentially irrelevant to human existence. The desire to obliterate one side or the other is to me the mark of burgeoning totalitarianism. To take the example clearest to hand: reports by a variety of journalists and academics of working conditions inside of Google itself do not appear, to me, to paint a picture of a robust, rights-respecting, participatory culture. It is not a sweatshop or coal mine, and it pays very well, but in many ways the work culture of Google looks to me like the kind of totally-surveilled, conformity-enforcing (in the name of "merit") work-place imagined in dystopian films like *Gattaca*, and the fact that many Google employees honestly think they know what is good for the rest of society better than society itself does is very trou-bling. A healthy democratic society needs a variety of strong viewpoints in active conversation and even (political) conflict; too much of what happens today appears particularly directed toward eliminating these fundamental components of what I con-sider freedom.

RS: Before the Internet became available for private and commercial use it was administered by the university. Today one has the impression the university is no longer on top of development in this domain. How should academic institutions have responded to the upheaval of new media? How should they become more involved today?

DG: Just as a point of fact, I believe universities were among several kinds of institutions that administered the Internet. On the one hand, referring back to the kind of democratic oversight of technological development that I have advocated above, I think universities have backed away from this and could and should do much more, and that in general it is quite difficult to find critical questions about digital technology being raised on US universities today with the same vigor they are raised about other cultural practices—although this is absolutely the kind of awareness and thought I try to encourage in my own teaching. On the other hand, that lack of criticism means that in another sense universities are too involved with computerization—they have, in many different ways, become active and often uncritical promoters of the technology industries, and somewhat often even act as salespeople for technology products.

Political forces in the US have worked hard to diminish any sense of civic or public good (to the extent that this is replaced with a kind of "open source" commons, it has become a vitiated and atrophied concept, one that is all about making resources available to the major information profiteers, like Google). My belief is that the Internet should never have been commercialized to the extent it has been, and this is not a matter for universities alone but for society as a whole. My view is also that higher education itself has been so compromised both by the attack on public goods and by intrusion of capital into spheres from which it was formally barred before, again largely without the consent of most of us involved in higher education, that we have been in many ways unable to provide the civic, intellectual, political and historical contexts that would have been necessary to form an adequate response to overwhelming technological change. Even

in the 1990s I don't think most of us imagined in any serious way
that global capital could so overwhelm nearly every important
institution of civic and public welfare in society, and it is hard to
be surprised that academics, who often rightly remain focused
on their narrow areas of study, were neither prepared nor really
even in a position to mitigate these changes.

Notes

1. Making airspace available for 'permissionless in-
    novation', The Technology Liberation Front April
    23, 2013 - http://techliberation.com/2013/04/23/
    making-airspace-available-for-permissionless-innovation

2. Terence Blake has done an admirable job translat-
    ing the often dense proceedings of this seminar into
    English (http://terenceblake.wordpress.com/2012/06/24/
    translations-of-bernard-stieglers-seminar).

Network Societies 2.0: The extension of computing into the social and human environment

Ulrik Ekman

Ulrik Ekman is well known in the field of digital studies as editor of the 2013 MIT Press compendium *Throughout: Art and Culture Emerging with Ubiquitous Computing* and co-editor of the 2015 Routledge anthology *Ubiquitous Computing, Complexity and Culture.* His main research interests are in the fields of cybernetics and ICT, the network society, new media art, critical design and aesthetics, as well as recent cultural theory. His publications include research articles and chapters such as "Editorial: Interaction Designs for Ubicomp Cultures" (*Fibreculture* 19), "Design as Topology: U-City" (*Media Art and the Urban Environment*; Springer 2015), and "Of Transductive Speed – Stiegler" (*Parallax* 13.4). Ulrik Ekman is a trained computer scientist who worked for years as a systems programmer and systems planner before studying in the humanities (languages, the arts, literary theory, philosophy, cultural studies). He works now

as Associate Professor at the Department of Arts and
Cultural Studies at the University of Copenhagen.

Ulrik Ekman discusses the (assumed) democratic potential of
digital technology and social media, the haunting of Turing's
ghost, the third wave of computing as its extension into the
social and human environment and externalization of psychological individuation in techniques. He talks about the role of
algorithms as means of personalization and foreclosure, the
affirmative and subversive energy of surveillance art, the transdisciplinary call of media literacy and the 'interpellative' aspect
of participatory culture.

Prelude

Roberto Simanowski: If you could go back in history of new
media and digital culture in order to prevent something from
happening or somebody from doing something, what or who
would it be?

Ulrik Ekman: It would be quite interesting to have been in
a position to insert some kind of critical wedge in a relatively
important situation back in the 1930s when Turing came up with
the model of the computer as a universal machine. This notion
of a universal machine with the potential to simulate all other
machines and their programs almost founds and certainly forms
the context for what can be called "digital media studies" and
"digital culture." It has been incredibly influential, first as an
idea, then as a model and a sort of blueprint, and then not least
for the making of ever so many real computers. If I wanted to
make different noise and disturbance here, this is motivated by
the tensions in Turing's thought, the tendential idealization of
the modern computer, as well as by the questions raised by contemporary developments in the culture of ubiquitous computing.
I continue to question the tensions between the finite and the
infinite, the discrete and the continuous in Turing's work. One
cannot but note the tension: all real computers must by necessity
remain finite and discrete, but in order to take on all computation

they must have infinite and continuous memory. A disturbance here would almost certainly have deconstructed the ideality so as to afford openings of different epistemologies of computation. These, or some of these, would be less than universal, perhaps general, perhaps particular, perhaps oriented towards the singularity of computation. Some of them would surely also deviate from ideality towards questions of various real embodiments of computation in machines.

RS: What would have changed through such a disturbance?

UE: In a sense, my wish to disturb stems from having just one apparently simple question in mind: are the computational units of current developments in the culture of ubiquitous computing still modern computers of which one could say that they are truly Turing heirs? If the heuristic idea of ubicomp today is supposed to be one of computation qua embodied virtuality in operation, if the diagram today is supposed to be a human-oriented, context-aware, and calm computing, and if such a diagram maps out in practical concretizations as multitudes of wired and wireless computational infrastructures with decentralized distributions of sometimes highly specialized units demonstrating mobility and ad hoc networking... are we then still talking about modern computers? Do you still want to think of the link between a sensor and an actuator in a dynamically connective and mobile network dealing only with the temperatures of 200 square feet in a forest or a field as something involving a universal machine? So, my wish to make different noise with and against Turing has quite a bit to do with seeing a need for a revised set-up of theoretical ideas. I also see a need for recognizing another set of existing blueprints or diagrams for computation and computers. Not least I affirm a need to observe that saying "digital culture" today often implies that we are already living with an enormous and growing set of real computers that might be becoming different together and have us exist differently, too. I am still not done with the intricacies of Turing machines, but perhaps we can return to this later.

Politics and Government

RS: From early on the Internet has been attributed with democratic value as a new public sphere of radically liberated communication, an update of Habermas' model of deliberative democracy. With the Web 2.0 the promise even increased with keywords such as participation and transparency. During the last years, however, a critical turn in digital media studies has pointed out the perils rather than the promises of the Internet, Web 2.0, and mobile media. How do you see this matter?

UE: How can it be that one can come across arguments during the 1990s that the 'information society' and 'cyberspace' are more or less inherently 'democratic,' that they in and of themselves offer a new kind of 'community' in a way that earlier social and cultural studies had apparently left as an unresolved matter; and that they give us the kind of 'public sphere' presumably requested in the wake of the semi-demise of much Frankfurt School theoretical work? I am still amazed that critical engagements with these kinds of lines of argument have either tended to be too absent or to peter out relatively fast. One of the things behind my wish to have been inserted as a critical wedge at some relevant point in this broad discursive development is that it seems to repeat itself without enough of a difference that makes a difference. When we get to the period around 2005, we see much the same kind of statements being made, only now it is in the main a question of the positive potential versus pitfalls of social media, blogging, micro-blogging, and then mobile media.

Of course, it is not that critical efforts are entirely absent – I recall self-reflexive efforts in the media and in journalism, alongside research articles discussing this critically, and a number of reconsiderations of the work of Durkheim, Raymond Williams, Habermas, Giddens, Castells, and more. However, these efforts were inconclusive, did not lead to any consensus, and dwindled away within a five-year period. In the next cycle, from 2005 onward, the critical engagement is actually much weaker, smaller in scale, and even less influential. Considering the demise of the Left, the broad socio-historical developments

after 1989, and the impact of liberalisms on globalization processes in a broad sense, this is hardly surprising. Nonetheless,
I would still like to have disturbed this tendential silencing of
critical or alternative or differential thoughts.

RS: Maybe it was even this, the declared end of Grand Narratives
and of History, as competition between different socio-political
models, that made all desire for a better world emigrate into new
media, hoping technology would save us from post modern and
post historical frustration.

UE: I think we agree on now being able to identify a certain
historical and theoretical rupture here. Perhaps you are right
that some of the perceived losses in this have fueled some of the
remarkably strong interest in new media as well as science and
technology studies. It might be an exaggeration, however, to say
that all desire and all hope emigrated to these fields. Perhaps
it would be more accurate to say that one finds here a rather
strong tendency to idealize and emphasize rather one-sidedly
what appeared to many as the positive potential in these developments. To my mind this still calls for different critical reevalu-
ations. Today it remains interesting and non-trivial to ask in
what senses computers, computer science, and cybernetics as
the discipline of steering and control could be said to afford
media, mediations, and communicational platforms for 'democracy,' 'community,' and 'public spheres.' Something analogous
goes for the ethico-political potential of networks, network (dis)
organizations, and network protocols to be 'democratic,' 'social,'
and capably open to differentiated debates with a certain rea-
sonableness and egalitarian influence. Network societies, decentralized networks, and the overriding concern with security and
control of infrastructure and information with a view to survival
originated not least in post-WWII military-industrial complexes
alongside a small number of university research centers in the
Western hemisphere. The numerous ethico-political and socio-
cultural tensions and differences inherent in this have neither
been resolved nor yet been treated thoroughly and convinc-
ingly in existing research nor in the media, in my opinion. If that

were the case, we could not today be witnessing in the media a late outcome of the post-9/11 ethico-political coupling in 'democratic' network societies of terror, security, and surveillance. I am thinking not just of the quiet acceptance or affirmation of the 'need' for surveillance by the people in many 'democratic' nations, nor just of much needed momentary alternate wake-up calls like Snowdon's, but of how disturbingly exceptional it is to see influential prime ministers object publicly to foreign intelligence services tapping their cellphones.

RS: If you allude to the German Chancellor Angela Merkel, I am less surprised than you that she abstained from serious reproaching her ally United States – in contrast for example to the Brazilian president Dilma Russeff who used her objection against the U.S. to overcome the *Vemprarua*-turbulence in her own country. While in the 1990s, regarding the Internet, the government in the Western World experienced itself "at war with our own products," as Klaus Lenk put it in the 1997 edition *The Governance of Cyberspace*, today all governments of the world are certainly relieved that the anarchy of the early days has morphed into the regulation and control we experience now. 9/11 is only an excuse for what was already clear after Perry Barlow's 1996 *Declaration of the Independence of Cyberspace*: That the "Governments of the Industrial World" will *not* leave alone "the new home of mind" as Barlow describes the cyberspace.

UE: In my earlier remarks my focus was somewhat more limited. My attention was on one part of the political axis, notably the post-9/11 developments concerning intimate linkages among terror, national security, and surveillance – up to and including the current operations of the NSA. Today some of the more critical and heated exchanges among the U.S. and several European nations concerning the politics of surveillance appear to have worrisome potential outcomes. The messages from Germany, France, and others make it clear that the Internet and the WWW as we have known them should perhaps not be taken for granted. We might see the reappearance of strictly regional and not least strictly national politics of informational security and surveillance that will imply so many deconstructions of the very idea of a decentralized global network of networks such as the Internet. Of course, such politics have always been there, but increasingly strong general strictures of this national sort would still mean an incredible loss of potential for the development of network societies on a global and more cosmopolitan scale. The "new home of the mind" that you mention could very well come to stay much closer to your physical national territory and its political governance.

RS: As for the "new home of mind" these 15 years later, your collection of essays *Throughout. Art and Culture Emerging with Ubiquitous Computing* 2013 with MIT Press presents almost 700 pages with essays by more than 40 leading researchers on digital media and cultural theory from a vast array of academic fields with quite different perspectives on the promises and perils of computing. What are the most interesting or challenging aspects to you about this topic?

UE: During the period we have worked on the book (it started in 2008 via a Danish but very internationally oriented research network), ubicomp, pervasive computing, ambient intelligence, things that think, and the Internet of Things have become much more of an empirical fact. Enough so that we have net addresses and a net protocol with the capacity to deal with the billions of computational units involved, enough so that these major lines of development are becoming solid parts of the latest editions of the standard textbooks in computer science, hardware engineering, software development, and HCI. And enough so that a great many people in the world are beginning to notice that the ground is shifting here and there underneath network societies that now begin to move from a phase one to a phase two, expanding and intensifying networking problematics along the way.

RS: Can you illustrate this shift to a phase two and the problems it contains?

UE: For example, even in a very small country like Denmark one finds a handful of research groups at work on 'pervasive healthcare,' something whose massive distribution and use of smart computational things and wirelessness might well soon alter our notion of the home, healthcare, and how to address the elderly in nations with a demography tilting in that direction. Or consider the first dozen intelligent cities, smart cities, and u-cities now being built with some kinds of ubicomp capacity from the ground up. These are experimental projects in South-East Asia mostly, but also factual developments in an epoch with an intensive interest in the development of edge cities, megacities, and new kinds of urban regions. But I should still start by stressing that on the other side of the initial visions from Mark Weiser and his Xerox Parc colleagues along with many others in Europe and Asia, multitudes of technical issues remain unresolved. The cultural dimension remains very much more underdeveloped both in research and in cultural practices. This is an asymmetry that this book is trying to address and change a bit by focusing somewhat more on the cultural and human sides of this.

RS: Ubiquitous computing furthers the information society we live in by extending the presentation and processing of information beyond computers. The new buzzwords, you already said it, are *Internet of things* or *programmable world* referring to objects that talk to each other and process information even without presenting themselves to us. Advocates speak of the swimming pool that heats up when it sees there is a Barbecue on the calendar, they project the fridge that automatically restocks, and they hope for sensors attached to asthma inhalers mapping their usage to communicate areas of risk as part of that 'pervasive healthcare' you mentioned. Skeptics, on the other side, warn of even more loss of privacy as well as of malicious hacks into shopping lists, cars, and pacemakers. How do you see this development? Are the perils worth the benefits?

UE: Thank you for your insistence on pressing these issues of critical evaluation. I hear more than a faint echo of your last question here, so let me return to the interesting and the challenging, the benefits and the perils... Perhaps there is only one issue, perhaps Simondon saw this already. It might be he was right that the organization of complexity is a phylogenetic aim which belongs to biological species but finds interesting analogies in the way technical objects and systems exist. The most interesting and the most challenging, the benefits and the perils are but flip sides of this: ubicomp cultures design complexity and this is their frontier. Technically speaking, the passage of time and all the repeated design processes make ubicomp objects and systems pass through successive modifications. This tends to have them develop from more abstract and diagrammatic states to more concrete states, something we are approaching today in rudimentary ways. The benefit-peril here is that ubicomp systems are called upon to move from a more or less self-referential performance structure (not entirely unlike what you tend to find in Turing machines) to one that is hetero-referential.

RS: That means the systems are open to their environments?

UE: Ubicomp systems are precisely not to remain disconnected from the context but are to become gradually *more* contextualized in a process of mutual adaptation of system and context or environment. This is a route that leads towards the more complex – the solution of complexity is a phylogenetic aim, as Simondon liked to say. It is interesting-challenging that adaptation to context is still truly difficult for computational systems, and that 'context' here tends to mean both the real/virtual environment *and* its human inhabitants. There is a reason for the nicknaming of these main lines of development (ubiquitous, pervasive, ambient, etc.): they are all taking names to suggest the expanded character of computation and computing. So, pressed by your questions I would point to these two main sources of beneficial-perilous complexification: context-awareness and adaptation to the *anthropos*, both of which will demand the production and recognition of meaning.

RS: As for the expanded character of computing, this reminds me of McLuhan's take on media as extension of man. Since the computer is already such an extension, are we then talking about the extension of extension and should we, since McLuhan considered such an extension at the same time an amputation of human capacity, also talk about the expansion of amputation? With the words I used before: What about malfunctions and hacks in complex context-oriented computational systems?

UE: One large part of computing in the expanded field concerns such extensions of man. But perhaps your remarks stay a little too close to the anthropocentric. For approaching current developments along this path might often lead to blindness or forgetting of the more singularly technical relationalities, including those of autonomous agents communicating among themselves without any human interception. Naturally, this might be what you have in mind when referring to McLuhan's notion of amputations of human capacity. To my mind, the use of this term would then tend towards a too one-sided and negatively critical approach. Moves towards autonomous technical individuations also involve inventions of the other that might be less of an amputation than an augmentation, for technical as well as human systems. So, amputation is obviously one important dimension in this, but only one of them. Something similar goes for malfunctions and hacks. It is obvious that an increase in complexity of human and technical systems and their interrelations paves the way for what can become an exponential rise in the number of malfunctions and possibilities of hacking. Moreover, if the ideas of the invisible computer and calm or embedded computing are privileged in research and development, malfunctions and hacks can become extraordinarily difficult to recognize and counteract as such. Nonetheless, all malfunctions and hacks come freighted with potentials for invention and positive improvement.

I would like to affirm the initiatives to move towards a human-oriented computing, and I am excited about the challenges and difficulties of having technical and human context-awareness co-develop. Still, I am deeply unsettled and disturbed by a range of the ethico-political implications in both the visions for this and in a range of the kinds of implementation we can already find and follow today. It should be obvious reason for concern that the ongoing work on new technical infrastructures with something like ubicomp processual capacity also means infrastructural and infraprocessual acceptance on a societal level of monitoring, surveillance, tracking and tracing, information gathering to a degree and with an intensity we have not yet known. The cultural theoretical uptake and the broader social debate are lagging behind or might be almost missing. But even the engineers and system planners know and make explicit that trust, security, privacy and the secret, ownership of information, and transparency remain major issues still to be dealt with. I look forward to seeing the development in tandem of the technical systems and the sociocultural dimensions to go with and against these.

RS: I completely agree with your notion about the lagging and lacking theoretical uptake of the technological development. Let me press you a bit more on the new technologies' ambivalence of great opportunities and unwanted but perhaps inevitable consequences in the ethico-political regard. Pervasive computing has found its own popular movement in what is known as Self Tracking, Quantified Self and Living by Numbers. Of course, the pervasive data aggregation in the name of self-knowledge and self-optimization facilitates big data mining and helps paving the way to pervasive control and algorithmic regulation. Here we encounter a problem similar to Simondon's phylogenetic desire for complexity: the desire for knowledge. A major method of gaining knowledge is to measure and survey, which in the age of digitization and datafication leads to a boost of empirical sociology beyond the academic field. The flipside of conducting measuring, however, is taking measures. No government, no health department, no insurance company or credit institute can afford not to react – or, better, take preemptive actions – if certain patterns and correlations of behavior are established. Knowledge obliges. The results are regulations justified by algorithmic analysis enforced by ubiquitous computing – unless society decides, for ethical reasons, to forbid certain knowledge or its utilization. But who would argue against the desire to know?

UE: It is obviously unrealistic, unnecessary, and also to a large extent undesirable to argue against a desire to know. Your question appears to me to be one respecting the status of the relation between current technics and the political economy of subjectivation and governmentality. This appears to be a question that is partly motivated by recent empirical developments, but also one posed in a theoretical vein not all that foreign to Deleuze's short text on control societies plus the last parts in his Foucault book, the work of the late Foucault, as well as a considerable body of sociological and critical theoretical work in recent surveillance studies picking up on this heritage. However, the empirical developments you mention are still far from being widespread and strong enough to be able to claim any kind of sociocultural significance. At most they are particular examples, perhaps some relatively weak social chains that may have generalizable potential a bit further down the road. This should itself warn against proceeding too fast, against drawing conclusions.

Second, I register a certain vacillation, or actually a slide in your question, moving from 'ambivalence' through 'facilitation' to 'control,' 'regulation,' as well as 'enforcement' by ubiquitous computing. It appears to me to make quite a difference whether you point to an undecidability, to a facilitation of actualizing a certain potential, to a normative mode of regulation, to a stronger notion of political control, or to something like a technological determinism. I am sure that a number of readers of Foucault and Foucauldian work, for example, will immediately recognize both the issue of how to distinguish among these and the ongoing difficulty of actually doing so in practice. I think all of these are in play in the parts of the history of the present that have to do with ubicomp and its enculturation via social and personal individuations – except the last one. That is, I do not subscribe to the notion of technological determinism that seems to lurk in your question.

RS: Your impression is correct. My question aims at the central issue in media studies: whether media have their own agenda or whether they are just tools serving the demands of people. Though I do not follow technological determinism à la Friedrich Kittler, I do share McLuhan's belief that the medium itself "shapes and controls the scale and form of human association and action." However, since we first shape technology and technology then shapes us, as McLuhan would say, I am especially alerted if representatives of a big technology company declare that technology is neutral but people are not. For example, this was claimed by the former Google-CEO Eric Schmidt and the current director of Google Ideas Jared Cohen in their 2013 book *The New Digital Age. Reshaping the Future of People, Nations, and Business.* I consider such an objection to technological determinism less a theoretical perspective than a strategic statement, a self-serving denial of any responsibility for the social and cultural changes that a mega player on the Internet such as Google no doubt brings to society. But you are right, if I slide from 'facilitation' to 'control' I am shifting from the message of the medium to the characteristic of social systems: Autopoiesis. I see the control and regulation I am addressing with respect to pervasive data aggregation as a means of the social system to regulate, stabilize, and reproduce itself – as discussed for example in Foucauld's concept of governmentality. Can we expect administrative and intelligence apparati not to use every technology available to improve their work?

UE: This substantiates your question considerably and makes it easier to address. We agree that neither human nor technical systems and agents are neutral. We are misunderstanding each other part of the way since you point towards media and I most often address questions of technics prior to discussing media. Moreover, however, I think we disagree as regards determinism and causation. I do not believe that we first shape technology only then to have technology shape us. I think of technics and the sociocultural as co-existing and co-developmental, and I tend to press this quite far towards a relational ontology, not unlike what you find in Simondon and his thought of transduction. This means I also very often, but not always, will parenthesize anthropocentrism (something at work also in Simondon's thought of the mode of existence of technical objects). Sometimes I do this by insisting that 'we' *are* relating as technological beings and entities (Leroi-Gourhan comes to mind), and that distinctions or binary oppositions such as human/machine, culture/technics, and lifeworld/system are always already off on the wrong kind of track. So, ubicomp is not really the technological Other (capital 'O') for 'us' humans but rather how we currently tend to exist and live on with technics, how technics exists with humans, among other things. To put it a bit provocatively: there is always something machinic in me that could be made operational, there is always something preindividually human in technics that could be put into operation.

RS: Agreed that the (technological) Other is somewhat part of us, agreed that technology is also the response to and result of certain socio-cultural patterns of behavior. However, society is not a uniform factor sharing the same values and ideas. We know that for example 'digital natives' see the issue of transparency and privacy quite differently as compared with older generations. Given that the younger generation is driving the development of the new technologies that sooner or later affect all of society, the Other may in fact less be a problem of the culture/technology-opposition than of differences within a culture or between cultures within a society respectively.

UE: I think we have less than a disagreement here and more of a misunderstanding of terms or conceptual armature. Perhaps I have failed to make clear the extensional reach as well as the interior character of my notion of technics. The differences within a culture and the differences among cultures that you gesture towards here always already involve technics and mediation, as does your gesture here (and any human gesture). If there is not really a culture/technology opposition, in my view, this is because human cultures exist technologically. This goes for relations concerning interior as well as exterior environments, and these involve social and cultural others as well as otherness more generally. It could well be that the main part of the misunderstanding here is due to my attempt to stick with the more general problematic of technics. Of course you are quite right to point to the need for a finely differentiated analysis of the socio-cultural values and ideas at stake in the development of current technics and I would be very interested to see this fleshed out in future work.

Let me try to get back to your earlier question concerning surveillance in an epoch with ubicomp. To my mind the techno-cultural potential of ubicomp is still undecidable, and there is nothing 'inevitable' about actualizations of self-surveillance – or, for that matter, sousveillance, or inverse surveillance. I do agree that an immanentist and critical approach to a history of the present is called for, but that still permits me to be at a remove not only from a determinism and a control, but also from pushing any notion of a normative regulation in one specific and more and less worrisome or negative direction. Your question is highly relevant and points to pressing concerns. But that does not prohibit me from affirming quite some faith both in a radical democracy and a cosmopolitanism to come *and* in existing democracies, their laws, institutions, and populations. Subjectivation with ubicomp, governmentality with ubicomp, -- these are extremely interesting questions. Nonetheless, general second-order self-control and massive, invisible, proactive code-regulation are not the only open doors here, nor even the most likely to be or stay actualized in the slightly longer run. Certainly they do not actualize the best value-systems, nor do they even pave the way for the stronger politics of sensation and mediaesthetics, the one with a better chance to survive with other means.

Algorithm and Censorship

RS: One buzzword of the present time is „smart things," objects such as my refrigerator, my coffee cup, and the windows in my building, that communicate among each other in order to process information that I had to take care of myself earlier. Hence, computers not only do more than just computing; they also do it with a much wider scope and have become much smaller than the computers of the 20th century. How do you see the future of computing?

UE: What a truly impossible question! But, in a sense, the impossible invention is the only one of interest, the only invention; so let me try to answer... I could just say to you that smart things and ubicomp will largely be the same as modern computing because computers are still modern. Or, I could say that ubicomp will certainly change modern computing and this decisively because smart things and smart materials are smaller, mobile, massively distributed, materially and environmentally embedded, wireless, context-aware, and ad hoc connective. But let me instead try to move alongside just one such formal and undecidable opening.

Actually, we were already moving towards something like this very early in our conversation when we discussed Turing's work. Perhaps smart materials, smart things, and ubicomp units already have altered the tendency to idealize the modern computer unduly. Even today, though, I am hearing Turing echoes: Turing machines are as powerful as real machines; they can execute any program that a real computer can; they can simulate all other computers, etc. These echoes remain – but perhaps they have in fact begun to die out. Smart things certainly remind us that real computers need electricity and run into unexpected conditions (just a little dust, or a user armed with a bottle of Coke). Smart materials have a finite number of configurations, have finite internal storage, and they are disturbed by input/output. Ubicomp systems can only manipulate a finite amount of data, remain delimited by processing time concerns, and solicit algorithms that are not general and indifferent to the actual limits imposed on memory... Or, inversely, ubiquitous computing systems do remind us of their difference from Turing machines because they do much more than permit of procedures: they are perhaps really good models of a great many important programs which assume continuous and unbounded input over time, and ongoing computation rather than halting. Perhaps the numerous units connecting and collaborating on and off in ubicomp environments are different enough to remind us that Turing machines should be *more* continuous and infinite. But that this should take place down along the more unpredictable and often complexity-generating axis of the context: peripherals, I/O, interfaces, and interaction design, meaningful human lives and their kinds of context-awareness...

When you are involved in, move through and engage with (consciously or, more often, unconsciously) mixed realities with multitudes of computational units dynamically organizing and disorganizing context-aware and human-oriented mixed reality environments around you, do you then still live with real computers reminiscent of Turing machines? If computation is increasingly embedded and increasingly becomes a question of microscopic MEMS, so that the very form and materiality of your cup, the texture of your clothing, the pigment of your wall and wallpaper are computational, does that bespeak a modern computer heritage?

My questions are sincere: I cannot decide, you cannot decide. At most one can begin to trace margins, cracks, some kind of openings that are on the edge of what remains to come in computing, if anything. I do think Turing machines are being marginally disturbed today. It is not just that they do not model continuous I/O and concurrency well, nor that computational complexity theory has begun to point out some problematic kinds of reductionist assumptions. Rather, new ideals, diagrams, and de facto implementations today disturb them. Not a little of this could perhaps be seen as a pull towards anthropological, biological, chemical, and physical 'logics' of computation. I am still with Turing's ghost: I tend to be tempted to ask Turing, not to decide, but how he opens up to thinking, diagramming, and living with human-computer emergence and the complexity of current technocultural (dis)organizations.

RS: The notion of living with*in* a computational environment instead of *with* computers as we knew them, is not undisturbing. Equally alarming is that smart things may conceal the difference that information is said to make, if we don't realize what information all the smart things process, and how. Do we need a new theory of information and communication?

UE: The concealment and the invisibility are not in and off themselves new – computers are doing this all the time, as they always did. The idealization of becoming *more* invisible, calm, and unobtrusive is perhaps partly new and should be scrutinized carefully, with ethico-political issues in mind. However, perhaps you are right to point towards the need for a new theory since the move towards a human-oriented and human-centered computing might disturb the currently hegemonic theorization.

Would it not have been of interest to disturb the work and the outcome of Shannon and Weaver's work on communication theory in the mid- to late 1940s, so that their notions of 'communication' and 'information' were made to pursue and include a few of those dimensions, lines, and points they clearly saw and knew about but still bracketed quite resolutely? Material machines, embodiment, life, animality, humanity, context, and semantics... the purposeful delimitations and reductions of all these must necessarily be scrutinized again today, considering the development of the third wave of computing and cybernetics. For example, can we stay with their influential work if we are to see a human-oriented, context-aware computing engaging dynamically with the more or less meaningful intentions and interactions of so many humans?

Naturally, this is a question that has been asked before, by Katherine Hayles for example, and so we have seen recent revisitations of the ghosts of Donald McKay's and Raymond Ruyer's competing theoretical work on information, communication, and meaning at the time.

RS: McKay and Ruyer against Shannon and Weaver? What would this contribute to a 'third wave' of computing?

UE: I am trying to point to the need in a third wave of computing for expanded notions of information and communication, notions not necessarily formalized as strictly in terms of mathematics and statistics as were those of Shannon and Weaver. One of the crucial hinges here is the approach to meaning and semantics. In my view, a context-aware and human-oriented third wave of computing must be able to deal differently with meaningful information and communication than did Shannon and Weaver's theory. Ruyer's work on living matter and its influence on Simondon,

Deleuze, and Guattari are largely forgotten today, as are his ideas in *La cybernétique et l'origine de l'information*. But here you actually find an attempt to think cybernetics and information in material, biological, and machinic terms, including an important role for organic productions of sense or meaning. In McKay's work on information, you do find a part that has to do with the value of the probability of its selection, but you also find a structural part which is to assure its correct *interpretation*, a semantic aspect to be decided via the changes effected in the recipient's mind. This more subjectively oriented and clearly semantic notion of information stayed alive for some time in the British school of information theory. But it must have appeared too inconsistent and at any rate too difficult to measure mathematically, judging from the way in which American cybernetics moved on in the 40s.

We never had just one theory of information and communication – there were always many. There is no doubt that also today a large number of researchers are drawing upon notions of information and communication that are considerably softer, looser, or more fuzzy than those formalized by Shannon and Weaver for efficient signal processing. Considering the current developments in network societies that move towards technical self-organization, embodied virtuality, and types of systemic context-awareness that are not just a question of GPS but must operate with a certain human semantic and semiotic reach, there are many good reasons for other notions of information as well as communication. These notions tend to reinscribe some kind of human language and cognition, but this often remains implicit or tacit in current research, and perhaps it is safe to say that these issues remain unresolved and only very partially addressed at this point in time.

Still, one can observe at least two common responses to this challenge. The first is to shy away, noting on the way that one of the seemingly uncircumventable facts is that Shannon and Weaver's theory is the wider and actually works. It has been quite exorbitantly successful as regards proving its worth, and today it infiltrates practically all communication whose operations and informational messages involve computers. One well-known further transdisciplinary move down this axis is Kittler's insistence, dehumanizing to some, that 'there is no software' – just the hardware objectification of an informational language. Then information works in terms of the probability of materializing certain numerical values of two variables: noise-free signal input and a separate source of noise... Just as the human subject and its agency are a structural function of advanced technical systems, one materialization of their statistics.

The second common response is to acknowledge and affirm the need today for another set of notions and a new mode of operation that can meet the call for a human-oriented and context-aware (smart, intelligent, ambient, pervasive, ubiquitous) computing with semantic and semiotic reach as in existing human languages and cognition. However, on the technical side of the systems involved this almost always means to go on using Shannon and Weaver's work. Only now one inserts on top of that base a higher level theory (program or algorithm) that simulates the solution called for. The vast majority of work in hardware engineering, network organization, and software development I have seen so far takes that kind of layering approach for granted, and an abstract, universal mathematical idealism or formalism tends to stay intact on top of this. The search for abstract invariants and the simplest, most elegant code or algorithm is still altogether hegemonic here.

Perhaps Herbert Simon was right when he argued that complexity often takes the form of hierarchical systems and that often one can be quite resolutely pragmatic about reductionism and remain with weak notions of emergence and complexity. I am not yet convinced, though, that this will altogether do with respect to the informational, communicational, semantic and semiotic dimensions of context-aware and self-organizing computing and their embodied virtualities of today. In addition, I find it interesting that important recent efforts in philosophy and systems theory can be seen to resist this kind of reductionism, quite insistently. Derrida's way of making cybernetic programs subservient to the trace is one such insistence – an insistence on a moving internal differential complication and complexification of human consciousness. Luhmann's work in social systems theory is another interesting example, one that actually echoes clearly McKay's work on information. I am thinking of Luhmann's argument to the effect that 'meaning' remains the basic concept of sociology. On his view, 'meaning' is a functional concept, one that must be presumed working in order for experience processing to be able to decide among different possible states or contents of consciousness. What does not get chosen here is not altogether eliminated but memorized and in some way kept accessible. For Luhmann, this made 'meaning' irreducible to 'information.' Its function is not to eliminate system-relative states of uncertainty about the world or environment. It is special and basic... It is not just that 'meaning' is a selective *relationship* between system and environment, but that it enables both reduction *and* preservation of complexity...

RS: Let me turn the question of information, meaning, and system to the experience of the Internet today. It is a known fact that Internet companies use personal data and personalizing algorithms to customize the websites they show us, the ads they send us, and the information they give us. One metaphor to describe the digital media age may therefore be 'narcissism' which in digital media studies translates to "daily me" (in Cass Sunstein's book *Republic.com*) or "you-loop" (in Eli Pariser's book *Filter Bubble*). The fate of Narcissus is well known. The personal and cultural cost of personalization in digital media is the loss of chance encounters, the preclusion of the unfamiliar, the removal of diversity and of what we are not (yet). The algorithm is the censor people more or less approve of and even desire. This becomes problematic once people are addressed not as consumers but as citizens expected to be open to others instead of cocooned in their bubble. Hence, personalization, driven by economic force, is political. Hence, are the actual policy makers in the digital media age those who program ego-loops, inadvertently undermining the foundation of a democratic society? Or is the alert regarding personalization hyperbolic and rather the clandestine update and comeback of the claim of critical theory that the cultural industry impedes citizens' release from their self-incurred tutelage?

UE: There is not all that much metaphorical about the narcissistic plane in this development – it is in a sense quite literal and real coding, something which makes your question all the more relevant. But I also have to admit that I tend to find this to have a more double face. I agree that in certain ways the corporations, the programmers, and the web designers deploying codes and algorithms are most often asymmetrically favored in medial as well as politico-economic terms, at least on obviously corporate sites. However, even though this most often goes for blogging and social media as well, here such asymmetries can be reversed to a certain extent, mostly on the medium-specific and communicational planes. Personalization becomes interactive in the other direction as well, and sometimes it becomes a genuinely social affair, so that Internet mediation also becomes socialized rather than just having people become 'personalized' and normatively 'socialized' by the web medium.

Algorithms exist on many planes in this, and altogether generally speaking I still find them to carry individual and social affordance-potential as well as potential for what you call 'censorship' plus loops and foreclosure (perhaps rather strong terms in a great many cases and contexts). I agree that the study of the role and status of algorithms and code is gradually becoming a much more pressing concern in contemporary network societies. I am truly glad to have seen a first little series of initiatives during the last five years or so to establish culture-oriented software studies as a legitimate sub-discipline. This is far too new a development that one can estimate its reach or outcome, but I am very glad to affirm it.

Let me return to your question. I think you are, much like Stiegler for instance, perhaps a little too worried and too critically disposed with respect to the socio-political and personal implications here. The tendencies with respect to normative personalization and socialization you are diagnosing are, of course, very recognizable to me and to many others. I do have critical questions here, but perhaps my focus tends to be on narcissistic processes other than the corporate normative overdetermination by algorithmic coding that you have singled out here.

RS: OK, let us come back to the myth of Narcissus that somehow also is about media literacy. The reason Narcissus dies is, according to one of the many sources, that he does not know that still water functions as a mirror and that he has no concept of a mirror. As a consequence, he falls in love with his own beauty after he just rejected the love of Echo who is doomed to only repeat the last words she heard, i.e. be a sonic mirror instead of a visual one. Thus, Narcissus' tragedy is actually that he was not content with being confined to himself. He was narcissistic against his own will and good. How is the situation with digital media?

UE: This myth is open to a great many readings and rewritings, including yours, and perhaps that is why it is so insistently with us today still. However, the speculum and the mirror stage are now surely somewhat differently externalized, not least via contemporary technics and their digital media platforms. Here I am particularly interested in the more insidious movements directed at using available algorithmic environments as the medium for potential self-surveillance, self-coding, and self-control. Most often this happens privately or in social silence, and it is usually not articulated or conceptualized as such. But quite frequently, especially the last five years in many countries, you find this turning into an explicit process of attempted medial self-presentation on coded and coding planes. Let me give you just one rather sharply delimited example: contemporary male and female self-portraits in the semi-nude, captured with a cellphone camera in a bathroom with a mirror, subsequently uploaded to a social media site. These you can today find on the Web in the hundreds, if not thousands. They solicit mediaesthetic analysis because they undertake partially experimental remediations and re-aestheticizations of the self-portrait as painting (van Eyck, Dürer, Michelangelo, Rembrandt…) and as photo (Brady, Nadar, Rimbaud, Eakins, Muybridge… Woodman, Sherman…). They typically draw upon hypermediation rather than the mirrorings in early painting, and they differ from photos taken in a mirror or taken with a camera held in front of oneself. They are rather to be approached as a new type of explicit staging of the cell-phone and the mirror and the social media site as the technical apparati for narcissistic processes. More importantly, I find here an expressive explicitation of the hastily increasing import of technics with mobile and social media-intimacy. This is becoming much more important for performative attempts at self-affective, self-sensing, and self-perceiving identity-formation.

Art and Aesthetics

RS: You give a great example of how new technology creates a new genre of aesthetic expression. It may be premature to call these bathroom-mirror-self-portraits art. However, it leads to the question of how technology and reflection relate to each other: Is art (or aesthetic expression for that matter) that is based on technology and draws attention to its procedures, also inevitably an act of reflection or education?

UE: Let me give you just one kind of example: urban software art involving surveillance in mixed realities. Urban software art most often draws upon programmers' competencies and hence remains a relative rarity. However, it follows a curve not unlike that of digital literacy and has begun to permeate cities in network societies. Like these, software art is now concerned with a third wave of cybernetics and its developments of ubiquitous or pervasive computing. Urban software art arrives in a multiplicity of variants. One of the more interesting is making itself felt at and as the critical edge of the surveillance programs and tracking systems already operating as augmentations of the public sphere.

At the Goethe Institute in Toronto you could be subjected to David Rokeby's *Sorting Daemon* installation, along with its display of so many finely differentiated profilings of other people on the street. In the contemporary urban environment of a South-East Asian megaregion, in the agglomerated global economic

command and control center of Tokyo, you might encounter
Christian Moeller's media art project *Nosy*. You then accompany
its robotic surveillance camera bitmapping what it captures onto
three nearby towers. On Trafalgquar Square in London, an old
European cultural city center, you might engage with Rafael
Lozano-Hemmer's *Under Scan* project. You and others gather
with its interactive video portraits and become embedded in an
advanced tracking and projection system. In a North American
suburban sprawl like L.A., you could step into Electroland's
Enteractive street level project. You move with its embedded sensors and actuators, its bright LED and video displays of human
movements. At the Barbican in London you might well engage
in *Rider Spoke*, one of Blast Theory's projects in pervasive gaming. You, your bike, and your handheld computer begin to help
co-author an urban mixed reality drama of hide and seek, invisibility and visibility.

Most of the time and in most of these places you will not be
conscious of the myriad software processes and wired or wireless movements of the third wave of computing. Today they
nevertheless operate with enough complex mediatory ubiquity-
effects to subtly influence your notion of reality. Software art
projects tend to make this influence a bit less subtle. Global
urbanization increases its complexity, undergoing extension
as well as intensification. In most urban situations and events
the operations of mainframes, servers, traffic and communication systems, personal computers, tablets, smartphones, and not
least new variants of out-of-the-box computing with networks
of sensors and actuators remain so many infrastructural invis-
ibilities. Urban software and surveillance art projects, however,
most often leave them less than unremarkable. They become
more than the silently present mediaesthetic contexts of the city
qua site, polis, and community.

RS: Tracking software art as a means of addressing the
ongoing but hardly noticed surveillance processes? In my 2008
book *Digitale Medien in der Erlebnisgesellschaft. Kultur – Kunst
– Utopie* (Digital Media in the Society of Event: Culture, Art,
Utopia), I devoted an extra chapter to the issue of digital art and

surveillance, with respect also to Rokeby's installations *Taken* and *Seen*. I was not criticizing Rokeby and others (Simon Biggs, Scott Snibbe) for employing surveillance. However, I was wondering to what extent such art also serves as a kind of beautification of and adaption to the culture of surveillance.

UE: To be sure, since they are partaking of a global market, a porous formation of states and regions, a set of post-industrial urban cultures, and not least cybernetics as a science of control and steering, such software art projects cannot but embrace surveillance. They do so as part of a spectacle of interactivity that appears organized to be superficial, distracting, enticing, and deceptive. It is all too likely that such art projects will remain 'merely' playful celebrations of branded products, part and parcel of leisure time consumption. Only now the spectacle includes individual, social, and ethico-political neutralization via a certain second-order surveillance and a competent overcoding of urban software code. However, perhaps this type of software art includes more. Dramatizing contemporary surveillance complexes is already an unusual feat, as are the interactive movements across limits of programmed urban screening and its visibility. Besides, there are efforts here to deconstruct the distinction between the everyday urban culture for the coded many (low) and the culture of systems design and programming for the elect (high) at work on coding control societies. So, such software art is on its way towards decoding 20th Century centralized state surveillance and its disciplinary panoptic spectacle for the modern city. It is decoding, coding, and recoding some parts of the more open system of control societies with their processes of free-floating soft modulations of coded dividuals on the move in the networks of the contemporary city.

However, it also touches upon another potential: critical edges immanent to software design and programming. A mixed reality pervasive gaming project such as Blast Theory's *I'd Hide You* is well on its way to have tracking processes become more: they involve technical implementation of bio-capacities such as synergy and emergence. Dynamic and mutual streaming video surveillance among a set of online players and a set of street players trying to obey an apparently simple rule: film other players without being filmed. This kind of programming with and for live play suffices to have inventions of the other arrive. You could say that this project morphogenetically and differentially constructs live an urban mixed reality to come and thus always already functions as a kind of city laboratory. It is an immanent urban transcendence qua a model mechanism or a set of dynamically superimposed maps of relations of urban forces internal to the concrete aggregates that will operationalize these relations. Such software art projects are in contact with a virtuality continuum so as to move towards a technical and human self-organization and emergence of mixed urban realities with tracking. They are not just giving rise to the coding of complexes and the complicated in surveillance. They have produced codings, recodings, and decodings of 'live' surveillant complexities. They are live and moving in the uncoded and the codable city. They are on the move as an entire differential series of diagrams qua embodied thought-experiments in which a simile of the being of the city to emerge may be glimpsed.

Media Literacy

RS: I agree with your observation of insufficient public discussion of the surveillance and privacy issue. I wonder, though, to what extent I need to understand programming in order to understand the "Real Privacy Problem" discussed from a cultural studies perspective like Evgeny Morozov's, to be found in his article of the same title in *MIT Technology Review* in October 2013. Sure, a technological issue can't be understood without technological insights. On the other hand, especially the matters of surveillance and privacy suggest the reason for the deficient discussion is not inadequate information but poor interest. This poor interest, it seems, is caused not primarily by the lack of understanding programming but by ignorance with respect to the cultural and ethical ramifications of technology.

UE: I hope that it has already become clear that I affirm, subscribe to, and also practice a quite transdisciplinary mode of work in a broad technocultural field. This means that I value and find necessary the kinds of insights provided by cultural studies, sociology, philosophy, semiotics, and critical theory, for example. It also means that I value and find necessary the insights stemming from computer science, human-computer interaction, interaction design, science and technology studies, media and communication studies. Such a transdisciplinary mode of work comes along with several obvious pitfalls and problems, including the great many disciplinary incompatibilities and the impossibility for any one person to master all this in any kind of real depth. However, it also affords a set of transversal movements, some of which I find to be lacking or underdeveloped in current research that very often pays its dues to hyper specialization in one or at most two fields or disciplines. I think this will simply not do with respect to the development we are discussing here – it remains a transdisciplinary project inching towards complexity all along. The corporations and their senior system planners know this all too well, and that is why we tend to see research groups composed of hardware engineers, programmers, anthropologists, psychologists, interaction designers, graphic designers, linguists, philosophers, etc. In the universities we are almost always just lagging behind, but that does not really change or remove the call for such a mode of operation.

All this means I work with a multiplicity of approaches and so consider it a little difficult to say what has primacy, what is the originary source of the problems with seeing to a more extended, well-informed, and critically reflexive discussion of surveillance and privacy. You are right, however, that I may tend to bring into play some of the disciplines in which I have had the more training – in this case computer science and software development. Of course this is not all or enough, but I still think that quite a case can be made for the need to see more of this in areas such as cultural studies and 'digital humanities.' For a great many people ignorance, lack of information, blind trust, indifference, powerlessness and more are all at play here, and this makes it difficult to approach.

My main reason for ongoing questioning down along the technical axis is the lack of information and the lack of rights plus capacity to do something about insight and ownership. This is very often due to the blockings of transparency via the extended use of hierarchies of privilege and access -- in technics generally, in intelligence and security, as well as in the political economy of information. Specifically, I find it a quite intolerable terror and tyranny that ubicomp projects are pursued with no or far too little misgivings, qualms, or scruples as to their systemic invisibility, inaccessibility, and their embedded 'surveillance' that will have no problems reaching right through your home, your mail, your phone, your clothes, your body posture and temperature, your face and emotional expressivity, your hearing aid, and your pacemaker.

The lack of information can very well be addressed from several angles. Programming is one good vantage point. Insight respecting hardware architectures and the cultural dimension is another. Treatment of interaction designs and their ramifications is yet another. Critical design approaches to digital media studies would be welcome. Generally, I welcome all these moves into deliberation, and even the overload ensuing, for this is already something quite different from taking for granted that informational invisibility, unawareness, inaccessibility, and expropriation is our code.

RS: Let us push the "terror and tyranny" of ubicomp projects a bit further. In a *Wired* article on the Programmable World (issue 21.06) Bill Wasik writes that once connected things become ubiquitous the world of everyday objects will be transformed "into a designable environment, a playground for coders and engineers." Since in a ubiquitous programmed world if-then-relationships are the "blood" of the system, the article also foresees a profitable market of if-then-apps. The result may be that we outsource the if-then-decision of our daily lives to the cultural standards of programmers and the commercial considerations of the app-industry. How would you approach this issue in a seminar on the social and philosophical implications of technological progress?

UE: Let me be somewhat blunt and provocative. When you press the light switch in your living room, the engineers, the designers, and the companies dealing with electrical systems have been out there for a long time profiting from your everyday cultural tactics and all the strategies relating to the use of electricity (lights turned on and off in this case). Your if-then decisions and the cultural standards with which you live have been technically, practically, economically, and politically pre-programmed in part by the strategies of industry, commerce, consensus re safety standards, political decisions as to infrastructure, etc. It is a real rarity today, however, to encounter strong sociopolitical criticism of technological 'progress' qua electricity and its implications, even though it remains possible and is perhaps becoming gradually more called for in view of our need to be differently concerned about energy, the environment, climate, and sustainability. Since you most often remain happily oblivious to the great many electrical strategies immanent to your everyday culture and form of life, why is it that a smart ubicomp environment should solicit a critically well-informed seminar on its social and philosophical implications?

RS: Maybe because in a smart ubicomp environment we even give up the *experience* of pressing the light switch which, until now, at least reminds us of the implicit if-then-structure of this device.

UE: No doubt you are right. Presumably something different must be at stake, something that does make such a critical seminar warranted. I would certainly agree, but I would then add that perhaps it is not altogether easy to demonstrate that this is a difference in kind rather than one of degree. For instance, both kinds of technological 'progress' depend on energy qua electricity, and they both depend on negotiating a human cultural habituation to a certain set of affordances, some kind of technical envelope or a curtain of technical objects (to echo

Leroi-Gourhan for a second). Still, I think one would be right to stay with the question.

Generally speaking I think the insistence on sensing a difference of import here derives from the drive towards solutions of complexity, as we talked about earlier. You have a sense that somehow a smart ubicomp environment is a far more complex affair than a light switch and electrical wiring and therefore perhaps more socially worrisome or politically more difficult to affirm. If so, the question would become one of thinking, and then evaluating, what is meant by 'more complex.' We evidently have multitudes of relata and relations in both cases, and the interactions among the relata are not altogether trivial, so in both cases we have good mereological questions. We also have in both cases quite some concern respecting complex topologies and temporalities, structural as well as functional complexity. However, something must be urging us to think that smart ubicomp environments do not permit of reductions of complexity as easily and do insist on further internal complication on our side. Is this just a matter of the fate of all inventions of the other (psyche and/or techné), all new phenomena to which we have not yet become habituated? I think you would be right to press the issue a bit further than that...

Actually, in order to fast-forward this some, we could note that we have recent and closely related precedents of this discussion. For instance, I remember being both surprised and interested to read a short, early text by Manovich treating of interactivity – in part unusual due to the explicit ethico-political engagement, in part due to its display of an affective plane with a mixture of fear, anger, and humor. I read this text on 'totalitarian interactivity' perhaps ten years ago, I think, a bit stunned by his analysis of new media art installations as representatives of a relatively advanced form of audience manipulation. Certainly, my attention was caught when he claimed that the spectator-subject-interactant is here placed in a structure reminiscent of a psychological laboratory or a high-tech torture chamber – the kind you might imagine yourself finding in the CIA or KGB.

Perhaps it is a little too easy to shrug this off as hyperbole and let its apparent exaggerations reside with the author's projections -- stemming from a certain pre-1989 period and a certain sociopolitical background proper to the Eastern Bloc. Perhaps this treatment of the interactivity of new media art actually deserves more and other than that, and it may well point towards the question of complexification we are trying to address. For Manovich saw in this an updated version of Althusser's Marxist socio-political concept of 'interpellation,' or the way in which ideology as embodied in major institutions and discourses always already constitutes subjects' identities by 'hailing' them in social interactions. Manovich made a series of observations remarkably similar to your question: engaging with interactive media art installations we are asked to follow pre-programmed, objectively existing associations – we are asked to mistake the structure of somebody else's mind for our own. According to him, this could be said to form a quite fitting kind of identity-formation for the information age. No longer so much that of early or late industrial society, being asked to identify with somebody else's body image (lifestyle, fashion, physical appearance). Rather that of a later epoch, one of cognitive labor: being asked to identify with somebody else's mind.

RS: The difference, though, would be that in an interactive art installation you are prompted to reflect on the interaction imposed on you (because the grammar of interaction presented is offered up for negotiation), while the application in an Internet of things-system does not aim at discussion but pragmatism and rather expects you to just follow the if-then-logic proposed.

UE: I am happy to agree that some interactive art installations offer such promptings, but this is not always the case, and besides, human interactants' behaviors often demonstrate quite some differences so that even explicit promptings may be ignored or turned into something else. Analogous remarks should be made with respect to interactive ubicomp systems and the Internet of Things: in some cases interactants are made very conscious of the implications of being in this context for interactivity and may have the chance to opt out; in other cases the interaction design and the system remain altogether calm, embedded, and invisible to humans as a technocultural infrastructure that must be taken for granted. Of course, we also have a whole series of shades of gray here, ranging from almost prompting human awareness (obtrusive ambience) to almost not doing so (vague ambience).

My point here, though, is that already with the Internet, mid-90s new media, and the first set of notions of interactivity we had the uncanny sense of coming together with technics, software, and interaction designs demonstrating a certain complexity. We have externalized modes of psychological and social individuations in technics; we are reimplanting these individually and socially, often (not always) without noticing this consciously or discussing it with others, often (not always) without making a difference that makes a difference ourselves.

More specifically, then, smart ubicomp environments would be uncannily complex in ways not entirely unlike this. Perhaps they are getting a good deal closer to the uncanny – insofar as they reach solutions of complexity qua externalizations of traits and processes we tend to associate with the human. The technical developers of such environments are ideally aiming at self-adapting and proactive systems with a context-awareness capable of dealing more or less intelligently with a wide range of human behavior, interaction, motivation, and intention. Again, we are extraordinarily far from seeing anything like this realized. Even so, it should already today be relatively obvious to many of us that we have begun to engage with systems that profile our identities in incredible informational detail. We are interacting with systems that register our whereabouts, activities, and objects or property. They recognize our physical appearance and ways of moving, our ethnic and national belongings, our facial expression and gestures. They register movement, pressure, wind, humidity, temperature, light, sound, radio waves, and they may alter our environment and its ambience or mood. And they may begin to make themselves felt, make themselves heard, display themselves, and speak to us.

RS: The argument that we are far from seeing anything like this realized may not appease those old enough to have seen what seemed to be fiction turned into a profitable product. The fact that already today systems profile our identities and determine the patterns of our actions is not comforting either. On the contrary, wouldn't it be naïve to assume that in a profitable if-then-app-market the individual keeps a say against all the well thought through if-then-solutions? I guess the issue is again one of technical determinism and individual choice. Let me illustrate my concern by switching from Manovich to Morozov who, in his new book on *Technological Solutionisms* (2013), gives the example of a smart kitchen that scientists at Kyoto Sangyo University work on: "the Japanese researchers have mounted cameras and projectors on the kitchen's ceiling so that they can project instructions – in the form of arrows, geometric shapes, and speech bubbles guiding the cook through each step – right onto the ingredients. Thus, if you are about to cut a fish, the system will project a virtual knife and mark where exactly that it ought to cut into the fish's body." Of course we still can neglect what the smart kitchen utters about cutting fish and follow the advice we got from our grandma. However, how much talk will there be with grandmas and other relatives or friends about fish and similar important things in life if well paid professionals know it all better and do not hesitate to tell us?

UE: I think we will have no trouble agreeing that it matters how our lifeworld exists technologically, how it is programmed, and what interaction designs are made operational in its mixed realities. We do seem to differ with respect to the priority granted in the relation of technics and culture, machinic and human system. Here I insist on mutual implication and co-development prior to any clear and strict asymmetries in favor of either technological determinism or free human orchestration. Interestingly, in this example concerning the smart kitchen my angle of approach appears to permit of more of a role for human and cultural agency than yours, although that is only one of the stakes.

Let me reiterate that this broad tendential development is happening most often in piecemeal fashion. This allows me to point out that my worry is partially different from yours and concerns the reach towards an ideal of living intelligence. We have yet to see more integrated systems at play in any one such smart environment. But the fact that things are moving in that direction might alert us to that goal of smart organization and not least smart self-organization. To the best of my knowledge no existing systems are self-adaptive, proactive, or genuinely self- and other-generative. In fact they are almost all of them annoyingly stupid rather than intelligent and smart (depending on how you wish to define these two terms). They malfunction and crash. They miss the point more often than not. They have any number of unintended and not exactly felicitous side-effects. But this should nonetheless still be enough to suggest that the tendential pull in R&D is vaguely reminiscent of some of the things also addressed earlier in AI and AL initiatives. Here it concerns a specific pull towards externalization of a considerable bundle of 'human' traits and processes, then a pull towards a more genuine co-development of human culture and technics.

If you are facing an artifactual mixed-reality ubicomp environment with such complexity, we should perhaps be discussing issues that remain different (in degree) from those associated with the light switch (even though this has agency too, as science and technology studies and actor-network theory like to remind us). Socially you are now also interacting with systems qua a multitude of dynamic mixed-reality quasi-personalities and quasi-socialities. Technically: as both Weiser and most engineers of software and hardware knew only too well, complex embedded systems without good interfaces are notoriously hard to maintain and repair – since it is hard even for the engineers to figure out what is wrong, what is working correctly but has really undesirable side-effects, etc. Ethically, definitions of human values plus mindbody schemes for individual and social identity formations are at stake, most often invisibly and tacitly, and most often without any right to database access, control, or deletion of so-called personal information. Economically, such an environment is truly excellent as regards supporting further development of experience and transformation economies. Technics may well help here with fine-grained registration over time of your profile -- on planes of affect, sensation, emotion, and perception – only then to engage you every so often prior to your conscious understanding and deliberation. Politically, individuals and social groupings most often remain powerless and uninformed about the 'humanoid' systems with which they interact. The concretization of the vision for billions and billions of computational units with mobility, context-awareness, and ad hoc networking connectivity on the micro- or molecular scale will have left modern notions of 'privacy' and the 'secret' far behind, just as it makes 'surveillance' a completely insufficient and misleading concept or term. It makes a kindergarten exercise of Huxley and Orwell's fictions, and even of the technical capacity of most existing intelligence services as we have known them.

If you have not sensed this already, I am extending the worst-case scenarios well into the incredible. We are very far indeed from seeing this happen, for any number of good reasons down along each one of these axes. And the complexity of the human, the animal, biological life forms include quite some good barriers and unknown membranes still for science and technics, computing included. I do have serious reservations, however, and these do run along lines somewhat similar to what I have just mentioned. At the same time, I will go on looking forward to further work on a human-oriented ubicomp environment. In all likelihood it has a lot to teach us about our relation to the environment, our sense of the world, and about our relation to ourselves and others. Every now and then I tend to try think of technics as our extended immune system. With ubicomp culture in mind I am again reminded how aggressively mastery-minded and appropriative this system is most of the time and in most of its processes. I am also reminded how often it displays processes that are obviously belonging to auto-immunity. I am almost always reminded how far our co-development with technics is from sustainability.

Enslaved by digital technology

Mihai Nadin

Mihai Nadin is a scholar and researcher in electrical engineering, computer science, aesthetics, semiotics, human-computer interaction, computational design, post-industrial society, and anticipatory systems. He developed several computer-aided educational aids prior to the widespread use of the Internet and was one of the first proponents in the United States of integrating computers in education. Nadin investigates in several publications the implication of the digital paradigm and discusses in depth the new civilization resulting from it in his 1997 book, *The Civilization of Illiteracy*. Mihai Nadin holds advanced degrees in Electrical Engineering and Computer Science and a post-doctoral degree in Philosophy, Logic and the Theory of Science; he has served as Endowed Professor at the University of Texas at Dallas since 2004.

Mihai Nadin sees the human condition at stake in the Gold Rush obsession of digital technology entrepreneurs; he considers big data the 'ultimate surrender to the technology of brute force' and the age of information 'by definition an age of total transparency.' He detects a new Faustian deal where Faust trades better judgment for perfect calculation; he unmasks social media as the 'background for conformity' and revolutionary technology as the underlying foundation of the ruling economic system.

Prelude

Roberto Simanowski: What is your favored neologism of digital media culture and why?

Mihai Nadin: "Followed"/"Follower:" It fully expresses how the past overtook the present. "Crowd" anything: self-delusional slogans for the daisy brain.

RS: If you could go back in the history of new media and digital culture in order to prevent something from happening or somebody from doing something, what or who would it be?

MN: I would eliminate any word that starts with "hyper" and "super," and every scoring facility. Alternatively, I would prevent Bill Gates from developing DOS, and Apple from giving up on its language (the IOS7 cries out as an example of failing to live up to the company's foundations). Yes, I would eliminate Term Coord, the European Union's attempt to standardize terminology.

More important: I would establish a framework for reciprocal responsibility. No company should be immunized against liability procedures. If your product causes damage due to sloppy design, insufficient testing, perpetuation of known defects, you are liable. Forget the legal disclaimers that protect disruptive technologies that disrupt our lives. And no user should be allowed to further the disruption. A simple analogy: Carmakers are liable for anything that systematically leads to accidents; drivers are liable for using cars irresponsibly. Does the analogy of the technology of the industrial age extend to that of the digital age? On an ethical level, of course. Innovation does not legitimize discarding ethics.

RS: What comes to mind if you hear "Digital Media Studies"?

MN: Opportunism. The unwillingness to think about a totally different age.

RS: If you were a minister of education, what would you do about media literacy?

MN: I would introduce "Literacies" (corresponding to all senses and to cognitive abilities) as the ubiquitous foundation of everyone's education. "Vive la différence" would be the common denominator.

Politics and Government

RS: While in the 1990s Internet pioneers such as John Perry Barlow declared the independence of Cyberspace from the governments of the old world, now it seems people hope for governments to protect privacy online and to intervene in the taking-over and commercialization of the Internet by huge corporations such as Google and Facebook?

MN: Pioneers are always mercenaries. Of course, to open a new path is a daring act—so much can go wrong. There is a lot of romanticism in what the Internet forerunners were saying. Most of the time, their words were far louder than their accomplishments were meaningful or significant. Declaring the Internet as an expression of independence from the government when you are actually captive to DARPA is comical at best. MILNET (split from ARPANet), further morphed into classified and non-classified Internet Protocol Router Networks, should have warned us all about what we will eventually surrender. Was Minitel (France, 1978) better? It offered little functionality, and was not dependent on the private data of its users. DOS—the operating system that even in our days underlies the world of PCs (since 1981)—was adopted without any consideration for the integrity of the individual. Apple stole from Xerox something that, even today, the company does not fully understand. But Xerox does data management in our days (it took over the tollways in Texas), and Apple sells music and whatnot—sometimes in collusion with publishers. You have to keep the competition vigilant. In the early years, everybody was in a hurry. This was the second coming of the California Gold Rush in which college dropouts found opportunity. Indeed, in no university, nobody—academic or not—knew enough about the future that the pioneers were promising to turn into paradise on Earth. When the blind lead the blind, you will never know when you arrive, because you really don't know where you are going.

RS: This is a strong, devastating statement: The pioneers of digital media and culture as mercenaries, comics, thieves, dropouts, and blind persons without ideas and beliefs?

MN: Without idealizing the past or demonizing the beginners, let's take note of the fact that Lullus understood that with new means of expression we can better understand the universe. And we can ask more interesting questions about the human being and its own understanding of the world. Pascal would not miss the value of feelings in the human perception of reality, and in the attempt to subject it to calculations. Leibniz, with whose name computation is associated, would seek no less than a universal language for making possible, for example, the understanding of history from a perspective of accomplishments. He was not interested in translating Chinese philosophy word-by-word. He was interested in ideas. (If you want to ask "What's that?"—i.e., what are "ideas"—this interview is not for you!)

College dropouts should not be vilified, but also not idealized. It helps to start something free of the constraints of cultural conventions. It does not help to realize that what is at stake is not a circuit board, a communication protocol, or a new piece of software, but the human condition. The spectacular success of those whom we associate with the beginnings lies in monetizing opportunities. They found gold! The spectacular failure lies in the emergence of individuals who accept a level of dependence on technology that is pitiful. This dependence explains why, instead of liberating the human being, digital technology has enslaved everyone—including those who might never touch a keyboard or look at a monitor. To complain about the lack of privacy is at best disingenuous. Those who rushed into the digital age gave it up!

In Web 2.0, profits were made not by producing anything, but in profiling everyone. The *nouvelle vague* activism of our days is a mantra for legitimizing new profitable transactions, not a form of resistance. If everyone really cared for their rights, we would have them back. All that everyone really wants is a bigger piece of the pie (while starting the nth diet).

RS: I am not sure about the diet but I completely agree that the implications of digital culture also affect those staying away from digital media, if such staying away is possible at all. But how guilty are those giving up privacy, their own and as a concept in general, by rushing into the digital age? Considering the conviction from the McLuhan camp that first we shape our tools and afterwards our tools shape us and that any medium has the power to impose its own assumptions on the unwary, I wonder how deliberate the acceptance of the new media's assumptions are. Hand in hand with the human being's unwariness goes triumph as *homo faber,* which Hans Jonas, in his book *The Imperative of Responsibility: In Search of an Ethics for the Technological Age*, calls the human fatality. We are entrapped by our success, Jonas states, in respect to the human's belief in technology. Our power over nature has become self-acting and made man into a "compulsive executer of his capacity." What would be required now is a power over that power. Did we really expect Gold Rush entrepreneurs to develop this kind of self-discipline?

MN: The echo chamber metaphor was used so far mainly to describe politics. It simply says that feedback of a narcissistic nature reinforces prejudices. Under Hitler, Stalin, Mao, and current Islamic extremism, masses tend towards hysterics. Self-induced delusions and political idolatry are twins. Does it look any different within the objective, rational domain of science and technology?

The expectation of objectivity is sometimes rewarded: there are scientific and technological developments of authentic novelty. But let's be clear: revolution means to turn things around, full circle, and in this respect, the information age is such a development. Technologically, this is a time of amazement.

Conceptually, it is rather the reinvention of the wheel in digital format. For a long time, no new idea has percolated. The innovators aligned themselves with those in power and those with money. When the profit potential of the typewriter—the front end of IBM computers in the attempt to be free of perforated cards—was exhausted, word processing emerged. The X-acto knife gave way to the cut-and-paste procedure. It was not a new way of thinking, but rather a continuation of old patterns.

I am deeply convinced that computation (not only in its digital format) will eventually open up new opportunities and break from the past. The self-discipline in your question—how to keep a lid on the obsession with profit at any price—should actually become the determination to give free rein to creativity. Under the pressure of profit-making, there is no authentic freedom. In the echo chamber of science, celebration of one adopted perspective—the deterministic machine—leads to the automatic rejection of any alternative.

RS: Big Data is the buzzword of our time and the title of many articles and books, such as *Big Data: A Revolution That Will Transform How We Live* by Viktor Meyer-Schönberger and Kenneth Cukler (2013). The embracing response to the digitization and datafication of everything is Data Love, as the 2011 title of the conference series NEXT reads, which informs the business world about 'how the consumer on the Internet will be evolving.' It is a well-known fact that big data mining undermines privacy. Is, however, that love mutual, given the acceptance and even cooperation of most of the people?

MN: Big data represents the ultimate surrender to the technology of brute force. Wars are big data endeavors, so are the economic wars, not to mention the obsession with power and total control of the so-called "free individual." Whether we like it or not, "information society" remains the closest description of the age of computers, networks, smartphones, sensors, and everything else that shapes life and work today. We are leaving behind huge amounts of data—some significant, some insignificant. Babbage's machine, like the first recording devices, like the abacus and so many pneumatic and hydraulic contraptions, are of documentary importance. I am sure that if entrepreneurs of our days could find any value in them, they would not hesitate to make them their own and add them to the IP portfolio of their new ventures. What cannot be monetized is the human condition expressed in such previous accomplishments. You cannot resuscitate Babbage or Peirce, except maybe for some Hollywood production or some new game.

Data becomes information *only* when it is associated with meaning. However, our age is one of unreflected data generation, not one of quest for meaning. Data production ("Give me the numbers!") is the new religion. Politics, economics, and science are all reduced to data production. Ownership of data replaced ownership of land, tools, and machines. Human interaction is also reduced to data production: what we buy, where we buy, whom we talk to, for how long, how often, etc. The Internet as the conduit for data is boring and deceiving. This is not what Vinton Cerf, to whose name the global transmission protocol TCP/IP is attached, had in mind. Instead of becoming a medium for interaction, the Internet got stuck in the model of pipes (sewage pipes, oil pipes, water pipes, and gas distribution pipes) and pumps (servers being engines that pump data from one place to another). Berners-Lee's world-wide web made it easier to become part of the network: the browser is the peephole through which anyone can peek and everyone's eyeballs become a commodity. Great pronouncements will not change this reality more than radical criticism (sometimes, I confess, a bit exaggerated). But we should at least know what we are referring to.

By the way: creative work—of artists, scientists, craftsmen (and women)—takes place on account of sparse data. Survival is a matter of minimal data, but of relevant information.

RS: Again, your account is quite radical and disillusioning, though not unjustified. In response, let me ask to what extent the browser reduces people to commodified eyeballs. Hasn't the Internet (or the Web 2.0) rather turned every viewer and listener into a potential sender thus weaving a network of "wreaders," as George P. Landow termed the reader-authors in hypertext in 1994, or "prosumers," as the corresponding Web 2.0 concept reads? Isn't this the spread of the microphone, to allude to Bertolt Brecht's demand in his radio essays 85 years ago? Isn't this dogma of interaction the actual problem?

MN: In the evolution from centralized computing (the "big iron" of the not so remote past) to workstations, to client server architecture, to the Cloud (real-time) re-centralization, we have not come close to establishing the premise for a human knowledge project. "The knowledge economy" is a slogan more than anything else. Computation made possible the replacement of living knowledge by automated procedures. However, most of the time, computation has remained in its syntax-dominated infancy. On a few occasions, it started to expand into the semantic space: consider the diligent work of the ontology engineers. The time for reaching the pragmatic level of authentic interactions has not yet come. The ontology engineers do not even realize that there is such a dimension. If and when it comes, we will end the infancy stage of computation. "Eyeballs" are not for interaction in meaningful activities, but rather for enticing consumers. Interaction engages more than what we see.

RS: One basic tool of data accumulation and mining is Google, which through every search query not only learns more about what people want and how society works, but also centralizes and controls knowledge through projects such as Google Books. How do you see this development?

MN: There is no tragedy in digitizing all the world's books, or making a library of all music, all movies, etc. After all, we want to gain access to them. This is their reason for being: to be read, listened to, experienced. The tragedy begins when the only reason for doing so is to monetize our desire to know and to do something with that knowledge. I remember shaking hands with that young fellow to whom Terry Winograd introduced me (May 1999). Larry Page was totally enthusiastic upon hearing from me about something called "semiotics." At that time (let me repeat, 1999) none of my friends knew what Google was, and even less how it worked. They knew of Mosaic (later Netscape Navigator), of the browser wars, even of AltaVista, Gopher, and Lycos (some survived until recently). Today, none can avoid "Googling." (Lucky us, we don't have to "Yahoo!") The act of searching is the beginning of pragmatics. Yes, we search in the first place because we want to do something (not only find quotes). Pragmatics is "doing" something, and in the process recruiting resources related to the purpose pursued. Larry Page is one of the many billionaires who deserve to be celebrated for opening new avenues through searches that are based on the intuitive notion that convergence (of interest) can be used in order to find out what is relevant. But nobody will tell him—as no one will tell Raymond Kurzweil—that the real challenge has yet to be addressed: to provide the pragmatic dimension.

The fact that Google "knows" when the flu season starts (check out searches related to flu) is good. But if you used this knowledge only for selling ads, you miss the opportunity to trigger meaningful activities. Seeking life everlasting is not really a Google endeavor. It is a passion for which many people (some smart, some half-witted) are willing to spend part of their fortunes. They can do what they want with their money. Period! But maybe somebody should tell them that it makes more sense to initiate a course of action focused on the betterment of the human condition. Or at least (if betterment sounds too socialist) for more awareness, for a higher sense of responsibility. Properly conceived, Facebook (or any of the many similar attempts) could have been one possible learning environment, way better adapted to education than the new fashionable MOOCs [massive open online courses]. Instead, it is an agent of a new form of addiction and human debasement.

Algorithms and Censorship

RS: Speaking of Facebook, here and in any social network where the amount of views, likes, and comments is counted the cultural consequence of computation seems to be comparison and ranking. Has communication shifted from ambiguous words to the excitement of who or what wins the competition?

MN: "Scoring" is the American obsession of the rather insecure beginnings projected upon the whole world. In the meaningless universe of scoring, your phone call with a provider is followed by the automatic message eliciting a score: "How did we do?" Less than 2% of users fall into the trap. The vast majority scores only when the experience was extremely bad—and way too often, it is bad. This is one example of how, in the age of communication (telling someone how to improve, for example), there is no communication: the score data is machine processed. The best we can do when we want to achieve something is to talk to a machine. The one-way only channels have replaced the two-way dialog that was meant to be the great opportunity of the digital age. We don't want to pay for talking with a human being. In reality, we don't want to pay for anything. As the scale expands, everything becomes cheap, but nothing has become really better. To speak about influence in social media, for example, is to be self-delusional. Scoring is not only inconsequential, but also meaningless.

Indeed, in this broad context, the human condition changes to the extent that the notion of responsibility vanishes. Consequences associated with our direct acts and decisions are by now projected at the end of a long chain of subsequent steps. At best, we only trigger processes: "Let's warm up a frozen pizza." You press a button; the rest is no longer your doing in any form or shape. More than ever before has the human being been rendered a captive receiver under the promise of being empowered. The variety of offerings has expanded to the extent that, instead of informed choices, we are left with the randomness of the instant. As a matter of fact, the "living" in the living is neutralized. The age of machines is making us behave more like machines than machines themselves. The excitement and energy of anticipation are replaced by quasi-instinctual reactions. By no means do I like to suggest an image of the end of humanity, or of humanness. There is so much to this age of information that one can only expect and predict the better. For the better to happen, we should realize that dependence on technology is not the same as empowerment through technology. The secular "Church of Computation" (as yet another Church of Machines) is at best an expression of ignorance. If you experience quantum computation, genetic computation, intelligent agents, or massive neural networks, you realize how limiting the deterministic view of the Turing machine is. And you learn something else: There is a price to everything we want or feel entitled to.

RS: During the debate of the NSA scandal in summer 2013, Evgeny Morozov titled an essay in the German newspaper Frankfurter Allgemeine Zeitung *The Price of Hypocrisy*, holding that not only the secret service or the government undermines the privacy of the citizen, but the citizens themselves by participating in information consumerism. Morozov points to the Internet of things that will require even more private information in order to work, i.e., to facilitate and automate processes in everyday life that until now we had to take upon ourselves. The price for this kind of extension of man's brain is its deterioration through the loss of use. On the other hand, some claim that if the swimming pool heats up automatically after discovering a BBQ scheduled in our calendar, our brains are freed up for more important things.

MN: Yes, we want to automate everything—under the illusion that this will free us from being responsible for our own lives. For those shocked by the revelation that there is no privacy on the Internet of data, I can only say: This is a good measure of your level of ignorance, and acceptance of a condition in which we surrender to the system. Walk into *Taste Tea* in San Francisco, where the credit card app "Square" registers your iPhone presence and logs into your account. This is not government intrusion, but the convenience of automated payment. We cannot have it both ways—privacy and no privacy at all. Fundamentally, the age of information is by definition an age of total transparency. That *Internet imaginaire* that some pioneers crowed about—it will make us all more creative, freer than ever, more concerned about each other—was only in their heads. And not even there. The "innocents" were already in bed with the government—and with the big money.

It is not the government that betrayed the Internet. The "innocents" volunteered back doors as they became the world's largest contracting workforce for spy agencies. The *hotness IQ* ranking for university studies in our days (cybersecurity, anyone? data-mining?) reflects the situation described above: "Follow the money!" Total transparency is difficult. A new human condition that accepts total transparency will not miraculously emerge, neither in San Francisco, nor in India, China, or Singapore. Government will have to be transparent. Who is prepared for this giant step? The government could make it clear: We observe you all (and they do, regardless of whether they make it known or not). Those hiding something will try to outsmart the system. The rest will probably be entitled to ask the Government: Since you are keeping track of everything, why not provide a service? My files are lost, you have them, provide help when I need it. We pay for being observed, why not get something in return?

RS: Lets talk more about automated decisions and vanishing responsibility that is a central topic of your work during the last decade. In your article "Antecapere ergo sum: what price knowledge" you foresee a rather bleak future in which responsibility is transferred from humans to machines by calculation and algorithmic datamining. You also speak of a new Faustian deal where Faust conjures the Universal Computer: "I am willing to give up better Judgment for the Calculation that will make the future the present of all my wishes and desires fulfilled." How do anticipation, computation, Goethe's *Faust* and Descartes' *ergo sum* relate to each other?

MN: In order to understand the profound consequences of the Information Revolution, one has to juxtapose the characteristics of previous pragmatic frameworks. I did this in my book, *The Civilization of Illiteracy* (a work begun in 1981 and published in 1997), available for free download on the Internet. There are books that age fast (almost before publication); others that age well, and others waiting for reality to catch up. Look at the cover of my book. I conceived that image as part of the book in 1996/97: something that might remind you of Google books and of what many years later became the iPad. The image from the Vatican Library is indicative of what my book describes in detail: that is, make available the libraries of the world to everyone.

This book is more than ever the book of our time. I don't want to rehash ideas from the book, but I'd like to make as many people as possible aware of the fact that we are transitioning from a pragmatics of centralism, hierarchy, sequentiality, and linearity to a framework in which configuration, distribution, parallelism, and non-linearity become *necessary*. The theocracy of determinism (cause¬effect) gives way to non-determinism (cause¬effect¬cause). It is not an easy process because, for a long time we (in western civilization, at least) have been shaped by views of a deterministic nature.

To understand the transition, we must get our hands dirty in pulling things apart—pretty much like children trying to figure out how toys work. Well, some of those toys are no longer the cars and trains that my generation broke to pieces, convinced that what made them run was hidden down there, in the screws and gears forming part of their physical makeup. Search engines, algorithms, and rankings—the new toys of our time—are only epiphenomenal aspects. At this moment, nobody can stop people from Googling (or from tearing apart the code behind Google), and even less from believing that what the search comes up with is what they are looking for.

We rarely, if ever, learn from the success of a bigger machine, a larger database, a more functional robot, or a more engaging game. We usually learn from breakdowns. It is in this respect that any medium becomes social to the extent that it is "social-ized." The so-called "social media" are top-down phenomena. None is the outcome of social phenomena characteristic of what we know as "revolutions" (scientific, technological, political, economic, etc.). They are the victory of "We can" over "What do we want?" or "Why?" And as usual, I go for questions instead of appropriating the slogans of others.

RS: As a remark on how we capitulate to our capabilities: During the anti-NSA protests in summer 2013, somebody presented a poster stating "Yes we scan." This of course alluded to the famous slogan in Obama's election campaign, articulating disappointment in the new president and perhaps also calling for a new movement. Read together, both slogans symbolize the determinism at least of this technological part of society: We scan because we can.

MN: Without accepting even a hint of a dark plot, we need to understand what is called "social media" as an outcome of the transaction economy. It was embodied in, among other things, new businesses. *Uber* and *Lyft* disrupt taxi services; *airbnb* and *HomeAway* disrupt the hotel business. The disruption had many dimensions, for instance, efficiency but also ethics. In the transaction economy ethics is most of the time compromised. The transaction economy replaces the industrial model, even the post-industrial model. To stick to the toy metaphor: Someone decided that we are all entitled to our little cars, fire engines, and trucks. We get them because they are deemed good for us. And before we even start being curious, the next batch replaces what we just started to examine. It is no longer our time, as inquisitive children, that counts. Others prescribe the rhythm for our inquisitive instincts. And for this they redistribute wealth. In rich and poor countries, phones are given away. You need to keep the automated machines busy. Money is not made on the phones but on the transmission of data. This is a new age in the evolution of humankind. Its definitory entity is the *transaction*, carried out with the expectation of faster cycles of change, but not because we are smarter and less inert; rather because our existence depends on consuming more of everything, even if that means sacrificing integrity.

The faster things move around, the faster the cycle of producing for the sake of consumption. Each cycle is motivated by profit-making. The huge server farms—the toys of those controlling our economic or political identity—are really not at all different from the financial transaction engines. Nothing is produced. A continuous wager on the most primitive instincts is all that happens. Thousands of followers post sexually explicit messages and invitations to mob activity; they trade in gossip and selling illusions. Ignorance sells better and more easily than anything else. Not only copper bracelets, cheap Viagra, diet pills, and everything else that succeeds in a large-scale market. If you Google, you first get what those who have paid for it want you to see, sometimes to the detriment of other (maybe better) options. Fake crowds are engineered for those living in the delusion of crowd sourcing.

The transaction economy, with all its high-risk speculation, is the brain-child of Silicon Valley. San Francisco is far more powerful than Washington DC, New York, and even Hollywood. Chamat Palihapitiya put it bluntly: We're in this really interesting shift. The center of power is here, make no mistake. I think we've known it now for probably four or five years. But it's becoming excruciatingly, obviously clear to everyone else that where value is created is no longer in New York, it's no longer in Washington, it's no longer in LA. It's in San Francisco and the Bay Area. (Palihapitiya is one among many bigwigs going public on such a subject.)

RS: Speaking of the replacement of Hollywood by Silicon Valley, Adorno once accused the culture industry of liberating people from thinking as negation, as addressing the status quo. Being busy *learning* the status quo, i.e., finding out how all the new toys work—politically upgraded and camouflaged by euphemistic concepts such as "social" and "interactive"—seems to be a clever strategy to achieve the same result. Your new book, *Are You Stupid?* describes stupidity as the outcome of a system faking change because it is afraid of it. Who rules that system? Who is behind that strategy?

MN: Let us be very clear: the revolutionary technology that was seen as liberating in so many ways actually became the underlying foundation of the transaction economy. Never before has the public been forced into the rental economy model as much as the digital revolution has done. You no longer own what you buy, but rent the usage, to be screwed by the "landlord" (who makes more money by selling your identity than by providing you with a viable product). And even that is not straightforward. It has become impossible to connect to the Internet without being forced into a new version or a new patch. It has all gone so far that to buy a cell phone means to become captive to a provider. In the USA, a law had to be promulgated in order to allow a person to unlock "your" phone! (Remember: this is the age of the rent economy, of transactions not production.) Profits have grown exponentially; service never lives up to promises made and to the shamelessly high prices charged. In this context, social media has become not an opportunity for diversity and resistance, but rather a background for conformity. Once upon a time, within the office model, it was not unusual that women working together noticed that their menstrual periods synchronized. Check out the "Friends" on various social media: They now all "think" the same way, or have the same opinion. That is, they align to fashion and trends, they have their "period" synchronized. All at the lowest common denominator.

In making reference to such aspects of the "social" media, I might sound more critical than their investors would prefer. But as long as we continue to idealize a technology of disenfranchisement and impotence, we will not overcome the limitations of obsession with data to the detriment of information. The toy train reduced to meaningless pieces entirely lost its meaning. Remember trying to make it move as it did before curiosity took the better of it? Information eventually grew from playing with toys: the realization that things belong together, that the wheel has a special function, etc. Given the fact that in the digital embodiment knowledge is actually hidden, replaced by data, the human condition that results is one of dependence. There is no citizenry in the obsession with the newest gadget, bought on credit and discarded as soon as the next version makes the headlines. The *Netizen* that we dreamed of is more a sucker than an agent of change.

RS: The discussion of stupidity in the light of new technology associates Nicholas Carr's 2008 article *Is Google making us stupid?* and brings up the question to what extent a search engine leaves the time to inquiring and acquire (or take apart and play with) knowledge. How do you see the role that search engines such as Google play in society?

MN: In everything individuals do, they influence the world—and are influenced by the world. Within an authentic democracy, this is an authentic two-way street: you elect and you can be elected. Google, or any other search engine for that matter, reflects the skewed relation between individuals and reality. Some own more than the other(s). This ownership is not just economic. It can take many other forms. If you search for the same word on various sites and at various times, the return will be different. In the naïve phase of data searching, way back in the 90s of the last century, relevance counted most. In the transaction economy, search itself is monetized: many businesses offer SEO [search engine optimization] functions. It pays to "find" data associated with higher rewards. Such rewards are advertisement, political recognition, technical ability, etc. In other words, through the search, a cognitive economic, political, etc. reality is engineered as the "engine" forces the searcher to receive it.

Of course, social media relies on search engines, because instead of empowering participants, it engineers the nature of their relations. This remark is not meant to demonize anyone. Rather, it is to establish the fact that in post-industrial capitalism, profit-making is accelerated as a condition for economic success. Those who do not keep up with the speed of fast transactions turn into the stories of wasted venture capital and failed start-ups. The cemetery of failed attempts to work for the common good is rarely visited. America, but to a certain extent Germany, England, and France, sucks up talent from the rest of the world, instead of rethinking education for the new context of life and work in the information society. When the world learned about the worrisome depth at which privacy was emptied of any meaning, by government and business, it was difficult to distinguish between admiration and uproar.

The fascinating Silicon Valley ecology deserves better than unreserved admiration. It is time to debunk the mythology of self-made millionaires and billionaires—and even more the aura of foundations *à la* Gates, which are mostly self-serving. America has encouraged the rush to the new gold not because it loves the new science and technology, but rather because it recognized new forms of profit-making. Unfortunately, the human condition associated with the information society continues to be ignored. At the scale at which profits are multiplying, crime is also multiplying.

The more recent wars that the USA has carried on are not possible without computers and the technology developed for waging them. Moreover, the profoundly dangerous undermining of democracy through vast surveillance of citizens is also the product of digital know-how bordering on the infamous. Computer science programs in many universities are nothing but training facilities for businesses at taxpayer expense. Research is very often a service to the military and the intelligence community, not an avenue towards new science, and even less an expression of ethical responsibility for the long-term consequences of new technologies. We teach the young and less young of our nation (and of other nations) the violence of games, and then wonder why America is the world champion in crime.

Media Literacy

RS: Let me come back to your book *The Civilization of Illiteracy* where you depict a civilization unfolding in which media complement literacy, and literacy—the way it is conceptualized in the Gutenberg Galaxy—is undermined by new literacies demanded and developed by digital technology. The general tone of the book is one of excitement and the invitation to be ready for the new challenges. Your answers in this interview so far indicate that this has changed.

MN: Fifteen years after *The Civilization of Illiteracy* was published (and almost 30 years since I started writing it), I cannot be more optimistic than I was at the time it was published. I already mentioned that I am convinced that it is the book of our time: new developments are still catching up with some of its predictions. It is an 890-page book, which I thought would be the last book of the civilization of literacy. I do not see anything terrifying in the reality that the human condition changes. It is not a curse, but a blessing. Corresponding to the new pragmatic framework, we are all experiencing the need to adapt more rapidly, and sometimes to trade depth for breadth. We do not have enough courage to discard everything that is still based on the structure of the previous pragmatic framework. The program in which I teach just built a new arts and technology teaching and learning facility: the same factory model; the same centralized, hierarchic structure. In reality, such a building should not have been erected. On the one hand, there are the big pronouncements regarding the state of science and technology; on the other, captivity to the past. Conflict does not scare me. I see in conflict the possibility of an authentic revolution in education and in many other societal activities. What scares me is the deeply ingrained conformity to the medieval model of teaching and learning. And the demagoguery associated with monetizing all there is. The Faustian trade-off is skewed: I will give you the illusion of eternity in exchange for your abdicating your desire to discover what it means to live.

RS: How do you see this Faustian trade-off (coming) in place? Are you talking about the computational, digital turn in the Humanities?

MN: A recent book on *Digital Humanities* (Anne Burdick, Johann Drucker, Peter Lunenfeld, Todd Presner, Jeffrey Schnapp, MIT Press 2012) claims that 'Digital Humanities is born of the encounter between traditional humanities and computational methods.' Of course 'recent' does not qualify as 'significant.' We learn from the text (and the comments it triggered) that 'Digital Humanities is a generative practice,' and that it 'contributes to the "screen culture"' of the 21st century. But we do not gain access to the questions of the human condition. We learn about design, but not from an informed perspective of the activity, rather on account of a reactive process of design that lacks a visionary dimension. McLuhan is quoted (again, the echo chamber metaphor is quite well illustrated in the tone of the writing); so are John Berger, Scott McCloud (on comics), and even Charles and Ray Eames. In respect to computation, the discourse is even more muddled. The words are often right; missing is the deeper understanding of the dynamics of human existence and activity. The applied aspect made the book a good candidate for adoption—and explains why it was funded: it promotes a notion of humanity congruent with that of technology.

In reality, "Humanities" is the expression of resistance. Those involved in humanities probe the science and technology instead of automatically accepting them. These remarks should not be construed as a book review. I use the book as an opportunity to recognize those honestly interested in understanding what is happening in our days, but also to point out that the endeavor is complicated by the fact that we are part of the process. You don't have insight into the earthquake that reshapes the landscape. The hype over big data is of the same nature as the hype over the digital (sic!) humanities. Humanities—i.e., the many disciplines that fit under this heading—is rushing into a territory of methods and perspectives defined for purposes different from those of the humanities. To give up the long view for the immediacy of results is not a good trade-off. I am amused by those great "humanists" who seek out programmers for testing their own ideas. Smiling, we bid farewell to the past (some might recognize behind this formulation an author who saw part of this coming).

RS: Let me bring in another aspect of this. Computation—or algorithmic reading—has been a tool of research in the humanities for some time. Digital Humanities aims at the application of digital processes and resources for text and image analysis, large data mining, and data visualization. The rationale behind it: Machines are better in processing data than humans.

However, the reading that algorithms carry out is "distant" in contrast to the close reading by humans. Your comment to Digital Humanities above is quite straight and critical. In the same spirit you state in your article "Reassessing the Foundations of Semiotics:" Quantity does not automatically lead to improved comprehension. The challenging semiotic project is, as you continue, not only to find information in big data, but also meaning in information. What do you expect from Digital Humanities in terms of reassessed semiotics?

MN: The great assumption is that there is a universal machine: the Turing machine. This assumption has led to the spread of the most insidious forms of determinism. Algorithmic computation became the magic formula for fighting disease, making art, and building rockets. It is forgotten that Turing defined only a specific form of automated mathematics. Universities, as centers of inquiry, were only too happy to replace the thinking of previous ages with the inquiry associated with virtual machines. They housed the big mainframe machines. Everything became Turing computational, and at the same time, as circular as the underlying premise. If you can describe an activity—that is, if you have an algorithm—algorithmic computation would perform that particular operation as many times as you wished, and in every place where that operation is involved. As long as the focus is on algorithmic descriptions, computation is assumed to be universal. Indeed, the arithmetic behind selling tomatoes in a market or exploring the moon became the same.

It turns out that quite a number of problems—the most interesting ones, actually—are not algorithmic. Protein folding, essential in living processes, is one example. So is computer graphics, involving interactive elements. Furthermore, adaptive processes can not be described through algorithmic rules. More important, anticipatory processes refuse to fit into neat algorithmic schemes. At the time when I advanced the notion that the computer is a semiotic engine, my enthusiasm was way ahead of my ability to understand that the so-called universal machine is actually one of many others. Today we know of DNA programming, neural network computation, machine learning (including deep learning), and membrane computation, some equivalent to a Turing machine, some not.

We are not yet fully aware that the knowledge domain covered by the universal computation model (the Turing machine) is relatively small. We are less aware of the fact that specific forms of computation are at work in the expression of the complexity characteristic of the living. The university is still "married" to the deterministic model of computation because that's where the money is. If you want to control individuals, determinism is what you want to instill in everything: machines, people, groups. Once upon a time, the university contributed to a good understanding of the networks. Today, it only delivers the trades-people for all those start-ups that shape the human condition through their disruptive technologies way more than universities do. Working on a new foundation for semiotics, I am inclined to see semiotics as foundational for the information age. But that is a different subject. If and when my work is done, I would gladly continue the dialog.

Self-monitoring and corporate interests

Nick Montfort

Nick Montfort develops computational poetry and art, is a frequent collaborator at the intersection of digital media and literature and associate professor of digital media at MIT, where he has served as faculty adviser for the Electronic Literature Organization. He is the coeditor of *The New Media Reader* (2003) and *The Electronic Literature Collection 1* (2006) as well as the author of *Twisty Little Passages: An Approach to Interactive Fiction* (2003) and *Exploratory Programming for the Arts and Humanities* (2016).

Nick Montfort ponders about the fate of buzzwords in the history of digital media, praises the Internet for supporting intellectual advancement, and does not expect a for-profit organization such as Google to serve the intellectual community or nonprofit organization. He addresses self-monitoring systems as corporate monitoring systems, he assumes authorship over a text resulting from a program he wrote including legal responsibility in case this text incited a riot, and he doesn't fear the quantitative turn of Digital Humanities but hopes for a "digital media DH".

Prelude

Roberto Simanowski: What is your favored neologism of digital media culture and why?

Nick Montfort: "Blog" is a pretty good one that works well as a noun and verb and describes a non-proprietary, user-controlled, system for a new sort of writing. Remember blogs? But I think one of the most telling neologisms is "ghay" (or "ghey"), which is an intentional misspelling of the word "gay" originally developed to circumvent lexical filters and allow people (boys and young men) to insult one another in a homophobic manner. This term's existence shows how negativity, including that based on identity, persists in online cultures, even if 'on the Internet, no one knows you're a dog,' even though new groups of people are connected by computing, and even though we built systems to try to block disparaging forms of speech. It appears not only because people want to use a particular slur, but also because a silly, ineffective way of preventing that slur from being used was put in place. And usage has evolved: Some people now use the term in the sense of "I wish to insult you, but don't worry, even though I am using a slur of this sort I don't mean to say that homosexuality is bad." What progress.

RS: Interesting to see how the arrival of effective search and filter engines have impeded free speech and how people found their way to work around it. Which leads to the next question: If you could go back in history of new media and digital culture in order to prevent something from happening or somebody from doing something, what or who would it be?

NM: I don't think free speech online has been impeded very directly, at least from my perspective in the United States. One might have a different idea in considering China, of course, and there are chilling effects and other indirect means of suppressing expression. But I find that many of the speech-related problems that I see are from trolls, spammers, haters, and other people who speak freely and in anti-social ways. We don't need to make all such speech illegal. We would, however, like to have a world in which those who want to communicate with one another can do so.

With regard to your question about what to prevent, the easy choices here would be ones that keep bad things from happening (for instance, the release of *Spore* or *Duke Nukem Forever,* games that were much better when we were imagining them) or ones that keep good things from ending (for instance, classic games are revived in new editions). To look on the positive side, I'd be interested in keeping the Digital Arts and Culture conference series going past its final 2009 conference. I wish there were some conference series of this sort today, spanning the arts, including theory and practice, and allowing for humanistic work that is technically serious.

RS: We will come back to the issue of humanistic work and digital technology. First this question: If you were a minister of education, what would you do about media literacy?

NM: When it comes to media literacy in general as well as programming, students should be invited to be creative and to learn by doing. I'd work, and would continue to work as I do in my role as a teacher (rather than government official), to allow more media practice and media making. This is a major aspect of my next book, *Exploratory Programming for the Arts and Humanities,* but is also part of all the classes I teach at MIT. I'm not saying that practice and media-making is the *only* way to learn, but I do find it to be an *essential* way to learn.

Politics and Government

RS: Some of the buzzwords of critical as well as euphoric discussions of the current and future state of digital media are "big data", "Internet of things", "algorithmic regulation". How would you discuss those words in a class on the cultural implications of digital media?

NM: Terms like these do represent underlying ideas and concepts, and they are worth discussing. But the ascendancy of the term "big data" doesn't mean it is truly a more effective and

powerful idea than is "distant reading" or "cultural analytics."
I think it's useful to discuss today's popular terms in the context of other famous terms from the past such as "push media"
and "cyberspace." Obviously these are terms that sound very
outmoded now, but I don't mean to be dismissive when I refer
to them; some of those underlying ideas have been important
and remain so, and yet, obviously, everything promised by such
terms did not persist (or never came to be in the first place). How
do terms such as these represent hopes, imaginations, fascination, and also misconceptions?

RS: If we ask Google Ngram, we learn that the term "big data",
of which "distant reading" can be seen as an offspring, occupies
discussions much more than "push media". We will come back
to big data and distant reading later. For now it may be good to
remind of this other term famous in the past and somehow forgotten in present time. Why do you think "push media" and its
antipode "pull media" did not persist?

NM: Without looking at the relevant big data, I am sure that
"push media" is a term strongly associated with the Web boom
of around 1996 and 1997. PointCast was a company, founded in
1996, that garnered a huge amount of buzz for "pushing" information to client computers, reversing the way the Web works.
Practically everybody had the Pointcast screensaver, which
displayed news headlines and such. In March 1997 the cover of
Wired featured a hand and the word "PUSH!" and instructed
readers to "kiss your browser goodbye." Why did PointCast
go out of business and why did talk of "push media" subside?
Because the concept, as exciting as it was, was almost totally
wrong. People did not want to turn their computers into print
newspapers or TV sets, at least on these terms, even though they
would later gladly use services like YouTube to access video.
They wanted to post their own content, search and surf in different ways, and write comments (even if the comments on YouTube
do not seem highly meaningful). Sure, there are types of information that people want "pushed" to their computers and devices
– weather information, software updates, posts and tweets from

feeds/accounts that they've subscribed to. But putting those in place didn't fundamentally reverse the Web. We didn't kiss our browsers goodbye.

The reason I bring up this term is simple. In late 1996, "push media" was the next big thing, generating tremendous excitement. Except, like "Infobahn," it wasn't the right concept or a truly relevant term. In 2014, "big data" is obviously a hot topic, the next big thing. Except maybe it isn't. Maybe by 2020 it will sound about as relevant as the Infobahn does today. In the case of big data, I think the reasons for the obsolescence of the term (and I am sure it will become obsolete) will be quite different. We really are facing what seems to us today like massive amounts of data related to communication, writing, media – and we have data from a huge number of sensors as well. We don't yet have the methods to analyze this data as we would like, and we *certainly* lack the means to contextualize it within our cultures, societies, and economies. But this data isn't inherently "big." It only seems big because we have been focused on much smaller data sets. Our discussion of "big data" does not pertain to how much data there is, but rather what our traditional means of data collection and analysis have led us to expect. When those expectations change, what seems like "big data" now will no longer seem big. It will just be data.

RS: Web 2.0 culture seems to have tamed and commodified the wild, anarchistic Internet of the 1990s when people played with identity in IRCs and MUDs and built their own websites in idiosyncratic ways. Remember John Perry Barlow's declaration of the independence of Cyberspace from the governments of the old world? Today, it seems people hope for governments to intervene in the taking-over and commercialization of the Internet by huge corporations such as Google and Facebook.

NM: Government has always played a huge role in online communications. Even before there was much popular access to the Internet, when people used BBSs run on individual's home computers and phone lines, the technical development of both the computer and the phone system was strongly supported by the government. Obviously the US government had a lot to do with the development of the Internet, too. The problem now is that corporations have found a way to profitably insinuate themselves into personal publishing, communication, and information exchange, to make themselves essential to the communications we used to manage ourselves. As individuals we used to run BBSs, websites, blogs, forums, archives of material for people to download, and so on. Now, partly for certain technical reasons and partly because we've just capitulated, most people rely on Facebook, Twitter, Instagram, Google, and so on.

RS: Capitulation is a strong word; stronger than technical or cultural reason. It associates the claims of activists to stand up against the danger of surveillance and commercialization for a "free, open and truly global Internet" as, for example, expressed in Tim Berners-Lee's campaign *The Web We Want*. Such claim certainly deserves consent. However, the notion the Internet has gone the wrong way reminds us of philosophers such as Adorno who considered, against the perspective of the majority of the people, the social system we live in as wrong. Isn't the claim of a better Internet similar to the utopian notion of a better society? To rephrase my earlier question: What would have been the alternative to the actual development of the Internet? And how do you see the interdependence of technological agenda and cultural demand in this regard?

NM: This is an extremely interesting and important issue. Often, we act as if we want the Internet to live up to the positive nature of our society. Consistent with the various media panics we have undergone, we assume that new technologies will be threats to the social order. Because of this, we want our familiar society to win out over these new threats. But in fact, while new technologies certainly have their relationships to communication and creativity, being influenced by the past and influencing what will come, they are part of society. As you've said, our current social norms are not always correct or ideal. We shouldn't just be hoping to uphold them, but to improve our societies, whether one wants to call that impulse progressive, utopian, or whatever else.

Of course our current social system is wrong, or, to be a bit more gentle, not optimal. Should we try to "fix" the Internet or digital media more generally so that it better replicates the dominant social treatment of immigrants, trans people, youth, and other disadvantaged and oppressed groups? Of course not! We should be working to improve social justice, and we should certainly use and shape our technologies to help us accomplish that.

You've asked for an alternative to the Internet, so let me provide an alternative that would be worse than what we have: An oligopoly of hegemonic corporate services that replicate the mainstream values seen in classic network television and the policies of retail stores. You can only hang around if you might buy something. You need a credit card (so you can't be a young person) and/or documentation that is effectively proof of citizenship. Don't expect alternative gender identities or other means of self-representation to even be discussed, much less implemented. Even cumbersome and seldom-adopted means of enhancing privacy (PGP, Tor) are absent, as of course are practical tools for ad blocking and spam filtering.

Access to digital information and conversation via the Internet isn't perfect, but it is better than this nightmare. Today, there are people who work on alternative DNS servers and other infrastructural improvements to the core technologies of the Internet. But from your and my standpoint, and the standpoint of most of our readers, I think that trying out practical ways of collaborating, sharing information, and fostering access and conversation can offer tremendous benefits. You could have started a conventional, closed-access journal 1999, but instead you created *Dichtung Digital,* a bilingual publication, which you made available online for free and later developed into a peer-reviewed journal. I have been blogging for many years and have used Web systems to collaborate on and publish freely-available work, working with people of different sorts internationally. These are the things we need to do to provide an alternative to monolithic discourse, whether corporate, retail, or institutional in some other ways. We need to build the structures that will support positive conversations, intellectual advancement, and empowerment. And we need to continually be part of these conversations.

RS: In his book *The Googlization of Everything (And Why We Should Worry)*, Siva Vaidhyanathan speaks of Google's "infrastructural imperialism" and notes that Google has been crowding out imagination of alternatives, not the least of which by its reputation for building systems that are open and customizable -- so far. Should we mistrust the positive record and worry? Should –and could– the US government or the European Union carry out something like Google's book project and run a search engine free of advertisement?

NM: Siva is absolutely right. Just hoping that Google will provide flexible, general-purpose search, search that does exactly what everyone in the world wants and needs, as a public service, is not a sound idea. While the government can lead the way in information access (for instance, the Library of Congress is a pretty good institution that does this, as is the British Library) I also don't expect new Web systems such as search engines to be government initiatives. Let me be more explicit about those institutions I mentioned, though: The Library of Congress, in addition to being a major library in the US, developed a non-proprietary classification system that is used throughout the US and in some other countries. The British Library has also made many general contributions and has more items in its holdings than any other library in the world. So some of our large governmental institutions that deal with information are very influential, and in very positive ways.

Building a large search engine is a hard task that few undertake. Currently, in English, I understand that there are only two sizable indexes of the Web; Google's and the one used by both Bing and Yahoo. It's Coke and Pepsi, but for our access to the universe of inscribed knowledge. The search capability we have is pretty good for commerce and for just "surfing" for entertainment; for doing scholarly research or getting medical information it is atrocious – sometimes it seems that you might as well simply go to Wal-Mart and try to find what you need there. But it is considered a hilarious idea to try to build a new index of the Web. We think that only Google can do it for us.

There probably are suitable uses of government regulation and suitable new government projects in this area, but the main response here should be to expand our imagination and undertake new efforts to build alternative systems. For instance, why are we waiting for Google to give us an excellent search facility for scholarly works? Google is not involved in the intellectual community of scholars, academic conferences, teaching, advising students, and so on. The research they are conducting is, by the very nature of their organization as a corporation, for the purpose of enriching their shareholders. That by itself doesn't make Google "evil," but the company is simply not going to solve the scholarly community's problems, or anyone else's problems, unless it results in profit for them. A regulation won't fix this; we, as scholars, should take responsibility and address the issue. To see a case where a nonprofit organization has done a better service than any company has, by the way, consider the Internet Archive. Obviously there is Wikipedia, too. Neither is perfect; they're just the best systems of their sort in the world.

Algorithm and Censorship

RS: As I learnt in the interview with Erick Felinto, Brazilian's most progressive former minister of culture, Gilberto Gil, once said: "I'm a hacker, a minister-hacker". Felinto continues, in a time when big corporations are increasingly colonizing cyberspace, we need to imbue people with the hacker ethics of freedom, creativity and experimentation. David Golumbia, on the other hand, holds that "hackers" are bizarrely celebrated as both libertarian and leftist political agitators. To Golumbia, "political activism" by "hacker" groups such as Anonymous is more easily parsed as right-wing than as left-wing activism, for their issues are usually ones on the agenda of the far right: the dissolution of the state, the celebration of individual freedoms over social equality, and a diminished focus on the dangers of concentrated capital. How do you see the role of hackers and hacktivism in the cultural and political environment of digital media?

NM: "Hacker" is a very loaded term, to leave aside "hacktivism," which is loaded in other ways. To some it means breaking into other people's systems, to some it means working to protect those systems, and to some it means building those systems. I think the political valence of destruction is different than that of construction, and that working for organized crime to infiltrate other people's computers and build botnets is also significantly different than opposing Scientology or (to get old school) the Communications Decency Act. It's certainly different than creating and maintaining Python, a Linux distribution, the Linux kernel, or other systems. To consider hacking in the sense of programming and in the constructive system-building sense, particularly in free software, I see that there is a liberal aspect to the activity, even if undertaken by political conservatives. (Perhaps like George W. Bush's artistic practice as a painter, which allows him to sensitively and strikingly portray Putin?) "Hacking" in this way involves adding code, and the concepts that code embodies, to the world, allowing others to use these additions they like, fork them if they like, or forget them if they like. I'm not saying hackers (specifically, free software hackers) are always virtuous in every way or that they are exactly what we expect them to be politically. For that matter, I don't mean to suggest that doing destructive things isn't appropriate and useful at times. Still, the basic activity of hackers (as I think of them) is constructive and the outcomes are offered to the world to improve the way computational systems work and the way we think about information.

RS: Since Internet companies use data and algorithms to customize the website they show us, the ads they send us, and the information they give us, one metaphor to describe the digital media age may be narcissism. In digital media studies the term translates to "daily me" (in Cass Sunstein's book *Republic.com*) or "you-loop" (in Eli Pariser's book *Filter Bubble*). To Sunstein, Pariser and others alike, the personal and cultural cost of personalization in digital media is the loss of chance encounters, the preclusion of the unfamiliar, the removal of diversity and of what we are not (yet). A valid concern or a hyperbolic alarmism?

NM: There are a lot of dimensions to personalization and self-monitoring beyond the narcissistic ones. You could use information about yourself to better contextualize what you read, to relate news in other parts of the world to your own city or experiences, or to get recommendations that broaden your perspective. I don't think that I would call a person with diabetes, monitoring his or her blood sugar levels, a narcissist simply because more information about the self is being observed in this case and this person is concerned with that information. When unseen algorithms isolate people by their purported world-views, of course, that is problematic. But let's not flatten every use of personal data to that.

RS: I agree. So lets take self-monitoring: What is your perspective here?

NM: I do admit that there are dangers in taking a Fordist/Taylorist perspective on oneself (and one's productivity). But I think individuals in culture today can work through the problems associated with self-monitoring. I'm more concerned that what we call self-monitoring is almost always mediated by corporations. The types of monitoring we can do are dictated by corporate, for-profit interests, just as the interfaces we use are developed by corporations. And of course the data we accumulate about ourselves, even if we look at it only on our phone or only on our local computer where it is captured, is almost always transmitted to corporations that are obliged to use it in any way that can increase their profits. It doesn't have to be this way, but we need to change things if it is to be otherwise.

Fitness monitoring is an interesting case. Fitbit's monitoring devices are popular ones, providing information about how the wearer's body vibrates throughout the day, an extraordinarily detailed sequence of sensor data that pertains not just to general activity level but to all physical activities being undertaken. Fitbit's system is not a self-monitoring system. It is a corporate monitoring system: the data is sent to Fitbit. The corporation then shares the data it obtains from a particular user with that user, via its website. Other users get some information, too. Years ago, it was noted that the sexual activity of some users was visible in their posted data. Fitbit responded by making certain data private by default. "Private" of course just means that the data is not posted on the Web for all users to see. The company Fitbit, based in San Francisco and founded by James Park and Eric Friedman, can still tell when its users are engaging in sexual activity. Fitbit has been taking on other companies as clients and is monitoring the activities of those companies' employees. I don't know whether your HR department gets to track how much sex you're having, but there is no technical barrier to this.

My point is that if you want to know how many steps you're taking each day, you can just get a pedometer. There's no need to get a corporation (or several) involved. If you want to plot the data and have it look pretty, there's no technical barrier to doing that on a computer or mobile phone without sending the data to anyone else. Why wait until people start getting fired for their tracked activities outside of work: walking too little, for instance, or having too much sex on their own time?

RS: I absolutely agree, if I want to track myself why do the data have to be on a corporate website. Your explanation suggests that it is actually laziness and incompetence (to go the extra mile and find ways to collect, analyze and visualize data without falling for the convenient app of a corporation) that eventually will allow employers to control their employees. However, we should not forget that the new cultural technique of self-tracking is intertwined with the meanwhile quite established cultural technique of sharing. It is not inevitable but very much suggested that my running becomes a 'social running' by sharing the data of my activities online. Plus, in this case the sharing has even more reason than the infamous sharing of what I am doing right now or what kind of food I ordered. According to the Hawthorne effect people work harder – and run faster – if monitored by others. Transparency boosts motivation and will push a lazy person into action. Jawbone's VP of product development once phrased it this way: 'The number one correlate with your weight is what your friends are doing.' Hence, it is very unlikely that self-tracking works the way it does without a social-networking feature.

NM: Actually, the 2007 Journal of the American Medical Association article "Using Pedometers to Increase Physical Activity and Improve Health," which considered pedometer use without data sharing, reported 'The results suggest that the use of a pedometer is associated with significant increases in physical activity and significant decreases in body mass index and blood pressure. Whether these changes are durable over the long term is undetermined.' So there is peer-reviewed medical research that people having their own (not shared) pedometer data is beneficial. Of course, for medical advice and information, I would go to the top American medical journal before an offhand statement from an executive of an interested company. Beyond that, I'll note that if you want to get into a sharing situation where social pressure helps you enhance your fitness, there are other ways to do it – join a gym, for instance.

Although I don't see it as critical to fitness success, I do understand why people wish to share exercise data with others. It may be, for instance, to try to connect to other people via data instead of via conversation. Is it really very socially significant that I walked 16,396 steps on Saturday? It's more than usual, and I suppose it could possibly prompt a conversation or make some of my friends more socially aware of me in some ways. But if the goal is social sharing, wouldn't it be much more significant to write something on my blog, or even briefly tweet, about where I walked, why, with whom, and what the weather was like? For some people, sharing raw data may indeed serve this social purpose, so I don't mean to suggest that data sharing is wrong. But it seems that it could just as easily substitute for deeper social interaction, rather than enhancing it.

RS: This brings us closer to the actual issue here: The increasing public sharing of personal data may in fact represent the decrease of social interactions. Could it be that people have become too lazy to write about their life and prefer outsourcing the task to technology which automatically both turns the report from words to numbers (or images if we include Snapchat and other social media of self presentation) and distributes it to as many people as wanted at once. This of course raises the inevitable question why people follow Facebook's imperative to share as much personal information as possible and why younger generations don't seem to care about privacy.

NM: I don't buy either the stereotypical privacy concerns that people have about, for instance, teens (refuted in danah boyd's book *It's Complicated*) or the "digital native" concept (with odd colonial valences among many other problems). Essentially, I would say that young people, as with any group of people, are neither fully aware of technology and complete masters of it in every way, nor are they rubes who fail to think about their own interests and who don't understand the social implications of technology. Young people do not need to learn the social norms of the use of technology from their elders. But they are also not total experts who are ready to chart the future of the Internet for everyone in the world. We should be respectful of the perspective and values that youth have; we should also respect the fact that their expertise and vision is not the only expertise and vision, nor is it the best in every way.

I have to point out that Facebook is not in favor of 'the sharing of as much personal information as possible.' Facebook is in favor of having as much personal information as possible fed into their own corporate systems, for others to see, certainly, but ultimately for their own use. In fact if all the information on Facebook were available in some other system that was at least equally convenient to use, the company would have a severe problem. So trustworthy branding, a trendy company, buying other prominent and successful startups, and so on is also critical from Facebook's standpoint. What Facebook really wants is for your social life to be impossible without them.

Finally, I don't think people are just being too lazy generally. They're inventing new forms and genres online, communicating and creating in radical new ways. It's just that there are a lot of complexities to the social, cultural, and political dimensions of digital media and the specific systems (often corporate ones) that are arising. In fact the problem is probably not laziness at all, but that people are moving too fast and are overlooking things that, with a better understanding of history and more time to contemplate them, they would be able to deal with in much better ways.

RS: This is exactly what should alarm us. More so since Facebook is so successful in accomplishing its goal. If boyd's message is that the kids are all right, we may add that – and some would say, for this reason – the society is not. Younger generations have basically adapted to the regime of sharing and look forward with excitement rather than discomfort to the Internet of smart things that will know everything about us and may pass it on to others who also like to know. I wonder how much they understand the social implications of technology if even people with more education and experience don't really know where this road of sharing will lead us. Not only Facebook but almost every app today wants to have as much personal information as possible. As we know, personal information sum up to societal information which is wanted by the intelligence apparatus and governments as well as by scientists and companies. Isn't the actual problem of big data mining rather than the more or less conscious compromise of privacy the looming of algorithmic analytics and regulation?

NM: I don't think these can be easily separated. There are some types of big data work that are hard to see as a threat to privacy: astronomical data and data from monitoring air quality, for instance. But much of the excitement about big data has been regarding data about people – cultural, economic, medical, and so on. Or of course reading people's email (or whatever Google wants to call its algorithmic analysis), initially to serve up ads but perhaps for many other interesting reasons. I say these are difficult to separate because there is no reason to amass huge amounts of data, which classically would be private, unless this data can eventually be analyzed, either by the collector or by a company to which it is sold, or can be used to regulate human or machine behavior in profitable ways. So I wouldn't locate the problem in the analytic stage. The collection stage very strongly prompts analysis and use.

Two analogies: In a criminal trial in the US, the judge works to avoid inadmissible evidence being shown to the jury in the first place. That evidence isn't shown at first and then retracted later. Also, in a hiring process, if you're not legally allowed to discriminate based on age, it works well if you don't ask applicants to provide their age. So instead of trying to block analysis, I'd suggest that we only give data to companies if, at the very least, there is actually some benefit to us. But really, the benefit should be worth the cost of giving up that data – it should pay us appropriately for how much the data is worth. And of course we don't know how much the data is worth.

RS: Indeed, we don't know and even if we knew that it is worth a lot it shouldn't be up to us to sell it because not only do personal information sum up to societal information, the personal approach to information can also produce societal pressure. Imagine fifty percent of the applicants in a hiring process volunteering their age, their ethnicity, and their Facebook password assuming that it is beneficial to them. What chances do you think the other fifty percent will have of getting hired if there is only one job for ten applicants? We have to be stricter: It should not only not be up to companies alone what kind of data they can collect and analyze but also not to the individuals alone what data they can share and provide. The decision should be in the hands of the society as a whole after it has discussed the possible implications of certain data sharing and reviewed the acceptability of such implications. In this context it is remarkable that in December 2015 the European Parliament agreed on a proposed Data Protection Reform that foresees the appointment of 'data protection officers' in order to 'help the competent authorities to ensure compliance with the data protection rules' as well as the adoption of 'impact assessment' carried out by the competent authorities with respect to certain uncertain data processing. Hence, maybe we have to think much bigger about the privacy issue, as an issue that, similar to that of social welfare and medical benefits, requires public debate and governmental regulation.

Art and Aesthetics

RS: In the 1990s there was a lot of talk about the "death of authors" and the empowerment of the reader in hypertext. Although in the discussion of hypertext today the role of the author is understood in a way that is much more complex, the death of the author remains an issue with respect to text automatically created by a computer program. Ironically, in contrast to the author's hasty discharge in the early hypertext debate, the trope of the death or disempowerment of the author is now not at all played out in the way one would have expected. Rather than considering the author as being replaced by software, a number of theorists and practitioners regard the author as present in the software. You have experimented a lot with computer-generated text and "poetic computing" as one of your lectures is entitled and discuss this issue in your book *Exploratory Programming for the Arts and Humanities* that will be published in 2016 with MIT Press. How much authorship do you claim in a text resulting from a program?

NM: When I write a text-generating program – and let me restrict myself right now to the "self-contained" kind that doesn't accept seed or source texts – I consider myself to be the author of the program and therefore implicated in the output the program produces. I wouldn't say, and I don't say, that I wrote the output. It was produced by the program, which I wrote. I make my programs available under free software licenses as free/libre/open source software, so anyone can run them and generate texts with them. I don't claim ownership of the texts that result when other people run the program. It is perfectly legal for someone to go and publish such outputs, and the system itself, without my permission, although it's nice for people to let me know when that happens. Now, I think it very likely that if one of my programs generated some text that, for instance, advocated the overthrow of the government and incited a riot, I could be found to be legally responsible for this. And, in the sense of moral author-ship, I certainly get some credit (or blame) for the poems others generate with my programs.

RS: Given that you don't claim ownership of the text resulting from somebody using your program, would then, if the text turns out to be lawless, the other guy be jailed? To hold you responsible in court or build you a memorial for the overthrow, wouldn't the idea then have to be communicated within the code itself, i.e. before the outcome of any text? As I understand it, you program a system with certain rules of communication while the concrete application of the rules, the communicated, is not in your control. Like langue and parol in linguistics, or the camera and the pho-tograph in media studies.

NM: Analogies to better-known domains may be helpful. IBM's chess computer Deep Blue defeated Gary Kasparov in a water-shed moment for human-computer relations. One can imagine the team of programmers saying "We beat Kasparov!" after this happened. This is an instance of metonymy, however; it isn't literally true. Kasparov could easily defeat any or all members of this team, playing in any configuration, if the game were between people. The programmers didn't beat him; they wrote a computer program that beat him. Sergy Brin and Larry Page don't find people's search results for them; the search engine they developed (and that many others contributed to) does. When you typed "I hate Jaws" into the Google search engine several years ago, the system would helpfully suggest: "Did you mean: *I hate Jews*?" Brin and Page didn't create this result, of course, but they and their company developed the system that produced this result. Just as the Deep Blue programmers can take credit for Kasparov's defeat, although they didn't personally defeat him, Brin, Page, and Google would have to be the ones blamed for that suggestion that the search engine made – and also the ones who get credit when the system works well.

RS: I agree with your conclusion but wonder about the premise. Deep Blue won because of the computing power, and only after it was upgraded to Deeper Blue so it could base its moves on the analysis of thousands of master games and the evaluating of 200 million positions per second. Google acts on the base of probability. These are qualities of the computer humans deliberately make use of. Their good making use of it certainly deserves them authorship. But of course, Brin and Page are not the authors of the line *I hate Jews*; only of the mechanism of autocompletion.

NM: That's a good point, and I think it does inflect mine in an important way. In both of these cases the system (Deep Blue, Google search) works not only because of smart programmers but because of well-curated data that is used to train the system. Even when there's not a mass of data to train on, those who develop such systems draw on experience "manually" to devise rules. In any case we have to look beyond the developers/programmers to, in many cases, data, and, in all cases, the culture and contexts in which these systems are developed.

RS: You also wrote a book about interactive fiction (*Twisty Little Passages* of 2003) describing the development of an online interactive fiction community in the 1990s and examining the concept of the "active reader" in contrast to the passive reader in traditional text from gaming and literary perspectives. What are your main points in the book? What would you rewrite more than a dozen years later?

NM: A significant change is the increasing amount of work that isn't "parser-based." When I looked at IF critically, and when I thought about it myself as an IF author, I considered that natural-language input (in the form of short commands: *get lamp, ask the librarian about the freeway, take inventory*) was very important. It was giving the player a chance to be a maker of language and to respond, even if in a limited way, in the same medium that the game was using to present the simulated, fictional world. Recently, there has been a great deal of interesting work in hypertext (mainly using the system Twine) and in "choice-based" games where one selects from a short menu of options. Meanwhile the visual novel, a form much beloved in Japan, is also gaining some ground in the US. These interfaces still don't appeal to me as much as that of parser-based IF does, but there is some very intriguing writing, including radical and experimental writing that goes in some very compelling new directions, that is happening in these forms. I've also written my own interactive fiction system, used these days for research purposes rather than widespread creation of IF, since writing *Twisty Little Passages*. I wouldn't try to document this system in an updated edition, but I would try to enrich the discussion of IF platforms and their influence on and relationship to creative work. That's of course also a topic that grows out of my work as a series editor of the MIT Press *Platform Studies* series.

Media Literacy

RS: In 2003 you edited, together with Noah Wardrip-Fruin, *The New Media Reader* collecting important texts about and projects of the than still emerging field of new media. If you look back at this book and forward to the probable future of new media (i.e. smart objects, big data, self tracking), what subjects have proved essential, what subjects need revision, what subjects would you add to the New Media Reader 2?

NM: Actually there is essentially nothing I would change about the texts we selected in *The New Media Reader*. We tried to determine the readings that would explain the history of the field, from World War II to the World Wide Web, and with the input of our many advisors I think we did that well. We could certainly substitute a reading here or there, but I think it would be a detail and not indicative of a need for a major revision. We could update the introductions, too, if that seemed valuable to readers. If there were any change I would strongly advocate for a new edition of *The New Media Reader,* it would be to eliminate the CD-ROM. Certainly not because I dislike the contents of the CD, which I think are rather important and which I worked to assemble very earnestly, but because in practical terms there are few people who even have CD drives in their computers and who make use of the CD. For practical use in classes, we should get as much as possible online (some of it already is) and allow people to access these resources over the network. I guess it's typical that the major changes needed are not in the book's content but are due to changes in platforms and storage media (or network access to resources).

RS: Digital Humanities seem to be the new buzzword in the Humanities. Some fear with Digital Humanities the quantitative turn taking place in contemporary society finally infects even the disciplines supposed to reflect and interpret society's development and turns it into a branch of the science department. Others hold that "algorithmic criticism" doesn't aim at verifying and stabilizing meaning through replacing interpretation by counting. On the contrary, "algorithmic criticism" and "distant reading" offer new insights in the way knowledge or data respectively is organized and opens up new opportunities for close reading and interpretation. What do you fear or hope from Digital Humanities and how do you see their relationship to Digital Media Studies?

NM: Fear of quantitative study by a computer is about as silly as fearing writing as a humanistic method – because writing turns the humanities into a branch of rhetoric, or because writing is about stabilizing meaning, or whatever. Valuable insights from computational humanistic study have already been reached, and these should be displayed in response to such talk. I'm actually worried about a different type of intellectual limitation when it comes to the Digital Humanities. Many people think that DH can only be done on our venerable cultural heritage. We can study literary history from centuries past, the development of cities, older examples of art, music, and so on, but we can't study digital media using DH, because, I suppose, that's too many digitals at once. It's bizarre, because that part of our culture which is digital is particularly amenable to analysis using DH techniques: you don't have to digitize it, because it's already digital. And, those working with DH clearly don't find computers entirely disdainful; they can be used for analytical and critical purposes. Why not consider the cultural production that is being done with them, too?

I see a connection between the study of 17th, 18th, and 19th century art, literature, and culture and the study of what is happening today with digital art, electronic literature, and online culture and communication. So I'm certainly in favor of having "digital media DH" along with other kinds of DH. Such work, just like any other DH endeavor, could provide new insights into its objects of study while also offering general benefits to the digital humanities. In case this sounds like a minor concern in light of some of the more overtly political and urgent issues that we discussed earlier, let me state: Understanding that we, today, are part of history, and understanding *how* we are part of history, is not an irrelevant detail!

The age of print literacy and 'deep critical attention' is filled with war, genocide and environmental devastation

Rodney Jones

Rodney Jones is an applied linguist investigating computer mediated communication. He is particularly interested in how digital media affect the way people conduct social interactions and manage social identities from surveillance and self-representation on social network sites to crowd wisdom, self-tracking and algorithmic analysis. He is the co-author of the 2011 textbook *Understanding Digital Literacies: A Practical Introduction* which not only teaches how new media work but also how they affect social practices. Rodney is Professor of Sociolinguistics and Head of the Department of English Language and Applied Linguistics at the University of Reading.

Rodney Jones points out the collusion of governments and corporations in an unregulated internet, as well as the potential of participatory media for grassroots movements *and* surveillance. He examines the discursive economies of social network sites and their algorithms, the (partially justified) replacement of experts by crowd wisdom, the (historical) dialectic of quantification and narrativisation (especially in clinical medicine), the self-tracking movement, the self-presentation on Facebook, and the the current role of (media) literacy in the educational environment.

Prelude

Roberto Simanowski: What is your favorite neologism of digital media culture and why?

Rodney Jones: I love the term 'datasexual', the new brand of 'metrosexual' for whom the collection and display of personal data has become a new form of grooming and cultural capital. The term is both funny and scary, and perfectly fits the aesthetic of many quantified selfers: young, urban, hip, educated, geeky and slightly arrogant. Part of me sees some kind of poetic justice in this, having grown up at a time when being geeky was certainly not sexy — so the rise of the datasexual is kind of like 'the revenge of the nerds'. I'm also fascinated with the new ways data has become mixed up with sex and sexuality. This is of course not entirely new. Back in the 1990's I did research on personal ads, and a key ingredient was always one's 'stats' (age, height, weight, etc.). Digital technology, of course, has brought the datification of the sexual marketplace to a new level. We are in a state of constantly grooming our virtual selves in order to attract friends, mates, employers, etc.

RS: Datasexual is a quite productive neologism indeed. I can think of at least two more layers: 1. The data scientist is "The Sexiest Job of the 21st Century" as Thomas H. Davenport and D.J. Patil wrote in the October 2012 issue of the Harvard Business Review. 2. The obsession with data regarding diet and physical activity replaces the cliché of the overweight nerd getting up only to get pizza and coca cola by guys excited about quantifying self apps which inevitably provides them with a sexy body. The revenge of the nerd comes in two steps: First, they provide the technology for a wide-ranging datafication turning numbers into the central criterion of communication – at the expense of words with which they have never felt very comfortable to begin with. Secondly, they produce the apps and social network settings that provide the necessary motivation to get their own stats 'in shape.'

RJ: Yes, it's also interesting to see this in the context of the development of food and health culture in Silicon Valley, and the wider context of 'Californian' culture. So there's an interesting mixture of spiritualism and empiricism – I meditate, and then quantify how much I have done it for example with the *Meditation Time & Tracker*-App by Robin Barooah. In this regard I highly recommend a book by Anthropologist J. English Lueck called *Being and Well-Being: Health and the Working Bodies of Silicon Valley*. At the same time, before we get too worked up about this 'contradiction' it's good to remember that lots of ancient spiritual systems rely heavily on quantification. Tibetan Buddhists, for example, use beads to count how many times they have prostrated or said different mantras, and the texts are quite explicit about the numbers that need to be reached before the practitioner can go on to the next step. The most obsessive self-trackers I've ever met are Tibetan lamas.

RS: I would never have guessed that: Numbers at the basis of mediation. We will come back to the issue of quantification. Before a rather speculative question: If you could go back in history of new media and digital culture in order to prevent something from happening or somebody from doing something, what or who would it be?

RJ: I wouldn't dare. I've seen too many movies about people going back in time to change things and ending up suffering unintended consequences. I think the idea that history moves in a simple linear fashion and that discrete events can be blamed for discrete outcomes is probably wrong. The causes and consequences of events are usually very complex, and often hidden from us, especially in the realm of media which involve not just all sorts of complex, inter-related economic and political decisions, but also the aggregation of countless personal decisions of users (the 'market'). I don't think it's as easy as identifying where we have taken a 'wrong turn'. I also think this smacks slightly of technological determinism — if only this or that technology or this or that media policy had developed differently, everything would be all right.

RS: Your feeling is probably right. I in fact do believe that media have the power to change the situation of men and that without certain media the world would be different. I suspect without the smartphone most people would still watch their environment rather than escaping into another world as I always did with a book. But this is a question for further studies of media or digital media respectively. Which brings us to the next question: What comes to mind if you hear "Digital Media Studies"?

RJ: It's always difficult to name what we do, and no term is really ideal. The real purpose of these disciplinary names is to make our activities comprehensible to university administrations, government funding bodies and prospective students, but when you start interrogating the labels they are all deeply problematic. Are we studying media, or are we studying human behavior? What is the utility of separating 'digital media' from other kinds of media (the term already promotes a kind of 'discourse of disruption' that is often hyped by media companies)? People who identify with the label may come from wildly different intellectual traditions: anthropology, communication studies, cultural studies, literary studies, psychology, sociology, etc., and often what one 'digital media scholar' is doing may have no resemblance at all to what another is doing— they may not even speak the same language.

For my work I use the term 'digital literacies studies' (though I should probably say I'm just an applied linguist interested in things people are doing with digital technology). The problem with my label is that most people don't understand what I mean by 'literacies' (or even think its a typo), because they may not be familiar with developments in the 'new literacy studies' over the past fifty years. They may think 'literacy' is simply the ability to read and write, whereas when I use the term 'literacies' I am referring to all social practices associated with the deployment of semiotic systems, practices that are not just about encoding and decoding information, but also about negotiating relationships, distributing material and symbolic resources, and constructing social identities.

Politics and Government

RS: While in the 1990s Internet pioneers such as John Perry Barlow declared the independence of Cyberspace from the governments of the old world, now it seems people hope for governments to intervene in the taking-over and commercialization of the Internet by huge corporations such as Google and Facebook. Thus, web activists calling for the government to pass laws to protect privacy online, and politicians suggesting expiration dates for data on social networks appear to be activists in a battle for the rights of the individual. Have tables turned to that extent? Are we, once rejecting old government, now appealing to it for help?

RJ: I think the tables have turned, but this is not just true in the realm of media, but also in the realm of things like healthcare, transportation, environmental protection, advertising, etc. The shift happened with the rise of neo-liberalism in the 1980's, and the 'unregulated' internet proved fertile ground for it. Freedom from government intrusion means freedom for 'markets'— powerful corporations inevitably fill the power void and are much more difficult to challenge since their CEOs and directors are not elected. Meanwhile, elected officials, at least in the United States, are increasingly servants of these corporations which fund their campaigns. It's a horrible dilemma, especially since citizens who rail against big government and those who rail against big corporations often seem to want the same thing, but are pitted against each other (while the governments and corporations are actually colluding). Unfortunately, too much of the infrastructure of our daily existence (including the information infrastructure) is in the hands of forces that are beyond our control.

The big question for media scholars is the degree to which participatory media provides the tools for grassroots movements to challenge this hegemonic marriage of government and corporations. On a good day, I think it does, because I think any increased opportunities to communicate laterally and quickly mobilise social networks can be very powerful (I'm thinking, for example, of the recent protests in Hong Kong). I'm also optimistic because lots of young people are one step ahead of the technology companies (especially when it comes to things like digital piracy). I think that the persistence of torrents is a good sign that the 'machine' has an achilles heel. On a bad day, I'm pessimistic as I see that the very tools that facilitate the formation of grassroots social movements are also tools that facilitate unbelievable capacities for governments and corporations to exercise surveillance of private citizens and to manipulate their experiences of reality.

RS: Speaking of governments, corporations and the control of the internet: Google has become one of the symbols for the centralization of an important public good such as knowledge in the hands of a private company. It is not only the most effective and popular search engine, it also gave us an enormous pool of digitized books, which we like to consult whenever we need from wherever we are. Would the US government or the European Union ever have been able to carry out something like Google's book project? Should –and could– they run a search engine free of advertisement and with an algorithm visible to all who care?

RJ: This relates to the last question. Would any government necessarily be a better steward of such information than a private company? That would really depend on the resilience of democratic institutions in a society, and my experience is that they are rarely as resilient as we think. Another aspect of this question has to do with the resource implications. Information is not really free. It involves an enormous amount of labor to produce and distribute. Unfortunately, with the way the internet works now, the 'value' of information is hidden from us, because we are being 'charged' for it in ways that are not always apparent (by giving our own information in return). This, of course, is a point that Jaron Lanier makes very persuasively. Would we be comfortable with a government using the same model to fund it's 'human knowledge project'? If not, what other ways could they fund it? What's scary to me about Google is not its size or reach but the economic model that makes that size and reach possible in the first place.

RS: An important aspect of the Internet with respect to politics and government is the subversive role it plays towards what Foucault called the 'order of discourse'. With the opportunity to express oneself online and with easy access to a plethora of divergent utterances on everything, the old 'disciplinary apparatus' has lost its base and impact. The situation is sometimes celebrated as shift from expertocracy towards swarm intelligence, sometimes bemoaned as cult of the amateur. How does an applied linguist look at this matter?

RJ: I think that what we have here is a shift from Foucaultian 'orders of discourse' to Deleuzian 'societies of control'. Opportunities to 'express oneself' are just as constrained as before, only now by the discursive economies of sites like Facebook and YouTube. People have 'access' to divergent utterances, but the algorithms channel us into the same old discursive traps. People who get their news from the internet in 2014 are in some ways less likely to be exposed to divergent views than those who got their news from TV in the 1960's because of the 'filter bubble'. At the same time, I think you are right — the new ways information circulates has brought on a crisis of expertise. But part of this crisis also comes from the fact that many people feel that experts have failed us: doctors can't cure us, bankers destroy the economy, priests have sex with children, athletes take drugs, politicians are corrupt, and corporations cheat us and pollute the environment. Ironically, now people seem to put more trust in algorithms (which aggregate and interpret crowd sourced data) than they do in people. They seem to think that what they are getting is actually the 'wisdom of crowds', when what they are really getting is the interoperation of aggregated data by algorithms which were created by the very experts that they distrust and often reinforce the very same agendas.

What is interesting to me as an applied linguist is how people negotiate this new economy of knowledge. I don't think it's as simple as the 'wisdom of crowds'. We need more empirical research on how people search for and evaluate information online (when, for example, they are suffering from a health problem), how knowledge is collaboratively constructed and contested in social networks, how 'laypeople' work together to pool knowledge and challenge experts. For me, the power of applied linguistics is that it gives us a way to operationalise theories. So applied linguists in the 1990s (especially critical discourse analysts) operationalised the idea of 'orders of discourse' by discovering ways discourses are instantiated in things like grammatical structures and genres. Now applied linguists need to operationalise the idea of 'societies of control', to understand how discourse circulates in networks, how selves (as discursive constructions) become instantiated in webs, how the nodes and ties of networks are created and strengthened through the moment by moment conduct of social interaction, and how people 'talk' with algorithms.

Algorithm and Censorship

RS: One could argue that the order of discourse has been inverted: not simply to the extent that laypeople now replace experts, but also in a general dwindling willingness to engage with counter arguments or with anything that is difficult and demanding such as a complex consideration instead of a straight statement. What we may also lose when we dismiss experts are people who, because of their expertise and experience, know better than we what is good for us and (because of their ethos) force us to avoid the easier way: the journalist or editor of news on TV and of a newspaper who offers a complex analysis of a political issue, the curator who decides what art work the public should be exposed to, the teacher who makes students read what she thinks they should know. One result of such development is the trust in numbers as we can see with social media and other platforms online that focus on the counting of views and likes. At the same time, algorithmic analysis of big data seems to verify Lev Manovich's claim from more than a decade ago: the database as one model to make meaning out of the world (by representing the world as a list of items) is overcoming the narrative as another model (representing the world as a cause-and-effect trajectory of items). In your 2013 book *Health and Risk Communication* you mention the 'discursive turn' in social science and investigate how people reflect and communicate health and disease. How do you see the relation of numerical and narrative elements in this communication? What role does the quantified self-movement, whose slogan is "self knowledge through numbers," play in this new scenario?

RJ: The story of clinical medicine in the past 100 years or so has been the story of the tension between quantification and narrativisation. In the 19th century and before, narrative played a central role in diagnosis, with the doctor's main job being the elicitation of a comprehensible narrative from the patient and the interpretation of that narrative. With the development of clinical trials in the 20th century, along with all sorts of technologies for the measurement of bodily functions, diagnosis increasingly became a matter of interpreting numbers rather than stories. The patient's narrative and the doctor's intuition both came to be seen as unreliable. This reached it's height in the 1990s with the rise of 'evidence based medicine'. A lot of this shift was market driven— increasing quantification gave health care systems, insurance companies and pharmaceutical companies more efficient ways of rationalising resources, billing for services and marketing drugs. At the beginning of this century there was a backlash against this focus on 'treating the numbers'. With the rise of 'narrative based medicine' (as well as the focus on narrative in alternative therapies), over-quantification came to be seen as suspect. So where does the quantified self movement fit in with this? Does it mean a shift back towards quantification?

Ironically, I think the opposite is true. What practices of self quantification actually give to many patients are better resources for them to tell stories to doctors. In fact, there has always been a dialectical relationship between narrativisation and quantification in medicine. Clinical practice has always been about turning narratives into numbers (doctors turn patient's stories into diagnoses, drug dosages and treatment regimens), and about turning numbers into narratives (doctors need to explain the results of medical test or risk scenarios in terms that patients understand). In the past, this process was completely in the hands of doctors. Patients only had their narratives. Doctors had the power to turn them into numbers and then to make new narratives out of the numbers. Self-quantification, at its best, puts some of this power in the hands of patients and gives patients a role in generating and interpreting data about their health.

RS: This sounds like a twofold happy end: The cooperation of numbers and narratives, or, as Katherine Hayles puts is, database and narrative as "natural symbionts", as well as the collaboration of doctors and patients. Doesn't the obsession with numbers and this kind of self-applied 'dataveillance' also bring new problems with it?

RJ: In terms of actual health outcomes, I am still very optimistic about what this development means for patients and their relationship with physicians. There are, however, a lot of potential dangers to this. One is the danger that self-monitoring can give rise to new regimens of governmentality and surveillance. Another is that the rise of self-tracking allows governments and health care systems to devolve responsibility for health onto individuals.

RS: This would be the dark side of this ongoing trend to self-optimization. It is certainly not wrong if people are more aware about their physical activities and eating habits. However, if the resulting data determines peoples' entitlement to health care benefits then the self-applied, quantified 'bioveillance' would turn into a means of further expanding the neo-liberal perspective on society. A case in point of the prevalence of numbers over narratives is Google's PageRank which is based on statistical concerns beyond any hierarchical taxonomies and ontology based interpretation.

RJ: The biggest problem with self quantification is that, like any form of entextualization, the 'insights' we can get from it are determined by the semiotic categories that it is able to represent. So quantification translates everything into numbers, and numbers have the power to help us see these things in new ways, but at the same time, they limit our way of seeing things. But this is true of any semiotic mode or genre (what I call in my book, technologies of entextualization). So all modes of representation (numbers, words, pictures) are biased, ideological.

As for Google, of course it manipulates Page Rank and censors all sorts of things, but that's not the real problem. The real problem lies in the uninterrogated ideological assumptions behind Page Rank to begin with — the ideological assumptions supported by this 'technology of entextualization'—which includes the idea that 'value' and 'relevance' are determined by popularity and association. As academics we are all too familiar with the consequences of this way of valuing knowledge. Does the number of citations really measure the 'impact' of an article?

RS: We academics of course assume that it doesn't. Different to the senior management, we presuppose that popularity is a problematic criterion for evaluation as long as we value complexity and intellectual challenge. However, we all know from Facebook that a thoroughly crafted post is not likely to receive more likes than a cute picture. On the other hand, isn't the regime of numbers – which gives everybody an equal say regardless of her intellectual or political resources – the inevitable destiny of democracy? Put differently: Does the quantitative turn digital media and especially social bookmarking bring to society prompt us to reconsider our concepts of power, participation and public voice? Discuss

RJ: This is a complicated question, with lots of parts to it. I think if you speak to many users of Facebook (and especially Instagram) they'll tell you that they spend a lot of time crafting their status updates in order to maximize likes, and even pay attention to when they post them, knowing that people are more likely to look at their newsfeeds at certain times during the day. I'm not sure that 'cute' is enough to get likes anymore. People try to be clever. I admit to doing it myself. I sometimes use Facebook status updates as examples when I discuss multimodal discourse with my students, because they are often very carefully composed, with their 'success' depending on how the poster is able to create particular relationship between elements in the image, between the image and the words, and between themselves and the different (usually multiple) audience that they are targeting. I'm not saying this is high culture. It's popular culture, but popular culture can also have an artfulness. At the same time, we need to be careful about expecting any more from Facebook than we do from other forms of popular culture. Sometimes, though, you do get a serious and thoughtful post that will attract a lot of attention. It depends upon the sociohistorical context. I found for example during the Umbrella Revolution that my Facebook newsfeed became a site of rather sophisticated debates about constitutional reform.

But the question of power and participation is more complicated. My suspicion is that political ideas that are packaged in ways that appeal to people's prejudices and fears tend to get the most traction ('likes'), and this was certainly true before social media: so you get great populist leaders like Huey Long and Joe McCarthy and Adolph Hitler (and now, perhaps, Donald Trump). I think the difference is the network effect: that these ideas get spread much more quickly, and they are amplified within echo chambers (that are partly created by algorithms like Google's). Likes attract likes. The 'popular' posts or 'bookmarked' articles appear at the top of the list and are more likely to become more popular. More worrying is the way people's ideas get reinforced rather than challenged. So if someone types 'Is Obama a Muslim' into Google, and then clicks on pages that assert that he is, then the next time he types Obama into the search engine, he will likely receive results asserting that Obama is a Muslim, and so start to think that this is a 'fact' or at least mainstream opinion.

RS: Another question I have about Facebook concerns its contribution to a better world by way of the so-called transparency culture and sharing imperative. While the economic interests behind this data worship are undoubted and certainly need to be addressed, the question remains as to why younger generations don't seem to care about privacy but establish, using Facebook millionfold day-to-day, radical transparency as the new foundation of our culture. Critics of digital culture such as Siva Vaidhyanathans have called for a "dignity movement" that needs to address that having a certain level of anonymity and "breathing room" is part of both being human and being social.

RJ: There's, of course, another way to look at this. That is, to remember that much of what we think about as 'privacy' and 'dignity' are really Western bourgeois notions that have actually developed quite recently, and that these ideas also have certain consequences, notably the privatisation of the public sphere and the concentration of wealth into very few hands. It is also important to remember that, as danah boyd points out, young people have their own norms and literate practices for sharing and concealing information and manipulating their self-presentations online. In fact, most of my conversations with my own students reveal a host of very sophisticated techniques for determining who gets to see what about them. It's also naive to think that what people post online is really 'true'. Often status updates are very deliberate artifices designed as parts of carefully constructed public narratives that are intended for particular audiences. Too much thought goes into this to characterise it as a kind of 'information promiscuity'.

RS: I have no doubt that young people don't want everybody to read everything they share in social networks. They are, as dana boyd points out, especially concerned about 'surveillance from parents, teachers, and other immediate authority figures in their lives' rather than the possible access of governments and corporations to their data).[1] However, I am not sure I would agree with boyd that teens' engagement with social media is just a different interplay between privacy and publicity 'instead of signaling the end of privacy as we know it.' In particular, the shift from a 'private by default' to a 'public-by-default framework,' that boyd notes, indicates that we are experiencing a tremendous change in the traditional concept of privacy. As for the fact that privacy as we know it is a rather recent feature of Western civilization is often used to pave the way for the post-privacy stage our civilization is entering; most prevalent maybe by moral philosopher Peter Singer in his 2011 essay *Visible Man. Ethics in a world without secret*. However, if recency is an argument what about other constructs and concepts that materialized in Western civilization not long ago such as equal rights for women and equal opportunity stipulations for religious, ethnic, or sexual minorities? I see an interesting historic-philosophical shift applied here: Since enlightenment man considered history, including technological development, as progress to the better and expected 'non-enlighted' cultures to eventually catch up. Now it seems privacy as one of the results of the historical process – the German sociologist Georg Simmel once considered the secret one of man's greatest achievements – is devalued as something we also could and actually should do without.

RJ: Yes, I suppose it depends on privacy from *whom*. Kids are very good at being private from their parents and teachers, but not very good at being private from advertisers and the government, but they don't see advertisers or the government as threats (yet) the way they do their parents (who have immediate power over their lives). Interestingly, I think if you talk to kids about privacy (from their parents) they will likely frame it in political terms— it's about 'dignity', 'rights', 'autonomy', so I think Simmel's ideas are still pretty strong. I'm not arguing that privacy should be devalued because it's new. I'm arguing that it's still valued (or at least the ideas of autonomy and dignity behind it are). Finally, I think it's important to remember, as I said above, that, especially in this age of micro-celebrity, there is a big difference between the person and the persona. I don't think a lot of people regard the 'self' that they are constructing on Facebook to be their 'real self' (any more than they think Lady Gaga acts the same way in private as she does in public or on Facebook).

The relationship between the Western enlightenment and privacy is an interesting one, for the more privacy is valued, the more disclosure is also valued. So in Western countries a gay man *must* come out if he is to be regarded as 'authentic' and 'free'. In China, where there is little regard for privacy, one is expected to keep this a secret (even if other people implicitly know). The idea of privacy can't be separated from the development of western capitalism/individualism. Privacy creates democracy and 'freedom' (whatever that means), but that's not why it is so important in our societies. The important thing, from a capitalist perspective is that privacy *creates value*.

RS: Let me relate the issue at hand with the question of technical determinism we touched on before. One of the classes you teach is called "Digital literacies in the era of surveillance". It explores the kinds of choices people have in utilizing digital technologies in societies in which nearly every action they take with digital media is being recorded, logged, aggregated and analyzed. Those media theorists who subscribe to McLuhan's notion of the medium as the message are rather skeptical as to the extent to which humans are able to understand and reject the postulates media impose onto them. The hate-love relationship of many people with Facebook may be one example: despite the complaints about the burdens inflicted by this communication and self-manifestation 'machine,' one still isn't able to quit. Are we prisoners of our own devices, who can checkout any time, but never leave?

RJ: As for social media, what traps us is not the media part, but the social part. The media becomes the place where all our friends gather, and so we can't socialise unless we go there (not so different from the church and the public square in the past— in fact, the church is a good analogy for social media since it also imposes a kind of regime of confessional sociality). Sherry Turkle worries that media have become the architectures of our intimacies, but I don't think this is at all new. Technologies (and the social institutions they support) have always been the architectures of our intimacies. Architecture itself (the walls of private homes, churches, schools, shops) have been the architectures of our intimacies.

Media Literacy

RS: In 2011 you published the book *Understanding Digital Literacies: A Practical Introduction,* co-written with Christoph A. Hafner. The topics range from hypertextual organization over blogging and games to social networks. In contrast to other textbooks about new media literacy, you don't limit your explanations to how these new tools of communication work and can be used effectively but inquire how they affect cultural behavior and values. Given your perspective as a researcher and your experience as a teacher, what role should literacy about the cultural implications of new technologies play in the educational environment and what roles does it play today?

RJ: This gets back to a point I made in my earlier answer. The question is not just how media literacy should be taught, but about how all literacy should be taught. The problem with most approaches to literacy is that they focus on 'how things work' (whether they be written texts or websites or mobile devices) and teach literacy as something like the skill of a machine operator (encoding and decoding). Real literacy is more about "how *people* work" — how they use texts and media and semiotic systems to engage in situated social practices and enact situated social identities. So whether we are teaching students how to write essays or blog posts, the most important question we should have for them is — what are you doing when you use this media or this genre or this language, and, even more important, who are you being?

RS: There are many concerns inside and outside academia about what people do with new media and what new media do to people. One example is Nicholas Carr who in his 2008 article *Is Google making us stupid?* and later in his 2011 book *The Shallows – What the Internet is Doing to Our Brains,* discusses the consequences

of online media for literacy. From Carr's perspective, multitasking and power browsing online make people unlearn deep reading with the effects being carried offline, and with the result that
they also unlearn deep thinking. The shift from deep attention
to hyper attention has also been announced and bemoaned by
French philosopher Bernard Stiegler who even speaks of a threat
to social and cultural development caused by the destruction of
young people's ability to develop deep and critical attention to
the world around them. Is this academic nightmare justified? Or
is this just another reiteration of a well-known lamentation about
the terrifying ramifications of all new media?

RJ: I don't think it is justified, for several reasons. There is no
doubt that new media are giving rise to new kinds of 'attention
structures' just as writing did in the past, as well as radio and
television. In environments dominated by digital media people
will definitely distribute their attention differently, but I don't
think there is any evidence that this will result in less 'critical'
thinking. The problem with most of these discussions is that they
get stuck in simplistic metaphors about the mind (e.g. deep—
shallow) that I don't think do justice to the complexity of embodied situated cognition. Second, there is the question of what it
means to be 'critical'. In some ways, being able to successfully
traverse multiple texts also requires considerable critical thinking, just of a different sort. Third, the assumption that we are
losing our ability to 'read deeply' confers value on a particular
type of text and a particular type of writing— writing that follows linear forms of argumentation. Texts that people write in
the future will be less linear and more hypertexual, and more
algorithmic, and demand different kinds of reading skills, and
different forms of criticality (forms that we desperately need to
learn how to teach).

   Finally, I don't think shallow reading is replacing 'deep reading'. What it's mostly replacing is television. There is absolutely
no evidence that young people today are reading less than they
were in the 1960s when I grew up. In fact most of the evidence
(e.g. from PISA surveys, from book sales) indicates that young

people are reading more than before, more than adults, and, that they are reading longer texts. As for the claim that people are becoming more 'stupid', I can just imagine my students rolling their eyes at being called stupid by a generation that has created the economic, political, social and environmental catastrophe we now find ourselves in. The 'social and cultural development' and 'deep critical attention' of print literacy has brought us centuries of war, genocide and environmental devastation. New forms of literacy may not solve these problems, but the 'good old days' when everybody read deeply, pondered critically, and acted wisely simply never existed.

RS: In 2010 The Time's columnist Ben Macintyre compared the rapid and restless information gathering of the Web 2.0-generation with the fox who jumps from one idea to the next drawing inspiration from many sources while the hedgehog sees the world through the prism of a single overriding idea. Macintyre takes this analogy from Isaiah Berlin's 1953 essay *The Hedgehog and The Fox* and clearly favors the fox model, since to him it also opposes ideological fixation. What Carr, Stiegler and others perceive from a quite culture pessimistic perspective – power browsing, short attention span – is for Macintyre almost the promise of a better future. Should we, rather than bemoaning or doubting the waning of 'critical' print literature, more actively emphasize and discuss the hidden promises of the ongoing cultural change?

RJ: As long as we don't work ourselves up into an optimism that becomes just as constraining as Carr's pessimism. I do think that what is often happening is not just jumping from idea to idea to get inspiration, but making connections between disparate ideas, which can be very useful. But any mode of thinking is only as good as its execution. A person can read Georg Simmel and miss the connections between the ideas, even when the author makes them quite explicit. And one can similarly surf across the surface of the web, but not engage in creating any connections between one thing and another.

RS: Before the Internet became available for private and commercial use it was administered by the university. Today one has the impression the university is no longer on top of development in this domain. How should academic institutions have responded to the upheaval of new media? How should they become more involved today?

RJ: It depresses me sometimes to see how the universities are responding to new media, mostly as platforms to deliver old media genres like lectures. The problem is trying to fit old pedagogies into the new kinds of participation frameworks made possible by new media.

RS: Another problem may be to upgrade old research disciplines by new technologies as it is happening under the umbrella term of Digital Humanities. This could turn the Humanities into a branch of the science department or, via quantitative analysis open up new opportunities for close reading and interpretation. What do you fear or hope from Digital Humanities for your field of research?

RJ: I'm not a literary critic, but my view of the humanities is that their goal should be to help us understand what it means to be human in the face of any technology we interact with — to shed light on how we live in whatever kinds of buildings, societies, and virtual worlds we have built for ourselves. The bifurcation of the human and the technological is entirely artificial. The technological is the human—its what we've built for ourselves. The goal of the hsumanities is to make us critical and reflective about all the technologies we use, whether they be sonnets or iPhones.

Notes

1.   Dana Boyd: *It's Complicated. The social lives of networked teens*, New Haven, London 2014: 56. The following quotes pp. 57 and 61f.

Surfing the web, algorithmic criticism and Digital Humanities

Diane Favro, Kathleen Komar, Todd Presner, Willeke Wendrich

The participants of this interview are colleagues at the Humanities at UCLA and members of its Digital Humanities group. They apply the tools and methods of Digital Humanities in their research and teaching, write about Digital Humanities or study subjects of Digital Media Studies such as literature in and with new media. Diane Favro is professor at the Architecture and Urban Design department and Director of the UCLA Experiential Technologies Center; Kathleen Komar is professor at the Department of Comparative Literature, former President of the American Comparative Literature Association and Acting Co-Director of the Office of Instructional Development at UCLA; Todd Presner is Professor of Germanic Languages, Comparative Literature, and Jewish Studies and Chair of the Digital Humanities Program; Willeke Wendrich is Professor of Egyptian Archaeology and Digital Humanities, Editorial Director of the Cotsen Institute

of Archaeology Press and director of the Center for
Digital Humanities at UCLA.

The interviewees address the fear of 'derailment' on the digital
highway, the 'lack of deep thinking' among their students and the
worry of humanists (and especially the 'old folks') to be devalued as thinkers by technological advances. They speak about
the pluriformism of the Digital Humanities movement, about
visualized thinking and collaborative theorization, about the
connection between cultural criticism and Digital Humanities,
they share their mixed experiences with the Digital Humanities
program at UCLA, explain why most innovative work is done
by tenured faculty and muse about the ideal representative of
Digital Humanities.

Prelude

Roberto Simanowski: What is your favored neologism of digital
media culture and why?

Diane Favro: *Hackathon*: beyond the obvious associations with
marathon [the long race] and telethon [crowd sourcing], etc.,
such events capture key characteristics of digital humanities
work: collaborative, adventurous, nimble, and productive.

Willeke Wendrich: Twitter feed. It is supposed to mean access
to the output of Twitter, but it evokes images of sparrows focusing on the seeds directly in front of their beaks, and to me sym-
bolizes how many tweeters react instantly on other tweets,
rather than the world at large.

Kathleen Komar: I am taken with the phrases "digital immi-
grant" and "digital native" because they make so painfully clear
the difference between my use and understanding of technology
and that of my students. Students are so comfortable multitasking and web surfing. I still process information vertically while
they do it horizontally.

RS: If you could go back in history of new media and digital culture in order to prevent something from happening or somebody from doing something, what or who would it be?

WW: Google Earth for updating their API without allowing backward compatibility.

KK: I would stop pop-ups and ads. They succeed in distracting me much too often!

RS: If you were a minister of education, what would you do about media literacy?

DF: Literacy is essential, but involves more than texts. I would advocate students become adept at critically reading a range of information-conveying sources including words/languages, spaces, colors, movement, and people/cultures, and that they become adept at using the appropriate tools to do so.

WW: Involve students in an exciting project to produce a high quality work and see their name in "print"/on the screen while having learned everything from metadata, to mark up and copy rights with preferably a bit of programming as well.

KK: Make sure that technology is available to *every* child. The rest they will figure out for themselves. And institute a course on web ethics.

Todd Presner: I consider digital literacy to be a grand challenge of the 21st century. This involves understanding, among other things, how information is structured, presented, stored, and accessed; how computational processes create and organize data; how interfaces structure user experiences; how platforms embody certain world-views and encode culture more generally. Digital literacy is both critical and creative.

Digital Media

RS: With the critical turn in Digital Media Studies in the last 10 years, the notion of the Internet as an 'identity workshop,' as Sherry Turkle described it, or the new public sphere for free political discourse has widely been abandoned (cf. Golumbia's

Cultural Logic of Computation, Morosov's *Net Dellusion*, Turkle's *Alone Together*, Carr's *The Shallows*, Lovink's *Networks Without a Cause*, Pariser's *Filter Bubble*, Vaidhyanathan's *Googlization of Everything* etc.). Meanwhile there is also worry and warning outside the academic field regarding the spoiling of the Internet by commerce and surveillance, i.e. Tim Berners-Lee's *The Web We Want*-Campaign, Edward Snowden's appeal to rescue the Internet, to name only two popular figures in the Anglo-American discourse. How do you see the development of the Internet over the last 20 years? Which worries and warnings do you share, which do you find ill-founded?

DF: My greatest fear centers on derailment. We were given the keys to the car with very little driver's education. Able to go down too many different roads on the Internet at any given moment, users easily forget their targeted original destination. While undirected touring can be wonderful, it has overwhelmed other types of investigations and minimized deep, slow thinking. Without critical, serious training on how to use the Internet we are weakening our criticality. The fact that users are insulted by the notion of needing Internet training is indicative of the problem. The un-ending attempt to be technologically current (Do I have the fastest connection? Last upgrade? Newest browser? Best smart phone/computer with all the latest bells and whistles?) further derails us, consuming time and redirecting efforts to the tools rather than the substance of inquiry.

WW: The internet has, on the one hand, democratized and become available to many, which is a positive development. On the other hand, it has a strong focus on consuming, rather than producing, and an expectation that the information found online can be trusted.

KK: It might be the case that the early days of any field are filled with heady idealism. Early on we may have felt that the internet would make us free and allow us to communicate globally and instantly. Our assumption (on the optimistic side) was that that would be liberating. In some ways it has been. The function of social media in fueling revolutionary movements is a case in point. But we have also been contained in many ways by our technology. I see my students much less in a face-to-face setting now than I did before the digital revolution. They email and want instant and brief responses to very complex questions. I fear that they think too broadly and quickly and do not do the work of thinking deeply or in any sustained way. I also fear that we will become so digitalized that our "personal" existence will become public data to be consumed and used but not to get to understand us as individuals. Distance reading might become an analogy for distance relationships. No need to read the primary text—no need to know the actual person at all.

TP: Like all networking technologies that preceded the internet (from postal systems to railways and telephones), we see a persistent dialectic: technology enables certain things and prevents other things; technology is hailed as salvific and simultaneously apocalyptic; it can democratize and also be used to advance authoritarianism; it can be used to facilitate participation, and it can be used to control and monitor populations. No big surprise here! Technology always has a dialectical underbelly, as these authors have identified, and it can also be used in surprising, unanticipated, and creative ways that have the potential to advance democratic values. We need to move beyond the either/or binary, and consider both the risks and possibilities embodied in any technology. We must not give up on the *weakly* utopian possibilities (to rework Walter Benjamin's phrase) since without them, it becomes very hard to imagine alternatives, build better worlds, and foster ethical communities.

RS: According to Maryanne Wolf, Director of the Center for Reading and Language Research and Professor of Child Development at Tufts University, Somerville, Massachusetts, and her doctoral candidate Mirit Barzillai, 'an early immersion in reading that is largely online tends to reward certain cognitive skills, such as multitasking, and habituate the learner to immediate information gathering and quick attention shifts, rather than to deep reflection and original thought.' (http://204.200.153.100/ebeling/Deep_Reading.pdf) The shift from deep attention to hyper attention and the results of multitasking and power browsing have been announced and bemoaned by many intellectuals, and I hear similar comments here. Nicholas Carr made the loss of deep thinking (or: derailment) popular in his 2011 book *The Shallows – What the Internet is Doing to Our Brains*. Bernard Stiegler speaks of a threat to social and cultural development caused by the destruction of young people's ability to develop deep and critical attention to the world around them. Your work as an academic teacher is closely connected to the ability of deep reading. Kathleen already voiced her concern that the message of digital media – instant and brief responses to complex questions – does not foster deep thinking. To press you all on this issue: Do you share the worries listed above? How do you experience the relationship to reading in the younger generation of students?

DF: Students today do seem to have differently-wired brains than those of the previous generation. Rapid assimilation and highly developed curiosity are positive results of "distracted learning;" lack of sustained inquiry and deep thinking are among the negative. "Free" and easy access is resulting in a rise in collage scholarship as well as plagiarism. Particularly of concern is the shift away from sustained writing and reading. Students moan loudly if asked to do a 10-page paper, while in the past the moan-threshold was at 20 pages. Deep reading is increasingly viewed as an educational necessity, not something done outside the classroom, for pleasure or personal learning. In response to this changing reality I now develop projects (rather than assignments) that are more oriented toward hypothesis testing, object creation (digital model, thick map, etc.) involving multi-media, interdisciplinarity, and peer learning through collaboration. Students respond well to the competition presented by working in groups, in contrast to the results they produce from isolated researching on the Internet.

WW: What I have found is that students not only have a shorter concentration span, but also appreciate audio-visual information over reading. They would rather have something explained to them in short videos than by reading an article (which is something I cannot identify with at all. I'm usually bored to irritation with video explanations because they are slow and not very information dense). I do, however, not tend to worry about such changes, although I will not cater to them. There is not much point to try to hold back societal developments. My hope is that we will end up with a pluriformity of media, although with the increased commercialization of the internet that might not actually happen. Now THAT is a true cause for worry.

KK: Yes, I share this concern. My students are great at surfing the web to find the information they seek; but when confronted with a poem by Emily Dickinson or Wallace Stevens, they are confused by the need to read deeply and to consider each word in its poetic context. They are less attuned to unreliable narrators in novels as well. I think that the need to mull over a word or phrase—and to be able to argue a particular meaning among other possible meanings is increasingly difficult for them. They are also less aware of the history of literature or culture that informs a particular work of art or literature. They are not any less bright than earlier students; they have been conditioned to think differently. That gives them some advantages in this new world—but I would hate to see them lose other capacities of thought.

TP: I think the era of deep attention is largely a fantasy that has been projected backwards to romanticize a world that never existed. We've conjured up an image of a past world in which people could concentrate on a single task (like reading a Tolstoy novel from start to finish) in order to elevate certain cultural ideals, behaviors, and artifacts. But this binary makes little sense: first of all, film theorists in the early 20th century complained about film causing a "cult of distraction" among the masses and before that, critics complained about the genre of the novel being subversive (largely because it helped bring literacy to a much wider public). In both cases, prior media revolutions elicited the same critiques. Hyper-attention has probably always been around, just like deep attention still persists today: If you've ever watched teenagers play videogames, you would note their rapt attention, complex strategy making, and formidable attention to detail.

RS: There is a series of neologisms around of the basic elements of digital media: algorithmic criticism, algorithmic design, ethics of the algorithm, algorithmic analytics, algorithmic regulation. This abundance of new technical terms around the algorithm evidences its central role in coding and computing. The implications this role will have on culture and society in the age of digitization is still to be seen. Some welcome the algorithm as a tool of knowledge production by big data mining and distant reading. Others, however, see the algorithm as Pandora's box since it fosters a way of thinking and acting based on stiff if-then-rationales and on statistics and it outsources human agency. How do you look at algorithms?

DF: I personally like the rigor imposed by rule-based (algorithmic) thinking, in part because the approach parallels my own field of study. The meaning of the term, however, has become equated with "computing." As a result, I tend to use other descriptors.

WW: They certainly have their uses, and we should not do away with them. Big data analysis, however, is of a completely different use than detailed qualitative analysis or thick descriptions of phenomena. Algorithms actually are not really stiff if-then-rationales. Mostly what happens in big data analysis is the description of trends, without any attempt to explain these. They are mostly descriptive, rather than analytical or interpretational.

KK: If we see algorithms as a formal set of instructions to carry out a specific function, then I like the clarity of the operation. This might be couched in numbers or words (e.g., if you see an oncoming plane, veer right). So it isn't the formal process that is a problem for me; it is the assumption that this is always numerical and that it can provide ultimate answers to complex questions. Complexity and ambiguity are not always bad; they induce us to imagine other answers. I would hate to see this human capacity devalued in favor of illusory certainty. A single answer is not always the best way to go.

TP: I've used the phrase "the ethics of the algorithm" in a recent study of the Shoah Foundation's Visual History Archive, a digital archive of 52,000+ Holocaust testimonies, to describe the ways in which computational processing of data is hardly a neutral enterprise and, in fact, requires an attention to ethical issues at every stage. Other authors, like Stephen Ramsay, have begun developing the critical field of "algorithmic criticism," examining not only the ways in which code needs to be analyzed and interpreted for its assumptions and structures, but also how code can be used to engage in cultural critique. The code and database might, for example, be reordered, disassembled, and reassembled according to the constraints and possibilities of computational logic. This is the essence of algorithmic criticism.

RS: Let me just pick the two key phrases in Todd's answer to readdress the problems I see when it comes to the advance of the algorithm. The "ethics of the algorithm" can also be seen in terms of the famous article by computer scientist Robert Kowalski in 1979 *Algorithm = Logic + Control*. In my interview with David Golumbia, the author of *The Cultural Logic of Computation*, he differentiates between two philosophical approaches to life: Leibniz to whom everything in the mind and in society can be reduced to mathematical formulae and logical syllogisms and Voltaire whose "critical rationalism" includes phenomena like irony and skepticism. In light of increasing algorithmic reading and regulation of society I wonder how much room the future will offer Voltaire if the future – including the Internet of things – is densely populated by computers as Leibniz' 'children'. My other question aims at Ramsay's concept of "algorithmic criticism." I absolutely support Ramsay in that computer-assisted text analysis should not be employed in the service of a heightened critical objectivity but deepened subjectivity. However, when Ramsey looks forward to the day "alogithmic criticism" is, as a practice, so firmly established that the term itself may seem as odd as "library based criticism". I am concerned about the insensibility towards the underlying media. While the library offers a specific collection of texts to a reader, the algorithm offers its reading of a (specific collection of) text(s) to the reader. The algorithm as a medium does not equal the library, nor does it substitute it, but complements it and establishes (by stepping between the given text and the reader) a very different pre-condition of criticism.

TP: I don't think we are in disagreement here. I would love to imagine and advance a kind of algorithmic criticism in which Voltaire's irony and skepticism unfolds in profound and even unpredictable ways, but I certainly recognize the lure and the dangers of the Leibnitz model. Again, we have both existing simultaneously, pulling us between logic and control, on the one hand, and artful subversion, on the other. The notion of an ethics of the algorithm is an attempt to inject ethical thought and humanistic values into computational processes at all levels, from the broader information architectures to the design of structured data and databases to the processes of capturing, analyzing, and interpreting that data.

Digital Humanities

RS: One neologism of the development of digital media is Digital Humanities, which meanwhile has been become the most important keyword in the Humanities. The debate on DH has itself coined a series of neologisms such as "fluid textuality," "ubiquitous scholarship," "animated archive," and "distributed knowledge production". What do those terms mean and what do they mean to you?

DF: I don't use the first terms, but would equate "ubiquitous scholarship" with pervasive access to scholarship that in turn promotes learning at many levels, including by citizen learners outside academia. I participate in a number of "distributed knowledge production" projects in which scholars in distant locations all work together in a truly interactive way. Such collaboration is dynamic and stimulating, as well as expedient.

WW: These terms are keyed by a specific section of DH practitioners. The interesting thing about DH is that it is very pluriform, with multiple disciplines working together, critiquing and using DH methods and tools. Often these critiques bridge the method and theory of DH as well as the practitioner's other scholarly backgrounds. In the case of archaeology and DH there is, for instance, a strong emphasis on theories of chronology and spatiality, critiquing how space and time are represented. Issues are, for instance, that chronologies differ depending on the geographical and archaeological context, a situation which does not lend itself easily to representation in standard western calendar structures.

KK: "Ubiquitous scholarship" and "distributed knowledge production" indicate a movement toward more collaborative work and towards more openly sharing research findings. I think these are good things in the Humanities—where we have been in the habit of going off to our own cubby holes and doing our own individual work. "Fluid textuality" implies a different area to me—one that involves electronic literature (on which I am currently doing research). It indicates the capacity of creating texts that are not fixed artifacts (like a book) but rather can be recombined or are interactive or may be authored by several individuals. So still collaboration of some kind. But also a fleeting characteristic. Texts can disappear or change rapidly in an electronic environment (websites or posts, for example).

TP: Together with my co-authors (Anne Burdick, Johanna Drucker, Peter Lunenfeld, and Jeffrey Schnapp), we introduced each of those terms in *Digital_Humanities*. They are not terms that people necessarily use in everyday discourse, even about the Digital Humanities, but are meant to conceptualize certain shifts in cultural production and humanistic inquiry enabled by the digital. In brief: fluid textuality refers to the malleable, fungible, and extensible environment for digital artifacts; animated archives are just that: archives that are no longer a bunch of "dead" and forgotten objects but ones that have been given a new lease on life in digital worlds, often through strategic curatorship and blended environments; distributed knowledge production refers to the world we work in, where collaborative research is prized and knowledge is spread across many locales, including academic and non-academic ones, not to mention slices of the broader public; and finally, ubiquitous scholarship refers to a future to come, in which the pervasive infrastructure of computing has also transformed the scholarly enterprise in a way that greatly enlarges its domain, reach, and impact.

RS: Besides new words, another contribution of this 2012 book to the discussion in the humanities is a different perspective on its present and future. Against the 'default position that the humanities are in "crisis",' the authors portray the computational turn in Humanities as a chance of bringing the 'values, representational and interpretative practices, meaning-making strategies, complexities, and ambiguities of being human into every realm of experience and knowledge of the world.' What would be an example for this extension of the values and strategies of the Humanities into other fields? How, on the other hand, do you see the 'dark side of the Digital Humanities' and 'where is cultural criticism in the Digital Humanities' (to allude to two popular and rather critical debates on DH at the MLA-convention 2011 and 2013)?

DF: At UCLA, the new Urban Humanities Initiative aims to integrate the criticality and values of humanists into the design and theorization of architecture and urban design and planning. At the same time, the UHI provokes humanists to experiment with the approaches of architects and urban designers, including hypothesis testing, visualized and spatial thinking, and collaborative theorization. In identifying a "dark side" for DH, we often forget that all fields have their own negative aspects since those of traditional fields have become masked by familiarity. Humans synthesize a myriad of actions, emphases, contradictions, and interpretive practices, yet these are often isolated in academia. By embracing ambiguity, simultaneity, fuzzy thinking, and interdisciplinary collaboration, DH is a positive provocation to the field compartmentalization that has increasingly hobbled academics pursuing new knowledge.

WW: Perhaps the most important contribution of DH is that it brings the understanding to computational approaches that data are not objective, often ambiguous, and context dependent. These are insights from the humanities that are seldom considered, let alone valued in the sciences, including computer science. I, therefore, don't think that there is a lack of cultural criticism in DH, although there are undoubtedly practitioners who use DH methods and tools uncritically (but then they would also write uncritical articles or books). In other words culture criticism, critical thinking, and social awareness are not inherently part of, nor inherently lacking in DH.

KK: The "humanities" began as those areas of study in which we examine achievements designed and executed by human beings—as opposed to natural phenomena. It is a study of human culture—which, at earlier moments in our history, would have included mathematics and engineering. So I see no inherent need to separate (or protect) the Humanities from other humanly generated systems of meaning such as mathematics. I think we should be chipping away at these separations rather than buttressing them. I believe it profits scientists to see their own work as a kind of narrative. However, I do not believe we should cede the arena of important intellectual achievements to the sciences—as many of our campuses have done recently. The speculative and critical thinking skills remain crucial in our society. Students (and colleagues) need to be able to examine cultural and political claims critically. This is the point of my undergraduate course on Kafka. Literature makes us think and rethink cultural currencies.

TP: The issue for me concerns the importance of the values, perspectives, methods, and content of the humanities at a time in which the humanities are under fire for their supposed irrelevance or secondary status. The humanities provides historical and comparative perspectives; it shows how knowledge is always "situated" in specific cultural, social, and economic contexts; it provides an ethical orientation and methods that seek to comprehend – not overcome – ambiguity, difference, uncertainty, and fuzziness. As I've written elsewhere, the connection between cultural criticism (*Kulturkritik*) and DH is crucial in this respect.

RS: I assume it is easy to agree that *all* fields have their "dark side" and that, though there is no shortage of cultural criticism in DH, DH can also be practiced uncritically. It is also absolutely understandable how DH can and should be critical regarding the 'givenness' of data and the structure of knowledge production and representation. Todd's discussion on DH as a kind of heir of cultural criticism and Critical Theory illustrates very well how "cultural-critical archive projects and platforms" undermine and overcome what Foucault defined as rules of exclusion by means of "citizen-scholars" and "participation without condition". The aim of such "historical documentation" or "database documentaries" seems to be the improvement of knowledge rather than its subversion. From a certain philosophical point of view, however, it is the subversion of knowledge that renders most the "ambiguities of being human". An example for this perspective is the German philosopher Odo Marquard who, in a 1986 essay on the inevitability of the Humanities ("Über die Unvermeidlichkeit der Geisteswissenschaften"), considers the function of Humanities in society to create a rhetoric of resistance not (only or first of all) towards institutions but (also and moreover) to signification and Truth. To Marquard the characteristic – and mission – of the Humanities is to irritate the business of understanding, to counterbalance the notion of reliable, objective knowledge in the natural sciences. The political importance of such deconstructive work becomes clear, as Marquard holds, with respect to confessional civil wars, which he terms 'hermeneutic civil wars': People killed each other over the right interpretation of a book. Such political view of the relationship of the Humanities to interpretation and knowledge may be surprising and foreign. However, it is mirrored by others if for example the Italian philosopher Gianni Vattimo, in his 1997 book *Beyond Interpretation: The Meaning of Hermeneutics for Philosophy*, speaks of a 'nihilistic vocation of hermeneutics' and welcomes it as 'the dissolution of fundamentalism of every kind.' Here the aim of interpretation is not the better, more complete, less manipulated understanding of reality but rather the understanding that the comprehension of reality is inevitably grounded in difference and irreconcilability. The vocation of DH may not be to present the Truth. But it also seems to be far from the nihilistic epistemology of postmodern perspectives.

Digital Literacy

RS: It is obvious that the humanities scholar of the future needs skills that exceed the traditional requests. Computational skills and statistical methods come to mind, as well as new ways of undertaking research and presenting the results. How does the ideal representative of Digital Humanities look like? What are the main obstacles you see in this regard?

DF: I would argue that there is no "ideal representative" of DH, as it is by nature interdisciplinary in approaches and practitioners. I believe that we are in a transitional phase of evolution in which new tools are stimulating dynamic methodologies that will gradually become the mainstream. Twenty years ago we had a separate academic program in my department called Architectural Computing; today computing is so pervasive in all aspects of teaching and research that program has been eliminated. I would imagine that likewise in the future the majority of humanistic inquiries will deploy the tools, theories, collaborative strategies, and interpretive practices of today's DHers and we will move on to other provocations.

WW: The ideal future humanities scholar will not necessarily need computational skills or a fluency in statistical methods. The training preparation and set of skills really depend on her particular research interest. Knowledge of relevant languages and disciplinary theories and methods will remain of great importance. Some of those languages could be, but don't necessarily have to be, computer languages. More important is the will and talent to work in interdisciplinary teams, take time and have the openness of mind to familiarize oneself in the background and methods of other team members, and have an appreciation of all team contributions. Developments are following each other in rapid order and rather than everybody in the academic organization trying to keep up with everything, we will have to divide tasks and play on our own and each other's strengths. Having said that, in general it works best if humanities scholars do try to familiarize themselves with a core suite of tools and programs, so that they are at least intelligent conversation partners. Similarly, the best designers and programmers have at least some understanding of what scholarly work is concerned with: the main questions, approaches and critiques.

KK: The main obstacle I see is fear. Humanists (myself included) fear being devalued as thinkers by the technological advances that seem to leave us behind. But every new app or piece of technology grows out of a narrative that can imagine a new way of doing things. Even pop culture such as science fiction and Star Trek have contributed to our technological developments. Many of us "old folks" fear that we cannot attain the necessary computational skills this late in our careers—and perhaps this is true. But the future generations may not see any problem. They are techno-savvy and unafraid of the challenges. My undergrads are excited about using computers to do their literary research. They are the future. But they still need the understanding of other cultures and languages and the critical-thinking skills to explore research outside of their immediate contexts. Working in collaborative teams (as many of the sciences have done for some time) is probably a strong need for future scholars.

RS: UCLA offers a graduate certificate in Digital Humanities Program which, as it reads at the website, 'prepares students to work in this new environment by providing them with knowledge about the tools, methods, and theoretical issues central to the emerging field and enabling them to ask specific research questions that harness new technologies.' What are the details of this program? What kinds of students enroll? What are the (administrative) obstacles you encounter?

TP: The graduate students come from a multiplicity of backgrounds across the humanities, social sciences, and arts, ranging from fields such as history, English and foreign literatures, comparative literature, art history, information studies, architecture, urban planning, archaeology, design media arts, and more. They are interested in how digital tools, methods, and technologies are transforming knowledge investigation, knowledge making, and knowledge dissemination in the 21st century as well as the ways in which their own fields can be drivers of these transformations. The DH certificate functions like a "minor" for graduate students and requires five courses, including an introductory seminar on DH and a capstone research experience in DH. The latter embeds graduate students in faculty-led team projects, often drawing on library and technical staff, undergraduates and other faculty members. Graduate students also produce a web portfolio of their research and present it publicly at the end of the program. More details about the program can be found online at: http://digitalhumanities.ucla.edu

WW: The students enroll in a core class, which has a focus on the theoretical aspects of DH, illustrated by looking at and analyzing existing projects. Practical work is an integrated part of the certificate, learning particular tools and basic programming, but with a focus on those approaches that might be of direct use to the type of research that they are doing. This can be database programming, three dimensional Virtual Reality reconstruction of ancient buildings, Geographic Information Systems to analyze spatial data, text analysis, gaming, statistical analysis, or big data. Rarely do students specialize in more than one or two of these large fields of interest. Students who enroll usually already have a strong interest in computer based research and they typically choose to do the certificate because they want to learn more in order to facilitate their own research, but also to give themselves an edge when applying for jobs. There don't seem to be major administrative hurdles to initiate and teach the program. It remains to be seen how well-accepted PhD theses will be that have a non-traditional structure or are strongly collaborative. In general advisors, even those who are DH proponents, will advise their students to err on the side of the traditional. The same is true for Assistant Professors who have a great interest in DH, but still feel they should produce a book with a respected publisher to safeguard tenure. Therefore for the coming decade or so, at least until DH work is more widely accepted by Academia, most innovative work is done by tenured faculty who can afford to take risks.

DF: The UCLA administration supports inter- or trans-disciplinarity, especially inquiries which have the potential to be transformative academically and in the world at large (this is specifically the aim of our new Urban Humanities Initiative). However, the barriers to working across fields, departments, and divisions within a rule-heavy, tradition-bound state institution remain significant. In addition to the administrative challenges presented (In what department does the program reside? Who pays for what? How can other divisions get "credit" for something named "Humanities"?), are the practical needs for digital access, storage, archiving, and space. The UCLA administration involves DH faculty and staff in committees dealing with digital infrastructural needs, but actual realization remains painfully slow. On the bright side, the UCLA library is a major partner in DH, providing expertise as well as space.

Opening the depths, not sliding on surfaces

N. Katherine Hayles

N. Katherine Hayles is a pioneer in the field of digital media and digital literature studies and the author various milestone studies. With books such as *How We Became Posthuman: Virtual Bodies in Cybernetics, Literature, and Informatics* (1999) and *My Mother Was a Computer: Digital Subjects and Literary Texts* (2005) she explores the liberal humanist concept of the "natural self" in the age of intelligent machines; with books such as *Writing Machines* (2002) and *Electronic Literature: New Horizons for the Literary* (2008) she draws attention to various forms of digital literature and offerey examples of its close reading; with her book *How We Think. Digital Media and Contemporary Technogenesis* (2012) and the co-edited collection *Comparative Textual Media. Transforming the Humanities in the Postprint Era* (2013) she discusses the issues of contemporary technogenesis and the future of Digital Humanities. N. Katherine Hayles is the James B. Duke Professor of Literature at Duke University.

N. Katherine Hayles discusses the advantages of social and algorithmic reading and reaffirms the value of deep reading; she doubts media literacy requires media abstinence; she underlines the importance of the Humanities for 'understanding and intervening' in society but questions the idolized 'rhetoric of "resistance"' and she weights the real problems facing the Digital Humanities against unfounded fears.

Roberto Simanowski: You have been writing extensively and from early on about digital or electronic literature combining a theoretical discussion with case studies. In addition you are the co-editor of *Electronic Literature Collection 1* published in 2006. How would you sum up the history of digital or electronic literature?

N. Katherine Hayles: Since I first became engaged with electronic literature in the early 1990's, the predominant tendency I have seen is its continuing diversity. As digital platforms and softwares have diversified and proliferated into cell phones, tablets, iPods, etc., so have the forms and content of digital literatures. The hybrid productions of Jason Nelson combining literary and game forms, the short fictions of M. A. Coverley written for the Excel format, the combination of real-world and fictional content by Shelley Jackson in *Skin* and by Scott Rettberg and Nick Montfort in *Implementation*, and many other experimental ventures indicate how robust and exciting digital literature has become, especially compared to its relative modest beginnings as Storyspace hypertexts. Social networks have provided other opportunities for experimentation, for example Twitter fictions that stretch over many tweets, functioning like electronic versions of the old BurmaShave signs along country roads.

RS: Since multi-linear writing within *Storyspace* in the early 1990s, the Internet and mobile media have further changed the way we read. Apps such as *readmill*, for example, allow immediate dialogue about a text amongst its readers; electronic books facilitate the analysis of how a reader reacts to a text: i.e. where she stops, what passages she skips, what notes she makes. How will social reading change the way we perceive literature in

electronic media? How will the algorithmic reading of such reading affect the writing of literature?

NKH: Social reading expands and facilitates reading practices
that have been going on for some time, in classrooms, book
clubs, blogs and elsewhere. I think it is an exciting development, as one can now share one's impressions of a text in close
to real time with colleagues across the world. Algorithmic reading is also exciting, since it allows us to ask questions impossible before, especially queries concerning large corpora of texts.
Nevertheless, we should not interpret algorithmic reading as
the death of interpretation. How one designs the software, and
even more, how one interprets and understands the patterns
that are revealed, remain very much interpretive activities.
Moreover, many algorithmic readings are carried out in tandem with hermeneutic interpretation in the traditional sense. An
example is the close reading that Allen Riddell and I give of Mark
Danielewski's *Only Revolutions* in my book *How We Think*.

RS: In his 2008 article 'Is Google making us stupid?' and later
in his 2011 book *The Shallows: What the Internet is Doing to
Our Brains*, Nicholas Carr discusses the consequences of online
media for literacy. From Carr's perspective, multitasking and
power browsing online make people unlearn deep reading with
the effects being carried offline, with the result that they also
unlearn deep thinking. The shift from deep attention to hyper
attention has been announced and bemoaned by many intellectuals. The French philosopher Bernard Stiegler even speaks of a
threat to social and cultural development caused by the destruction of young people's ability to develop deep and critical attention to the world around them. You take issue with Carr's conclusions in your book *How We Think*. On the other hand Stiegler, in
his 2010 book *Taking Care of Youth and the Generations*, refers
to your report that students are no longer able to engage in deep
reading. What role is the cultural technique of reading going
to play if power browsing, multitasking, and permanent online
connectivity make the long-established contemplative reading

session increasingly obsolete? How will and how should literature and literary studies react to this process?

NKH: As Carr acknowledges, the web brings powerful advantages, including to scholarship. I am old enough to remember
what it was like to do research when one had to rely on type-
writers and card catalogues; not for a minute would I want to
return to those methods! Even Stiegler, who in *Taking Care of
Youth and the Generations* has mostly a denunciatory tone, in his
newer *A New Critique of Political Economy* sees hyper attention
as a Derridean pharmakon, poison and cure together. Clearly
the problem here is how to maximize the web's potential for serious intellectual work and minimize its potential for superficial-
ity and distraction. Stiegler's position, as stated in a lecture he
gave at the SLSA conference in 2011, is that we should focus on
"adoption, not adaptation"—in other words, we should wherever
possible limit access to the "entertainment complex," including
the web, to prevent the kind of technogenetic changes I describe
in *How We Think*, especially for young people and children where
neural plasticity is the greatest.

RS: Media abstinence as part of media literacy in an Adornian
like way? Stiegler's proposal seems unlikely given the ubiquity
of digital media and entertainment. At least it appeals to parents
and teachers to oversee the younger generations's media use.

NKH: While Stiegler's approach of "adoption—no!" may be feasible for very young pre-schoolers, it becomes ineffective, and
probably impossible, for children older than five as they become
exposed to school, classmates, and other influences outside of
the home. Moreover, it assumes that media immersion is entirely
negative, and many researchers (Steven Johnson, James Paul
Gee) make persuasive cases for some good effects, from acquir-
ing hand-eye coordination to gaining a more sophisticated sense
of strategy and planning. If we now turn to deep attention, we
can see that from the beginning, the tradition of deep attention
required the support and nurturing of institutions—intellectual
discourse and an educated elite in classical Greece, monasteries
in the Middle Ages, debate and writing in the Renaissance, etc.

So it is in the contemporary period as well. The role of educators at every level, from kindergarten through graduate school, should be to make connections between contemporary practices, for example browsing and surfing the web, and the disciplined acquisition of knowledge. The difference is having an intellectual context for questions and seeking for all the rich resources that can contribute to understanding those questions more deeply, seeing their implications more fully, and moving tentatively toward answers adequate to these complexities. Instead of "adoption, not adaption," my slogan would be "opening the depths, not sliding on surfaces."

RS: In your book *How We Think* you discuss the future of the Humanities with respect to digital media. Your conclusion is that Traditional Humanities 'are at risk of becoming marginal to the main business of the contemporary academy and society.' Digital Humanities, on the other hand, you add 'are at risk of becoming a trade practice held captive by the interest of corporate capitalism.' This prospect about the future of Humanities sounds like a choice between Charybdis and Scylla. How can the Humanities survive the digital turn without dying?

NKH: The Humanities, as I understand them, are above all about understanding and intervening in the cultural, social, technological and intellectual contexts throughout history that have shaped what people want, what they consider important, and what moves them to action. These questions are as vitally necessary now as they have ever been. For the past few decades, as we know, the Humanities have been immersed in the critique of dominant institutions. While this has lead to important intellectual developments such as deconstruction, postmodernism, and posthumanism, it has also had deleterious effects as well, tending to isolate the Humanities from the wider culture and tending toward a rhetoric of "resistance" so widely accepted that the mere idea of "resistance" is idolized without thinking seriously about consequences and the assumptions undergirding it, including the ways in which humanists are complicit in the very practices they criticize.

One of the sites where these forces are currently in play is in the Digital Humanities. There are plenty of problems facing the Digital Humanities: technical (e.g., distinguishing patterns from chimeras in data analysis); cultural (e.g., defining significant problems rather than ones tailored to chasing grants); economic (being coopted by corporate funding to the extent that pedagogical and educational priorities are undercut); and ethical (e.g., power relations between professors and graduate students). However, when people talk about the "Dark Side of the Digital Humanities" (the subject of an MLA panel 2013), these kinds of problems are often not what they mean. Rather, what they more likely have in mind are the disparity in funding between the Traditional and Digital Humanities; the fear that data analysis may displace traditional criticism; and (as I heard Stanley Fish assert on a panel we shared) analysis without interpretation, as if data and text mining were simply machine functions without human understanding. In my view, these fears either reflect a misunderstanding of algorithmic methods (in Stanley Fish's case) or envy about the relatively abundant funding streams that the Digital Humanities enjoy, neither of which is a well-founded critique.

RS: The opposition of algorithmic analysis and interpretation may be shortsighted as is the competition between database and narrative for the 'exclusive right to make meaning out of the world' that Lev Manovich announced more than a decade ago. As you point out in your book, database and narrative are natural symbionts rather than natural enemies considering narratives 'the necessary others to database's ontology.' However, if Stephen Ramsay calls for "algorithmic criticism" as a way to supplement and balance algorithmic processing by hermeneutic activity, he also responds to Franco Moretti's provocative request to replace interpretation by data mining, i.e. close by distant reading. Also, there is a call for „engaged humanities" making a contribution to the quality of human life through productive knowledge (as for example in Cathy N. Davidson's and David Theo Goldberg's 2004 essay *Engaging the Humanities*).

This seems to counter the concept of humanities as a necessary correction of the positivistic paradigm of the natural and engineering sciences in society with the principle of ambiguity (as advocated for example by German philosopher Odo Marquard in his 1986 essay *On the inevitability of the humanities*). In Marquard's perspective the function of Humanities in society is a rhetoric of resistance not (only or first of all) towards institutions but (also and moreover) to signification and Truth. In this light, interpretation after data mining is mandatory not to verify meaning but rather to destabilize it. How valid, do you think, is this concept of the humanities still with respect to the ongoing quantitative turn in the Humanties?

NKH: I think the opposition between interpretation and data mining is somewhat misguided. Data mining is not devoid of interpretive decisions; how one designs the software has everything to do with underlying assumptions and presuppositions, which are forms of interpretive activity. Moreover, one should also not assume that data mining and text mining bear a simple relation to signification and truth. Often results are ambiguous, and judgment is needed to distinguish genuine patterns from chimera and other artifacts of the way the analysis was carried out. As for meaning, isn't it destabilized every time someone offers a new reading of a canonized text, or insists on the importance of a non-canonical one? I don't see meaning as an accomplishment over and done once and for all, but rather a continuing search that contains moments of meta-stability as well as moments of destabilizations. This kind of ferment is what keeps the humanities relevant and constantly renewing themselves. Would it even be possible constantly to destabilize, without ever positing or hoping for or arguing for some kind of stabilization? Even if one thinks destabilizations should be constant, isn't this a kind of stabilization in itself? In my view, we should think carefully about the kinds of problems mentioned above and their implications for pedagogy, for example, the necessity for a deeper understanding of statistical methods and their relation to the results of data and text mining. As the Humanities move into "Big Data," they might usefully engage with scientific disciplines that have been dealing with these problems for some time.

RS: So you rather see a *bright* side of the Digital Humanities?

NKH: As mentioned above, I find the prospects for asking new kinds of questions using data and text mining techniques exciting, and I am fascinated by what Jeffrey Schnapp and Todd Presner have called *Digital Humanities 2.0,* in which they call for a shift from analytical methods to an experiential focus. I can see their point, but in my view, the two approaches (analytical vs. experiential) are complementary to one another rather than antagonistic. I find the antagonism between the Traditional and Digital Humanities, understandable as it may be, also misplaced. In a collection of essays that I co-edited with Jessica Pressman, entitled *Comparative Textual Media: Transforming the Humanities in the Postprint Era* (2013), we suggest that a better way forward is to embrace a media framework as the basis for teaching and research rather than now-obsolete and cumbersome categories such as centuries, genres, and national languages. Such a transformation, focusing on the specificities of media and practice-based research combining hands-on experience with theoretical work, would re-energize traditional research as well as providing a basis on which scholars specializing in print, manuscript and orality could engage fruitfully with those specializing in digital methods.

From writing space to designing mirrors

Jay David Bolter

Jay David Bolter is well known as the author and co-author of important books on the subject of digital technology, culture and aesthetics: *Turing's Man: Western Culture in the Computer Age* (1984); *Writing Space: The Computer, Hypertext, and the History of Writing* (1991); *Remediation: Understanding New Media* (1999, with Richard Grusin); *Windows and Mirrors* (2003, with Diane Gromala). In addition to writing about new media, Bolter collaborates in the construction of new digital media forms and created, for example, together with Michael Joyce *Storyspace*, a pre WWW hypertext authoring system. Bolter is the Wesley Chair of New Media at the Georgia Institute of Technology and a co-Director of the Augmented Environments Lab. He works closely with Prof. Blair MacIntyre, Prof. Maria Engberg, and other AEL researchers on the design of augmented and mixed reality experiences for cultural heritage, informal education, and expression and entertainment.

Jay David Bolter talks about the (missing) embrace of digital media by the literary and academic community, about hypertext as a (failing) promise of a new kind of reflective praxis, about transparent (immediate) and reflected (hypermediate) technology. He compares the aesthetics of information with the aesthetics of spectacle in social media and notes the collapse of hierarchy and centrality in culture in the context of digital media.

Prelude

Roberto Simanowski: What is your favored neologism of digital media culture and why?

Jay David Bolter: I am not sure that I have a favorite neither in a positive or negative sense. Such neologisms as hacktivism, slacktivism and crowdsourcing are all in current circulation; they all represent contemporary views of our media culture. Insofar that is the case, we have to accept them (not necessarily of course to use them ourselves). Rather then selecting favorites, a more appropriate task would be to understand the underlying reasons why culture seems to need to create new vocabulary. One such term that I would nominate for study is "collective intelligence." It captures a major preoccupation today, the notion that as a networked digital culture we can achieve a level of knowledge production that is not possible for an individual and indeed is of a different order from the kind of knowledge that was produced in earlier media era.

RS: If you could go back in history of new media and digital culture in order to prevent something from happening or somebody from doing something, what or who would it be?

JDB: I am really not keen to rewrite the history of digital culture. I don't trust my own hindsight much more than I do my ability to anticipate future developments. When I think of the history of my own engagement with digital culture, however, it is clear that I often failed to grasp the importance of two key developments in digital media. The first was the advent of networked hypertext and the WWW, whose significance I didn't appreciate until it was well underway in the 1990s. The second was the advent of social media, where I was again late to the party. Both Web 1.0 and Web 2.0 were phenomena that I did not anticipate. My only consolation here is that many others failed to appreciate the significance of the digital even longer than I. For example, the literary community failed utterly to engage with digital media in the 1990s (despite the increasingly importance of the WWW). Indeed even today the literary community remains reluctant to explore the possibilities that digital media offer.

RS: This failure was indeed surprising given the fact that with its hypertextual and multimedial techniques digital media offered very interesting forms of experimental writing. But the new literary genre that was announced quite early in academic journals (I remember Richard Ziegfeld's essay *Interactive Fiction* in New Literary History in 1989) never really took off. You were one of the earliest academics to write about new technologies of reading and writing. In your 1991 book *Writing Space* you discuss hypertext as "both a visual and a verbal representation", not writing of a place, "but rather a writing *with* places" and you reveal the link between hypertext and the literary movement of concrete poetry, a kind of *poetry in space* („Poesie der Fläche") as its German proponent Franz Mon once called it. I remember how in the late 1990s at conferences people were convinced of a bright future of hyperfictions as a literary genre once it grew in popularity. However, soon academics – such as Marie-Laure Ryan in her 2001 book *Narrative as Virtual Reality. Immersion and Interactivity in Literature and Electronic Media* – addressed the internal aesthetic problem of multi-linear writing and recommended to "tame" hyperfiction by offering a more simple structure with more self-contained lexias, i.e. narrative episodes. The subversion of the cohesive structure of the text and the lack of authorial control over the readers' navigation was obviously too different from the thoroughly choreographed non-linear narration and unreliable narrators that the postmodern poetics at that time proposed. I remember how we both, over a drink at the Electronic Poetry Festival in Paris 2007, expected much more openness for experiments with digital technology from artists than from the literary community. Was it wrong to suppose the literary community to be more embracing towards digital media?

JDB: I think that even in the 1980s and 1990s the literary community was predisposed to be more aesthetically conservative than the art community. Look at the rather radical broadening of the definition of art in the decades since the 1960s: performance art, installation art, media art. The experiments of the historical avant-garde of the 1910s and 1920s and the neo-avant-garde in the 1950s and 1960s had eventually affected the community as a whole. In the case of literature, postmodern writers were seldom as radical in their aesthetic revolt from modernism as were the visual artists. There were of course the concrete poets, language poets, Oulipo, and so on. But such groups were never more than small avant-gardes. Postmodern writers such as Thomas Pynchon were after all quite traditional in comparison with performance artists such as Carolee Schneemann. Thus, even in the 1990s "serious" writers could not imagine rethinking the (print-based) assumptions that lay behind their work. Those assumptions included the fixity of the text and authorial control over the text, both of which hypertext challenged.

RS: In *Writing Space* you discuss the relationship between the new form of nonlinear writing and the theory of interpretation promoted by Wolfgang Iser and Stanley Fish in the 1960s and also point out a philosophical correlation: namely that between hypertext and postmodern theory, which your colleague George P. Landow from Brown University at the same time proclaimed in the subtitle of his book on hypertext as *Convergence of Contemporary Critical Theory and Technology*. A quarter of a century later postmodern theory has lost its appeal, its relativisms and transcendental homelessness are hard to endure, people yearn for reliable values and even Grand Narratives again. However, the 'postmodern technology' has remained and has fundamental effects on our individual and social life. How do you see the situation today with respect of your observations and expectations of 25 years ago?

JDB: When I look back at *Writing Space* and my work from that period I think I would have to characterize my position as innocent opportunistic. I was attempting to read the new possibilities of the digital technology into the framework of contemporary literary and critical analysis. I was doing this in an effort to talk to an academic community for whom that kind of analysis was the common currency. So it was natural enough to look at these new forms of non-linear writing that seemed to be promoted by digital hypertext in terms of reader response theory by Wolfgang Iser and Stanley Fish, in terms of even deconstruction or other forms of post-structuralist interpretation. Like George Landow in his book on hypertext I too felt that this was a legitimate way of understanding what hypertext was doing, because I myself was immersed in that same critical theoretical framework.

But that strategy didn't work very well at the time because the community was not really ready to accept the notion that digital technology could be a new medium of literary expression and academic analysis, that it could in some sense take a position aside the printed book. And therefore they saw the attempt to appropriate the reader response theory, deconstruction and so on a kind of misguided or even reductive understanding of what post-structuralist theory was trying to do. Ultimately they were right in a certain sense, because post-structuralism too was conditioned by the contemporary, still print-based media culture. The notions of the indeterminacy of the text, the death of the author, intertextuality and so on— all these notions depended for their ironic effect on the fact that text were fixed in print and did have identifiable authors and the authority of the publication system. In any case, and for whatever reason, the community refused to listen. Neither the academic community of literary scholars nor the community of writers found digital technology interesting. And neither of them saw that hypertext in particular could be a new communicative and expressive form they needed to engage with. So given that they weren't prepared to engage with the technology it was futile to try to provide a critical, theoretical basis for that engagement. The think that strikes me is that the literary community has still today refused to engage with the digital.

The whole line of argument that I was making in that period about hypertext has been superseded in a variety of ways by multiple forms of media that digital technology has developed into, by new modes of interaction and by the advent of a huge community of participants in media culture that didn't exist in the early 1990s. So with all those changes, looking back it doesn't seem as if there is much left of the notion that hypertext could be a new form of writing. To put it another way: The kind of literary hypertext culture we were envisioning never happened. On the other hand the popularization of hypertext in the form of the WWW and all the technologies that developed out of the WWW have been proven to be a tremendous success and have really changed our media culture in significant ways. That's a triumph of hypertext, but it is a triumph of hypertext not limited to or even addressed by the academic community.

Media Literacy

RS: An unexpected triumph and maybe an unwelcomed one. This at least is the question if one considers the contemporary concerns about hyper-reading which popular writers – such as Nicholas Carr in his 2011 book *The Shallows – What the Internet is Doing to Our Brains* – but also academics – for example Katherine N. Hayles in her 2007 article in *Profession* "Hyper and Deep Attention: The Generational Divide in Cognitive Modes" – address as a potential threat to deep reading. Doesn't the hypertextual technique – of multiple offers to leave the text at hand for another one – practice a form of nervous, inpatient reading unable to engage in one particular issue? Doesn't hyper-reading – if it discourages a sustained engagement with the text – ultimately also hinder deep thinking? This grim picture is quite the opposite of what was expected from hypertext technology in the 1990s when the structure of the variable cross-linkages not only was celebrated as liberation from the 'tyranny of the author' but also welcomed as destabilization of the signifier and as emphasis on the ambivalence and relativity of propositions. Hypertext was seen as an ally in the efforts to promote and practice reflection. Today hypertext technology and its cultural equivalent hyper-reading are rather seen – for instance by the French philosopher Bernard Stiegler – as collaborators of the culture industry. Did this promising technology betray us? Is Hypertext a Trojan Horse appearing as a tool of critical thinking while actually undermining it?

JDB: My view of this issue is more fatalistic or more accepting of the inevitability of certain kinds of cultural change. First of all, yes, the predictions hat we were making for hypertext as a new kind of reflective praxis didn't come true. Literary hypertext never became a generalized cultural form of expression. What we did get was the WWW, where linking was unidirectional and for many of the first generation hypertext writers a simplification and reduction that in fact didn't foster reflective practice. But it was tremendously successful incorporating visual and audio forms into writing as never before creating a much larger set of communities of writers and that was true even in the 1990s when writing on the web meant designing your own website and became exponentially more the case in the 2000s with the advent of social media.

So that is the fact of contemporary media culture. In response to this fact of extraordinary broadening of participation but also the changing of writing forms that constitute that participation we have a set of academics and popular writers who are deeply critical to what happened like Nicholas Carr's popularization of this point of view that writing and reading are changing our brains to make it less reflective. The academic community has agreed in its own way with this judgment, at least the older, more traditional academics, for example Stanley Fish, Jonathan Culler and many others have written negatively about the new form of reading that seems to be practiced in the digital realm nowadays.

I would say that the criticism is both right and wrong. Right in the sense that it certainly does seem to be the case that the kind of writing and reading that was highly valued in the age of print

were different and there was a kind of valorization of reflective or deep or close reading. That is clearly not being practiced
by the huge community of readers and writers on social media
today. But does this mean that close or reflective reading has
disappeared? No, there is still a community that practices that
form of writing and reading. It is still welcomed, indeed required
as a kind of ticket of entry into the literary academic community. But what happened is that this form of reflective reading
and writing no longer has the status and claim to centrality that
it had in the 20th century. So instead of a single community of
readers and writers we have an interlocking set of communities
of readers and writers, some much larger than others none of
which can claim a kind of centrality or importance that eclipses
the other. So what the critics really are complaining about is the
loss of centrality of certain ways of reading and writing.

RS: Your account of the situation may be fatalistic, as you said,
but doesn't strike me as very pessimistic. Rather you address the
claim of centrality and invite us to be open to several forms of
practices of reading and writing. However, if one formerly dominant mode becomes decentralized it is not certain that afterwards importance is equally distributed among more candidates
or cultural techniques. More often in history – of social movements as well as media development – we see a recentralization
of power and importance. Of course, for the issue at hand, even
this must not be bad. In fact, one could argue that a non-linear
reading which is more attuned to multi-tasking and serendipity
allows easier for productive (mis)understandings and intuitive
intelligence.

However, I have the feeling you are more concerned about the
loss of reflection in the culture of the 21st century than you are
willing to admit. This is at least my impression when looking at
your 2003 book *Windows and Mirrors: Interaction Design, Digital
Art, and the Myth of Transparency*, which you co-author with
your colleague at in the School of Literature, Communication,
and Culture at Georgia Tech University Diane Gromala. In this
book you describe the positions of the two professions of graphic

designers and HCI professionals with the metaphors window and mirror: the transparent versus the reflected technology. This extends the distinction between immediacy and hypermediacy from *Remediation*. *Understanding New Media* (1999), the book you co-wrote with Richard Grusin. Like Grusin, who since then has become increasingly critical towards the significance of digital technology to our culture (he speaks of a "dark side" of the Digital Humanities) you are equally skeptical of the possible pitfalls of digital media in *Windows and Mirrors* requesting an approach to design that turns digital media into an object of reflection rather than making them transparent. To play the ignorant: Why should we be afraid of the disappearance of the computer through transparent interfaces? Don't we also want letters to be invisible so we can reflect on what the text says rather than on how it looks like?

JDB: First let me say that I don't think there is any danger of the disappearance of the computer. The notion of the transparent interface and the disappearing computer is one that we can see most prevalent in interface design in the 1990s and indeed still today. But in fact what is happening belies the notion that our digital technologies are burying themselves into the world. The internet of things, ubiquitous computing, these are technological and cultural manifestations that are growing in importance. But the computer as a platform for media is in fact not disappearing at all. If we look around we see the last thing that people want to do is their technology to disappear. They want it to be seen. People buy the iPhone because it's a beautiful object which then can also be a status symbol that they can proudly present to others. We see these media devices everywhere and not at all burying themselves.

Secondly there has always been a dichotomy between visibility or invisibility, or what Richard and I called between hypermediacy and immediacy in the history of media culture. Even in the age of print after all we saw both manifestations. Indeed when the typography makes the medium as transparent as possible at the same time we have the tradition of the artist book, advertising, graphic design in which the way that a text looks *is* what the text says.

RS: Combining your first and second notion I would say: Yes, people also used (and some maybe still do) books as a status symbol furnishing their home with them but still preferring the book itself to be transparent so they have direct access to the world behind the interface. Art books are the exception in the world of books. Why should this be different in the realm of digital media?

JDB: Digital transmission and presentation is indeed used for all sorts of communication. Often the user does simply want to get the gist of the text or view an image. But a number of factors contribute to a stronger emphasis, at least at present, on hypermediacy in the digital realm. One of the most important (and most remarked) factors, is the tendency to process multiple channels at the same time. A typical user may be moving back and forth among open windows or multiple apps on her phone. While she is reading or interacting with one window or app, she may focus on the context displayed. But each time she moves from one to another, she becomes aware again of the multiplicity that her media environment offers her. The multitasking is of course exactly what traditionalists such as Nicholas Carr criticize about our use of computers, claiming that it destroys our ability to concentrate. Whether that is true or not, the critics are right in suggesting that this mode of consumption diverges from the traditional practice of reading in the age of print. In the age of print one did tend to read only one book, magazine, or newspaper at a time.

Art and Aesthetics

RS: *Windows and Mirrors* considers digital art as the corrective to the assumption that the computer should disappear. Hence, art seems to be an inevitable part of any media literacy precisely because, by its very nature, art draws attention to the language system it employs. Digital art thus makes us aware of how digital technology works on a semiotic as well as cultural level. Would you then, if you were a minister of education, make art to the center of any courses on media literacy?

JDB: Given the position that I take in my new book concerning the current state of media culture, it would be hypocritical of me as a minister of education to try to dictate anything about art and media literacy. I don't think there can be a coherent policy because such a policy would be predicated on an ultimate goal or standard to which our community as a whole could subscribe. There is no universal agreement on a standard. In the case of art, the term has become so vague as to be almost meaningless: it is now applied to most any activity of making. The kind of critical art that I discussed in *Windows and Mirrors* has significance only for a particular community.

RS: "The internet once belonged exclusively to the Structuralists", you write in *Windows and Mirrors*, describing this community as composed mostly of graduate students and professors in computer science with a culture "highly developed in mathematics but not in art". Many people may of course not see the lack of art as deficit. However, as somebody who, after the tenth grade, decided to let his mathematical skills die and rather pursued his interest in literature and art I am prone to agree with your perspective. Nevertheless, or rather for that reason, I want to play the devil's advocate by considering the opposition of structuralists and designers as one between information and spectacle. Let me explain what I mean by this and mention some sources that make me think this way.

My reference are three texts from the 1990 about the "breakout of the visual" in the digital world, as you - this is my first text - write in your 1996 essay "Ekphrasis, Virtual Reality, and the Future of Writing." In multimedia, you observe, the relationship between word and image is becoming as unstable as it is in the popular press, where images are no longer subordinate to the word and "we are no longer certain that words deserve the cultural authority they have been given". Three years later, Robert Coover, also a very early advocate of hypertext and hyperfiction, declared the passing of its golden age. The constant threat of hypermedia, Coover wrote, is "to suck the substance out of a work of lettered art, reduce it to surface spectacle." One element of this aesthetics of the spectacle is the "post-alphabetic text", a term which Matthew Kirschenbaum 1999 in a paper entitled *The Other End of Print: David Carson, Graphic Design, and the Aesthetics of Media* used to describe David Carson's design style that "refashions information as an aesthetic event." Carson represents the shift from the reader to the sensualist even before the takeoff of digital media in design and typography between the mid-1980s and the mid-1990s. His counterpart in the digital world may be Macromedia's Flash, the opposition to any iconoclastic position and the enemy of all hardcore structuralists.

The arrival of Flash may – despite Lev Manovich's description of the *Generation Flash* as neo-minimalists – be seen as the return of the baroque logic of mannerism, spectacle and sensory experiences also into the digital world, which had been announced by some scholars in the early 2000s, i.e. Andrew Darley (*Visual Digital Culture: Surface Play and Spectacle in New Media Genres*, 2000) or Angela Ndalianis (*Neo-Baroque Aesthetics and Contemporary Entertainment*, 2004). As *Windows and Mirrors* notes, in June 2002 even Nielsen declared his collaboration with Macromedia Flash and Norman muses about emotional design. Is this the overcoming of an unproductive opposition or rather the surrendering of text-purists to the power of the visual? You note in *Windows and Mirrors* that the goal is "to establish an appropriate rhythm between being transparent and reflective" and write: "No matter how flashy, every digital design must convey a message to its viewer and user." And to be sure, your book advertises the reflective rather than the sensory. How do you see the situation today? Did more Flash bring more mirrors?

JDB: Like all analytic dichotomies (since Hegel?), my dichotomy between structuralists and designers can at best serve to indicate the ends of more nuanced spectrum. What we see today in our media economy, and even on the Web and other Internet-media services is a range of relationships between information and spectacle. As we noted above, web-based practices have not rendered obsolete the desire for the transparency of information. If the spectrum of possible practices extends from pure information (whatever that might be) at one end to pure surface spectacle (again if that is possible) on the other, then we see an enormous range in the middle. Highly designed web sites still exist, but the templates of social networking sites such as Facebook constitute a messy compromise between information and spectacle. Even Nielsen was not entirely wrong when he predicted the return of textual interfaces. After all, text messages and Twitter are among the most popular digital practices today, and they consist of nothing but alphabetic symbols and links. The baroque impulse toward spectacle and sensory experience today seems to be in a state of permanent but productive tension with the impulse for structured representation and communication.

RS: Messy compromise between information and spectacle is a great description for what is going on on Facebook. I would even go further and consider most of the updates – even if textual – in the light of spectacle rather than information or "phatic communication" as the linguistic term reads communication for communication's sake. The deeper meaning of the shallow sharing, however, may be the desire to hand over the burden of experience to others to whom our experience naturally is no trouble at all but an information which can easily be 'processed' via likes, shares and one word comments. The psychological explanation for this outsourcing of experience is, I would argue, that we can't endure the present time because we can no longer anchor it within a timeline that connects our past and our future in a meaningful way – which in a way resembles the baroque experience of being out of center brought by the Copernican system. But this perspective is my own idiosyncratic approach which needs to be justified at length elsewhere. For our conversation at hand I want to move to your next book, *The Digital Plenitude*, planned for 2016 with MIT Press. This book discusses the status of art and culture in an era of digital media. What will be the main thesis of your book?

JDB: The goal of my book is to examine two developments in the second half of the 20ᵗʰ century that I think have helped to define our media culture in the 21ˢᵗ century. One of them is the advent of digital media, websites, video games, social media, mobile media and all the remediation of so called traditional media like film and print that now appear in digital form. Digital media are everywhere and they provoke our constant interest and attention. The other development is the end of our collective belief in Culture with a capital c. The collapse of the agreed on hierarchy in the visual arts, music, literature and scholarship and even politics. This collapse is a sort of open secret in the sense that we all know implicitly that it is happening. But many of us are unwilling to acknowledge the consequences of it. Many of us write about media culture today in a way that seems to be determined to ignore that history, taking extreme positions seeing digital media either as utopia or dystopia and utopias and dystopias are always measured in terms of implicit cultural standards. So when we examine the period that with digital culture has arisen we see that this change in our attitude towards culture interacts in very interesting ways with digital media. I think we can see the breakdown of hierarchy and centrality in culture is happening throughout the 20ᵗʰ century, accelerating after the Second World War. At the same time that the computer is being invented but prior to the advent of digital media, in the 1950 and 1960s, we see strong forces to promote what was called popular culture. Not only the rise of the economic status of rock music, popular films, comic books, television shows but also an increasing sense that these media and cultural forms are legitimately important in ways that we used to accord only to high literary and high artistic forms.

These two important streams or phenomena – the rise of pop culture and the development of digital media – interact in all sorts of interesting ways today so that digital media become a matrix for this cultural condition that we have today in which instead of a center we have a plentitude of cultural communities each with their own sets of standards and practices, interlocking, overlapping, conflicting, competing in various ways. What

I want to do in this book is to explore some of the ramifications what it means to live in the age of such plentitude in which we can no longer say this is the right form of reading, this is the most important form of music, this is the function of art. All these kinds of assertions have moved from a discussion of our culture as a whole to a discussion within the communities.

RS: A very postmodern perspective, I think, that applies the insights of postmodern philosophy that there is not the one right way to see or do things to aesthetic taste and cultural techniques.

JDB: I think we can now see looking back that those were right who saw postmodernism as the continuation of modernism in other terms. The concerns that postmodernism had, even when postmodernists pretended to be incorporating popular culture into their analysis, it was still the case that postmodernism was really exploring the final gasp of elite modernist culture. And right now we see that that expiration has come to its conclusion, that we really are at the end of modernism. And this is what that end looks like, not the triumph of a new ism but a multiplicity – or cacophony from a modernist perspective – of different forms and aesthetics and assumptions about the function of art and cultural expressions that are not reconciled or reconcilable.

RS: I like your notion of the contamination of postmodernism with modernism. Even though the postmodern attitude – as Frederic Jameson holds in his 1988 essay *Postmodernism and Consumer Society* – replaced parody (which always implies to know it better) with irony and pastiche (as the helpless approval of "anything goes"), Lyotard's aesthetics of the sublime certainly still contains the idea of emancipation – and if only by stopping the consumption of meaning. Your answer makes me wonder whether if not hypertext has been the practical equivalent to postmodern theory, digital media at least turns out to be the fulfillment of the postmodern impulse? But let me come back to your notion of a plentitude of cultural communities each with their own sets of standards and practices. You say these communities overlap, conflict, and compete in various ways. There are academics who are concerned that digital media is shifting society more to the situation of closed communities that – as "echo chamber" and "daily we" – don't overlap and conflict with each other anymore but rather simply end the discussion about the right set of cultural values and practice that exist in modernism and even in postmodernism. Is the era of digital plenitude an era where "anything goes" consequently means "mind your own business"?

JDB: Let me say that this collapse of the center doesn't look the same to all communities. In fact for many communities the center is still there it happens to be co-extensive with the center of their own community. And if they look out at that confused media world they see chaos; they see the breakdown of culture as they understand it. That's exactly what people like Nicholas Carr on the popular level or some conservative academics on the scholarly level are concerned about when they complain about the loss of reflective reading or the ability to think and make arguments. So I don't believe that there is a future policy that can be pursued to direct or guide the development of this interplay of media and culture that we see today. I think we just have to understand that within our own communities we can still act coherently with assumption about what kind of standards we have to pursue. But we have to understand that outside our community this discourse isn't necessarily going to make much sense.

RS: I conclude that your book about digital plentitude is not a book about the abundance of data – or "big data" as the buzzword nowadays reads. I hence assume you see your work closer to "Digital Media Studies" than to "Digital Humanities"; provided you see a difference between both concepts.

JDB: For me the two terms denote different, though overlapping, fields and practices. DMS is connected with the longer tradition of media studies, as it was practiced by scholars such as Innis and McLuhan. That generation of writers and scholars educated the next generation, who explore the relationships among various technologies and forms in our complex media economy today, including but not limited to digital media. Media archeology is a branch of media studies. DH is a term that I associate with a longstanding project of employing the computer to facilitate humanistic research: literary studies, text traditions, lexicography, other kinds of archival work that had been done previously by hand. I realize that now DH has become a broad term for a whole range of different kinds of theoretical and practical engagements by humanists with digital media and digital culture activities.

Digital knowledge, obsessive computing, short-termism and need for a negentropic Web

Bernard Stiegler

Bernard Stiegler is one of the most inspiring and important continental thinkers of today, an heir to Nietzsche, Husserl, Heidegger, Foucault and Derrida, but also to Simondon and Adorno. He is best known for his three volume *Technics and Time* on technology and memory (in English 1998, 2009, 2010) but also for his other philosophical and political interventions in contemporary culture such as *States of Shock: Stupidity and Knowledge in the 21st Century* (Engl.2015), *What Makes Life Worth Living: On Pharmacology* (Engl. 2013), *For a New Critique of Political Economy* (Engl. 2010). With his new series *Automatic Society* (the English edition of part 1 *The Future of Work* will be released in the Summer of 2016) Stiegler systematically explores the social implications of digital technologies. Stiegler is the Director of the Department of Cultural Development at the Centre Georges-Pompidou and the founder of Ars Industrialis, a political and cultural group advocating an "industrial economy of spirit" against the short-termism of capitalist consumer culture. In 2010 he started his own philosophy school in the small French town of Épineuil-le-Fleuriel open for lycée students in the region and doctoral students from all over France.

Bernard speaks about digital tertiary retention and the need for an epistemological revolution as well as new forms of doctoral studies and discusses the practice of 'contributive categorization,' the 'organology of transindividuation,' 'transindividuation of knowledge' and individuation as negentropic activity. He calls for an 'economy of de-proletarianization' as an economy of care, compares the impact of the digital on the brain with heroin and expects the reorganization of the digital from the long-term civilization in the East.

Media Literacy

Roberto Simanowski: In his pageant play *The Rock* (1934) T.S. Eliot writes: "Where is the Life we have lost in living? / Where is the wisdom we have lost in knowledge? / Where is the knowledge we have lost in information?" These critical questions resonate with a common thread in many of your texts regarding the evacuation of knowledge (connaissance) and know-how (savoir-faire), and the substitution of *savoir vivre* by ability to consume. Eliot's complaint is informed by what Nietzsche called the death of God and Weber termed the disenchantment of the world. The next lines in the Eliot passage read: "The cycles of Heaven in twenty centuries / Bring us farther from God and nearer to the Dust." God is no criterion in your writing, dust somehow is. Rather than a return to religion you advertise a return to the critique of political economy and a re-reading of poststructuralism and its sources, Hegel and Marx. Schools and universities as institutions where knowledge is taught and reason is formed play an important role in this regard. However, these institutions are at war with old and new media for attention as you discuss in your new English book *States of Shock: Stupidity and Knowledge in the 21st Century*. Lets start with a very simple question: If you were the minister of education, what would be your first instruction?

Bernard Stiegler: First I would say, I need to become also the minister of science and research. Because first you have to change the way in which science is produced and the objects of science themselves. The problem is what I call tertiary retention and especially its new form: digital tertiary retention. Digital tertiary retention is transforming the conditions not only of the transmission of knowledge, but also of its elaboration and the tradition of scientific objects. All knowledge, including everyday life knowledge, what in French is called savoir vivre, as well as practical knowledge, savoir-faire, is now transformed by digitalization. I think that this is an enormous transformation for which a new organization of academic knowledge is needed. More practically, more precisely, it necessitates the creation of new forms of doctoral schools, new forms of high-level research.

RS: Tertiary retention is your term to describe exteriorization of long-term memory in mnemo-technical systems such as archives, libraries or even oral lore. How do you apply this to the digital?

BS: The way in which we create new theories and theoretical objects is conditioned by our instruments. Knowledge, particularly academic knowledge, is always conditioned by what I call the literal tertiary retention in the case of the knowledge of the West, for example the alphabet and writing as the condition of the possibility of apodictic geometry in the sense of Husserl. Today we have objects, biological, mathematical, physical, nanotechno-physical objects. Actually, every kind of object is produced by digital means that are not means in reality but are in fact the element of knowledge in the sense of Hegel: its new milieu. Therefore it is absolutely necessary to develop new forms of doctoral studies, which will not only produce new objects of knowledge but new instruments for producing rational objects.

RS: Given the agenda of your book *Digital Studies: Organologie des savoirs et technologies de la connaissance* of 2014 I take it that you are not talking about digital technologies as new instruments of knowledge production in the sense of Digital Humanities.

BS: What I mean is not Digital Humanities which considers digital instruments in a classical way. What I mean is digital studies which is very different. The question for people who use digital means for analyzing archives for history for example or archeology does not really changes their views on what is death, what is the role of linguistics etc. For me, to study digital text is to necessarily completely reconsider what language is - once digitized. It is also questioning what is the relationship between language and writing, how writing modified the evolution of language, made possible linguistics for example etc. What we need is an epistemological revolution.

RS: What does such an epistemological revolution look like?

BS: A laptop, a computer, is a device, an apparatus to produce categories or categorization through algorithms. The basis of the theory of knowledge for Aristotle is the question of categorization. What is happening with digitization is an enormous transformation of the basis of knowledge. And I think this needs a complete reconsideration of what is knowledge as such. I myself practice with my students what I call contributive categorization exploring what is the process of categorization for Aristotle but also by practicing the process of categorization with data.

The other important aspect is destruction: Innovation goes much more quickly now and knowledge arrives always too late. Not only in the sense of Hegel saying that Minerva is flying in the evening and that philosophy is always too late. We have today a transformation of technical milieu that goes extremely quickly and we need to practice the transindividuation of knowledge in a new way. To that end, we have to develop a contributive research that is based on the use of those processes of contributive categorization but that are also processes of contributive certification based on hermeneutic communities, realizing in such a way the method of what Kurt Lewin called "action research" where you can involve many people in a team who are not necessary academics but interested in the team's object: your own students but also, in PHD programs based on such a contributive research, forming communities of hermeneutic and networked action research

RS: Transindividuation is a central concept in your writing, one that is inspired by the philosopher Gilbert Simondon and aims at co-individuation within a preindividuated milieu. Individuation itself is an omnipresent and continuous transformation of the individual by information, knowledge, and tertiary retention, which is often carried out through the encounter with books, and nowadays increasingly through engagement with digital media. Transindividuation is the basis for all kinds of social transformation and is certainly vital to "action research" and "hermeneutic communities". Your notion of hermeneutic communities and the transindividuation of knowledge reminds me of Pierre Lévy's 1994 book *L'intelligence collective: Pour une anthropologie du cyberspace* and other concepts of knowledge production from below on the Internet as a kind of democratization of knowledge. Wikipedia is one example, the quantified self movement is another one. I also think of your discussion of the transindividuation of memory as a way to overcome the global and quotidian "mercantile production of memory". What role do you think the Internet and especially Web 2.0 can play in terms of the transindividuation of memory and knowledge?

BS: Knowledge itself is a process of transindividuation as it is based on controversy, on conflicts of interpretation, on processes of certification by critical means, by peer to peer critique. This was the basis for the Web in the beginning. At the beginning the Web was based on the process of transindividuation. But the Web was so successful immediately that the question was how shall we create data centers for being able to satisfy this traffic. This became a problem of investment, an industrial question in the sense of economics, industrial economy. This deeply modified the functioning of the Web itself. I know this also because I worked with the WWW Consortium. There was an enormous lobby by Silicon Valley for completely transforming the data format into computable formats dedicated to data economy, dedicated to computation. Today the platforms, the social networks and services like Amazon, Google or Facebook are only dedicated to the computation of and on data. This was not the role of the Web at the beginning. At the beginning the role of the Web was to track and trace and to make formalized, searchable and then comparable the singularities of the people producing webpages etc. So I think we need a reinvention of the Web.

RS: On the reinvention of the Web I would like to hear more in a moment. First I want to put knowledge, tertiary retention, and transindividuation into a broader political context. In your book *For a New Critique of Political Economy* you write: „The consumerist model has reached its limits because it has become systemically short-termist, because it has given rise to a *systemic stupidity* that *structurally prevents the reconstitution of a long-term horizon.*" Stupidity and the lack of courage or desire to use ones own understanding have been addressed in the Enlightenment and later by Critical Theory. Famous in this regard is Adorno's claim that amusement promises a liberation from thinking as negation. Your critique of the commodification of culture seems to return to both Adorno's severe critique of distraction and the Enlightenment's call to emergence from one's self-incurred immaturity. What has changed — since Adorno and after the Web 2.0 seems to have fulfilled Brecht's famous media utopia (with regard to radio) of putting a microphone in each listener's hand?

BS: The question is the pharmacology of the Web. I work a lot with Adorno and particularly on this question. But my problem with Adorno is that he couldn't understand that if he was to address these questions with reference to the Enlightenment he must transform the Kantian heritage concerning what Kant calls schematism and transcendental imagination. I have tried to show in *Technique and Time 3* that it is impossible to continue to follow Immanuel Kant on this question of precisely the process of categorization of the concepts of the understanding as a transcendental grip. It is not at all a transcendental grip but is produced by tertiary retentions. And this is the reason why we need to completely redefine the theory of categorization for today.

Not only with Aristotle but also with Kant. Moreover we have to pass through the theories of symbolic time by Ernst Cassirer and also by Durkheim explaining that categorization is produced for example in shamanic society through the totem.

This is the first question. The second question is how to deal with the pharmakon. If you don't use the pharmakon to produce therapies it will necessarily be a poison. To say we have completely to redefine education and put students not into the grammar school but in front of a computer, is wrong. I am absolutely opposed to the notion that the digital must become the first priority of education. Children should first be absolutely versed in grammar and orthography before they deal with computation. Education in school should follow the historical order of alteration of media, i.e. you begin with drawing, continue with writing, you go on to photography, for example, and then you use the computer which would not be before students are 15 or 16.

So the point is not to make all children use a computer but to make them understand what a computer is, which is completely different. If we don't create a new education the practice of the market will rule like the practices of a dealer. In a way the digital is as strong as heroin is for the brain. It has exactly the same effect on society as heroin has on the brain. When you use heroin or opium the capacity of your brain to produce endorphins decreases and there is a moment when you become completely dependent on its intoxication, and have no other way than using heroin. Now we are in such a situation with the digital tertiary retention. The reason is we don't know how to cap it, this pharmakon. It is prescribed by sellers of services, the dealers of digital technology. I don't mean to be providing a moral judgment here, but a purely pharmacological analysis. The problem is not that Google or other big Internet-companies have bad intentions but that we, the academics, don't make it our job to produce a digital pharmacology and organology.

RS: Your call to produce a digital organology reminds me of your notions on how music apparatuses such as the phonograph or radio have created a short-circuit in musical skills. Being able to play music should be a precondition for significant skill when listening to music. The obvious link to the digital would be that we don't understand the digital if we don't understand its apparatuses, i.e. operating systems, programs, applications. As you point out, before we acquire such understanding we have to be able to master reading and writing. This, however, seems to be jeopardized by the digital apparatuses which undermine the organology of transindividuation within book culture by compromising lasting attention, deep reading and complex thinking. In your book *Taking Care of Youth and the Generations* you refer to the neuroscientist Maryanne Wolf who holds that we are not born to read but have to undergo a cerebral rearrangement in order to achieve the skills of reading and writing, a cerebral rearrangement which is, as Wolf and others hold, nowadays jeopardized by digital media. In a later text, on *Web-Philosophy*, you cite Wolf's concern as a mother asking herself how the digital brain will be able to grow and withstand digital technologies without negative effects. You conclude: "If bodies like the World Wide Web Consortium do not take on this kind of question, these organizations cannot reach very far." What is it such institutional bodies could do but don't? And how can they help to reinvent the Web?

BS: I think they should produce negentropy. Now, the problem of negentropy is always the production of singularity. If you are to manage a huge flux of data through algorithms, that are automatic computations, you need to process a comparison between singularities to make them analyzable and understandable, and you transform this singularities into particularities. A singularity is self defined, and a particularity is defined by a set of which it is a part. Computation necessarily transforms singularities into particularities of such a set. Using digital technologies, you have to deal between negentropy and entropy or, to say it with Saussure and structuralism, between diachrony and synchrony. In the theory of systems, diachrony is the dynamic tendency that makes dynamic the system, and synchrony is another tendency that maintains the system meta-stable. I believe that it is today absolutely possible and necessary to redefine the architecture of the networks creating algorithms and big data dedicated to the traceability of singularities and to put these singularities into hermeneutic communities for creating dynamic communities of knowledge -with technologies for annotation, new types of data analysis algorithms and new kinds of social networks.

RS: Negentropy, i.e. negative entropy, can be understood as the export of entropy by a system in order to keep its own entropy low. You consider individuation as a negentropic activity. How would the Web achieve this?

BS: The Web is producing entropy not only in the sense of thermodynamics, but in the sense of information theory, cybernetics, theory of complex systems and what I call now neguanthropology. The Web is completely subject to computation and automation based only on computation. Now, through interactions with the practitioners of the web, helped by algorithms like bots on Wikipedia, these practitioners created negentropy - that I call also noodiversity. This is what is destroyed by the data economy, only based on computation. The question for the future, not only for the Web, but for human kind is to produce negentropy. The problem of climate change for example is a problem of increasing entropy. It is possible to create new systems dedicated to reduce the automata of algorithms for giving people the possibilities to trace, confront and co-individuate their differences, their singularities. I am working on a new theory of social networking not based on the network effect but based on the theory of collective individuation. The problem is not dedicated to a short-termist market but based on a long-term economy capable of producing a new type of development based on an economy of negentropy.

Politics and Government

RS: Let me respond to the issue of long-term economy and negentropy and the overdue transition from the Anthropocene or *Entropocene*, as you put it, into a new "general ecology" or, as you call it, *Neganthropocene*. In many of your texts you underline the destructive nature of the globalized industrial system, warning, as in your book *What Makes Life Worth Living: On Pharmacology*

(2013, French 2010), that "it is the future of terrestrial life that is at stake with unprecedented urgency" and calling for a "peaceful growth and development". Degrowth – which was first discussed in the 1979 book *Demain la Décroissance: Entropie-écologie-économie* by Nicholas Georgescu-Roegen, Jacques Grinevald, and Ivo Rens – is an imperative in many alternative, ecological economies today as for example the title of Serge Latouche's 2009 book *Farewell to Growth* indicates. However, when the German philosopher Hans Jonas, in his 1979 book *The Imperative of Responsibility: In Search of an Ethics for the Technological Age* entertains the same idea, he assumes that the rather unpopular concept of non-growth can only be implemented by a government that does not rely on its constituencies' approval. Ironically, this would, as Jonas notes, turn all the hope to totalitarian countries such as China or even Russia who today, however, are far away from compromising economic growth on behalf of ecological concerns. In this context it is remarkable that today governments in democratic countries such as Germany give themselves what they call a *Digital Agenda* in order to govern the development of digital media and its ramifications in society. This *Agenda* also addresses the risks and threats associated with the process of digitization such as privacy, dataveillance, as well as pattern recognition and prediction (and hence manipulation) of individual behavior through big data mining. It may come as little surprise that businessmen, such as the chairman of the German Federal Association for Information Technology, Telecommunications and New Media, criticize the high data protection regulations set by the government as a hindrance for new business models and Germany's success in the digital revolution and warn that we must not apply the rules of the analog world one to one in the digital economy but should review the concept of data thriftiness and become more daring. With respect to growth concerning industry 4.0 and with respect to what has been called data pollution one could say, while the government implements negentropic regulations, the business world rejects any interventions and calls for entropic freedom.

BS: Let me first answer the question about growth and de-growth. I disagree with the concept of de-growth. The problem is not growth as entropy. It is not possible to de-growth. What do we mean by growth? The definition of growth by Keynes is absolutely partial and insufficient if not contradictory - particularly with respect to his essay *Economic possibilities for our grand-children* of 1931. This is also the reason for which I follow today Amartya Sen and his new type of indicators for what growth is. He doesn't call this growth, he calls it human development. The problem is the development of what he calls "capacitation" and what I call myself knowledge. The problem is proletarianization. We need an economy of de-proletarianization which is also an economy of care. Because knowledge is a type of care. When you know how to do something you have knowledge for taking care for something. Knowledge was destroyed twice by a first and a second industrial revolution as prolerianization of manual workers loosing their knowing-how during the 19th century, and prolerianization of customers loosing their savoir vivre during the 20th century. And the digital revolution is now prolarianizing academic knowledge and sciences - with big data etc. Now I think we have to deproletarianise economy, and to put knowledge at the core of new modes of production and ways of life being the beginning of the real growth ... In the current situation, we are decreasing the capability of people to growth, that is to know how to live by taking care of life. We become more and more dependent on technology. The point is not to de-growth but to develop a new economy that is really producing a new type of investment. This new economy is what I call a growth of negentropy. But the problems for the current economy is that it is only capable to make money with what is purely computable, that is purely entropic. Negentropy is produced by bifurcations. The market is only based on computation, and the systemic bifurcations are never produced by computation. This is the problem.

As for Hans Jonas' considerations, yes, you are right, it is surprising to see that it is possible to discuss such questions in China. But it is not completely surprising. When I was in Nanjing the chancellor of the university told me: The West said it is impossible to have a Marxist revolution in China because it was not an industrial but a rural society. And you were right, we were not an industrial society. But now we are and now that transformation will happen. Of course, we have to be careful interpreting such discourse. But I think the statement is interesting and relevant because today there is a very critical situation on the geopolitical level in which you have a society, the United States of America, that is capable of controlling everything with a technology that is in itself entropic, which means: condemned to insolvency. Because entropy is creating an enormous insolvency. On the other side you have a country like China with enormous quantity of disposable money and capacity for investment, who is the main shareholder and banker of the United States. So I think there is a very interesting techno geopolitical question: How to find here the possibility of creating a new stage of the digital. We will not find such a possibility in the United States, even if I know many people in the U.S. who would be very positive about such a change and who believe in its necessity. But in the U.S. it is now too late. Because you have stakeholders who have a competitive advantage they don't want to lose. They cannot work this new type of business, the negentropic model, I believe, because behind them are shareholders who then won't make money. The transformation of Google to Alphabet is a symptom of this. The American economy has very big constraints. I don't believe that they are really capable of producing the new stage of the digital.

The digital is reaching a limit. This limit is expressed and reached by the big data as they increase the level of entropy into noetic life and systems, such as for example language, as shown by Frederic Kaplan ["Linguistic Capitalism and Algorithmic Mediation", Representations 27 (2014), 57-63] regarding the linguistic capitalism of Google, that eliminates exceptions that are the origin of evolutions of language. This is what Chris Anderson's "The end of theory" is incapable to understand. The computational conception of cognition is a new metaphysics of capitalism. In the United States you have very important economic and political agencies that have enormous possibilities for intervention but they don't have the technological perspectives in order to act properly. I believe it is possible to do things with China on this question. But I work also with other people — English, Italian, German — and try to create a world-wide consortium about this through the digital studies network. There is a new dynamic for addressing the question of the anthropocene, which is the actual topic we are discussing here.

RS: The belief in computation as a new metaphysics of capitalism! One may also call it – especially the theory of singularity as made fashionable by Ray Kurzweil – a new grand narrative in a paradoxical, non- or post-human Hegelian sense: The Spirit becomes self-aware in the form of artificial intelligence, the journey of human consciousness is fulfilled once it is given, passed on to machines. Would such extension of intelligence be the "purpose in nature" that Kant assumes behind the seemingly non-rational, aimless purpose and actions of men? And would this be — in case this development leads to mankind's extinction or suppression — the final destiny and inevitable providence of reason behind a seemingly unreasonable advancement? However, the question at hand is the relationship of such a technological telos to political or cultural systems. You seem to link the obsession with computation to Western capitalism and expect an alternative approach from the East. I assume that, when the chancellor of the University of Nanjing stated that now that China is industrialized transformation will happen, he didn't mean a Marxist revolution or at least socialist reformations. This assumption raises a question: The short-termism, that you claim needs to be overcome, is not only a phenomenon of the economy but also of contemporary culture as Douglas Rushkoff's 2013 book *Present Shock* demonstrates, and as Zygmunt Baumann pointed out already back in the late 20th century when he described the episodic rather than narrative identity of the modern individual who is wary of long-term commitments and "abolishes time in any other form but a flat collection or an arbitrary sequence of present moments; a *continuous present*." The ontogenetic short-termism somehow mirrors the end of grand narratives on the phylogenetic level: The Western world lacks the teleological notion (or: grand narrative) to be on its way to a better society (if we ignore the mantra from Silicon Valley Start Ups and their like that their apps, platforms, and services constantly create a better world). In your book *Uncontrollable Societies of Disaffected Individuals: Disbelief and Discredit* (2012, French 2006) you describe the "spiritual misery" that capitalism generates as "disappearance of every horizon of expectation and of all belief, whether religious, political, or libidinal". One may think: to the extent that contemporary China holds on to such a teleological notion or grand narrative it may be able to orient peoples' lives in longer terms. But is modern China still committed to such a cause? Is it able to produce, with its communist underpinnings, the "new spirit of capitalism" that you hope for in your book *The Re-enchantment of the World: The Value of Spirit Against Industrial Populism* (2014, French 2006)? Or is it, with its aggressively growing economy and reckless culture of consumption, yet another form of short-termist, runaway capitalism or, as you call it, a "drive-based organization of capitalism"?

BS: I don't think I am equipped to interpret the relationship between industrialisation and Marxism in China. Personally I don't believe the question is a Marxist revolution. I don't agree with what is called Marxism even in the sense of Marx himself. But I believe that in Marx, for example in the *Grundrisse*, you can find something else extremely important concerning automation and mechanical knowledge etc. I believe that the future belongs to those who are capable of producing a new theory of becoming and of creation of bifurcations into becoming creating futures, and I believe that new theory will not come from neo-liberalism. Because the reality of those theories is to ensure the efficiency of computation and the overcome of computation is bifurcation. I believe those theories will especially come out of Asia – but also of other countries everywhere in the world. Because Asia is, precisely, a long-term civilization. Of course, you are right, if you go to Beijing, Tokyo, Seoul, or Hong Kong, it is absolutely consumerist behavior that you will see. But I don't think at all that the change comes from the masses. I think the change comes from contradictions in the system. I also believe, the change in the Web that I referred to before is precisely based on the re-functionalisation of the digital differed time with the real time. It is a question today precisely of the reorganization of the digital. And it is in the interest of Asia and Europe to part ways with the Californian model of networking. And I think this is possible. There are very good thinkers and engineers in Europe. Europe and Asia will have to find a kind of agreement. Maybe they will not find it. I would even say, probably they will not find it. But if they don't, it will be a catastrophe. It will be a military and eco-logical catastrophe. We have no chance. My job is to create this opportunity, not against the United States of course, but from the point of view of China, Japan, Russia etc. it is a question not only of competition but opposition to the U.S. This is for Europe another question. We have to find rational ways to avoid these conflicts. I think this is possible. It is improbable, extremely improbable. But it is not absolutely impossible.